D1113959

THE VEST-POCKET GUIDE TO BUSINESS RATIOS

Michael R. Tyran

Compiled and edited by Fred Dahl

Prentice Hall
Englewood Cliffs, New Jersey 07632

Prentice-Hall International (UK) Limited, *London*
Prentice-Hall of Australia Pty. Limited, *Sydney*
Prentice-Hall Canada, Inc., *Toronto*
Prentice-Hall Hispanoamericana, S.A., *Mexico*
Prentice-Hall of India Private Limited, *New Delhi*
Prentice-Hall of Japan, Inc., *Tokyo*
Simon & Schuster Asia Pte. Ltd., *Singapore*
Editora Prentice-Hall do Brasil, Ltda., *Rio de Janeiro*

This publication is designed to provide accurate and authoritative
information in regard to the subject matter covered. It is sold
with the understanding that the publisher is not engaged in
rendering legal, accounting, or other professional service. If
legal advice or other expert assistance is required, the services of
a competent professional person should be sought.

*From a Declaration of Principles Jointly Adopted by a
Committee of the American Bar Association and a Committee of
Publishers and Associations*

ISBN 0-13-951948-3

10 9 8 7 6 5 4 3 2 1

Printed in the United States of America

Library of Congress Cataloging-in-Publication Data

Tyran, Michael R.
    The vest pocket guide to business ratios / Michael R. Tyran :
compiled and edited by Fred Dahl.
        p. cm.
    Adaptation of author's Handbook of business and financial
ratios. c1986.
    Includes index.
    ISBN 0-13-951948-3
    1. Ratio analysis. I. Dahl, Fred. II. Tyran, Michael R.
Handbook of business and financial ratios. III. Title.
HF5681.R25T975   1991
658.15'1—dc20   91-17279
                                                      CIP

PRENTICE HALL
BUSINESS & PROFESSIONAL DIVISION
A SIMON & SCHUSTER COMPANY

HOW THIS BOOK CAN HELP YOU

How do you know, during a busy day of decision making and meetings, whether your company or your part of the company is making a profit? Whether it is financially sound? Whether it will have the cash to meet its commitments this quarter? Whether costs are running away on you? Whether production is keeping pace with sales? Whether your clientele is paying their bills on time? In a word, how do you sustain control over all the many financial aspects of a small business, corporation, department, division, or nonprofit organization?

Ratios are key to control. Of the many helpful ratios in this vest pocket guide, you can select the ones that you feel will best support your efforts to maintain steady, ongoing control of your organization. Whether you are a CEO, CFO, corporate middle manager, small business owner, or financial adviser/consultant, the ratios in this book can help you meet your control objectives with a minimal drain on your time.

FRED DAHL

HOW TO USE THIS BOOK

Here's how the guide works. Each chapter focuses on an aspect of business management—profitability, financial status, sales, costs, cash inflow, cash outflow, production. Within each chapter is a series of ratios designed to enable you to isolate trends. (Note: Because some calculations apply to more than one area, certain ratios appear in more than one chapter. They are presented more than once for your convenience.)

Getting started is easy. Select the ratios that best suit your organization and objectives. Then incorporate those ratios into your accounting system, whether it is "do-it-yourself," handled by a staff or outside accountant, or automated. After a few periods (months or quarters), you benefit in several ways: First you quickly establish historically validated standard values for the ratios; you have a set of norms against which to compare future results. Second, even as the norms become fine-tuned over time, you see at a glance any significant deviation from the norm—and you can take action right away. Finally, after as little as a year of use, your organization's norms can be compared against those of your industry—an excellent way of determining how you are doing in comparison to the competition.

The requirements are simple. The guide assumes you know something about running a business and high school math. You do not need an accounting background. All relevant accounting terminology is defined at the beginning of each chapter and again at the end of the book. (For those who feel they need a primer, the appendix will be helpful.)

The format makes it easy for you to get the information you need—and understand it. The emphasis is on "here's how," not "here's why." Headings are in question form in anticipation of your questions:

What is cash flow?

For each heading, you will find, a simple, brief answer, followed by a formula:

Cash flow is the net amount when disbursements are deducted from cash receipts.

Cash flow = Cash receipts − Cash disbursements

Note: If disbursements are greater than receipts for period, cash flow can be negative.

An example then shows you how to make the calculation:

Example: First-quarter cash receipts for MNO Corp. are $136,900, and its cash disbursements are $144,200.

Cash flow = Cash receipts − Cash disbursements
$$= \$136,900 - \$144,200 = -\$7,300$$

In the first quarter, MNO had a negative cash flow of $7,300; that is, it paid out $7,300 more cash than it received.

Once you understand the ratio, you need only make it part of your accounting and reporting system, and then watch the trends.

Note: If you are uncertain of the importance of a calculation, a brief explanation generally follows:

What do cash ratios do for the accounts payable manager?

Cash ratios enable the accounts payable manager to determine the sources of greatest cash inflow and outflow, and possibly to take steps to improve the organization's overall cash position.

Example: Given MNO Corp.'s cash flow statement (see preceding example), several observations can be made:

- The company came dangerously close to a negative net cash position in the first quarter.

- Billed sales and progress payments represent the major portion (approximately 88%) of receipts. Remedial measures are probably best focused on these areas, as opposed to areas with lesser contributions to a positive cash position. Steps must be taken to increase billings and/or collections in the next quarter.

- Measures might also be considered that will limit or defer second-quarter disbursements.

- Borrowed funds to meet short-term cash needs are a possibility too.

Finding the ratio you want is easy. A detailed table of contents at the front of the book lists all the ratios in their order of appearance. Also, an extensive index at the end of the book lists the ratios and other subjects in alphabetical order, along with the numbers of pages on which they appear.

Note: Decimals and percentages are interchanged without explanation.

Example:

$$\text{Investors' capital-to-sales ratio} = \frac{\text{Stockholders' equity}}{\text{Sales}}$$

$$= \frac{\$57,000,000}{\$240,000,000} = 0.2404, \text{ or } 24.0\%$$

Stockholders' equity (investors' capital) represents 24% of ABC's sales in 19X0.

- To change a decimal to a percentage, move the decimal point two digits to the right.

Example: 0.2404 becomes 24.04%.

- To change a percentage to a decimal, move the decimal point two places to the left.

Example: 24.04% becomes 0.2404.

Note: Every effort has been made to publish an error-free book. Any errors that might have slipped through the authors and proofreaders are regretted. We apologize for any confusion that might result. Comments regarding content are welcome; they may be sent to Fred Dahl, CBEP, Prentice Hall, Englewood Cliffs, NJ 07632.

CONTENTS

Chapter 2
The Organization's Financial Status:
Analyzing the Balance Sheet, 38

Chapter 3
Analyzing the "Top Line":
Sales Management Ratios, 101

**Chapter 4
Containing Expenses:
Cost Analysis, 157**

CHAPTER 1

IS THE COMPANY MAKING MONEY? ANALYZING THE INCOME STATEMENT

WORDS TO KNOW

Bottom line. *See* Net income.

Capital. *See* Stockholders' (shareholders', owners') equity.

Cost of goods sold. *See* Cost of sales.

Cost of sales (cost of goods sold, direct costs). The cost of making or buying a product sold, or of providing a service rendered, consisting of direct personnel, direct materials (and other direct costs), and factory overhead.

Direct cost. *See* Cost of sales.

Direct labor. *See* Direct personnel cost.

Direct personnel (labor) cost. The portion of payroll that can be directly attributed to the making of the company product—e.g., assembly line workers.

Equity. *See* Stockholders' (shareholders', owners') equity.

G&A. *See* General and administrative expense.

General and administrative (G&A) expense. An indirect cost associated with running a business, other than production or sales.

Gross margin. *See* Gross profit.

Gross profit (margin). Sales less cost of sales (direct costs).

Income (earnings) before taxes. *See* Pretax earnings.

Income from operations. *See* Operating income.

Income (profit and loss) statement (P&L). A financial

statement showing a company's net income—the profit after deducting all expenses—over a period.

Indirect cost (operating expense). A cost that cannot be directly attributed to production, such as selling expenses or general and administrative (G&A) costs.

Investors' capital. *See* Stockholders' equity.

Net income (bottom line, net profit). Revenues less all expenses—direct, indirect, taxes, etc.

Net profit. *See* Net income.

Net sales. *See* Sales.

Operating expense. *See* Indirect cost.

Operating income (factory income, income from operations). Sales less cost of sales (direct costs) and operating (indirect) expenses. It excludes peripheral income, such as interest on investments, and nonoperating expenses, such as taxes.

Other direct costs. Costs, other than labor or materials, that are directly attributable to the making of the company product—e.g., factory-related expenses.

P&L. *See* Income statement.

Pretax earnings (income, profit, net before taxes). Earnings left after adding operating income to nonoperating income (e.g., interest earned on loans), and then deducting nonoperating expenses (e.g., extraordinary costs)—but not taxes.

Profit and loss statement. *See* Income statement.

Revenue (revenues). *See* Sales.

Sales (net sales, revenue, top line, total credit sales, etc.). Income from the sale of a company's product or service, less a deduction for returns and bad debt.

Selling expenses. An indirect cost associated with sales, selling expenses include the costs of marketing and contract administration.

Stockholders' (shareholders', owners') equity (investors' capital). The difference between a corporation's assets and liabilities, representing the investors' ownership interest in the company.

Top line. *See* Sales.

Total sales. *See* Sales.

Total credit sales. *See* Sales.

WHERE ARE SALES DOLLARS GOING?
VERTICAL ANALYSIS

What is vertical analysis of the income statement?

In vertical analysis of the income statement, each income entry in the statement is expressed as a ratio or percentage of total sales. The aim is to see how sales dollars are being spent.

The income entries are:

- Sales (Revenues)
- Gross profit
- Income from operations (or operating income)
- Pretax profit (or net income before taxes)
- Net income

Example: ABC Co.'s (nonitemized) income statement is as follows:

ABC Co.
Income Statement
19X0

	Amount	% Sales
Total sales	$ 240,000,000	100.00
Cost of sales	176,600,000	73.6
Gross profit	$ 63,400,000	26.4
G&A expense	$ 13,900,000	5.8
Selling expense	11,300,000	4.7
Subtotal	$ 25,200,000	10.5
Income from operations	$ 38,200,000	15.9
Other income	$ 48,000	0.2
Interest expense	72,000	0.3
Subtotal	$ (24,000)	(0.1)
Pretax profit	$ 37,960,000	15.8
Taxes (at 50%)	18,980,000	7.9
Net income	$ 18,980,000	7.9

Sales (The Top Line)

In addition to its role in vertical analysis, sales may be used in connection with certain balance sheet entries to evaluate an organization's profitability. (See Chapter 2 for balance sheet ratios.)

How may sales be related to fixed assets (a balance sheet entry)?

Sales (or revenues, the "top line" entry on the income statement) may be expressed as a multiple of the average value of fixed assets (a balance sheet entry).

$$\frac{\text{Fixed-assets-to}}{\text{sales ratio}} = \frac{\text{Sales}}{\text{Fixed assets}}$$

Example: With annual sales of $240,000,000, ABC Co. has fixed assets of $35,800,000.

Property, Plant, and Equipment	
Land	$ 2,300,000
Buildings/improvement	20,000,000
Machinery/equipment	31,400,000
Subtotal	$53,700,000
Less: Accumulated depr'n.	17,900,000
Net fixed assets	**$35,800,000**

$$\frac{\text{Fixed-assets-to}}{\text{sales ratio}} = \frac{\text{Sales}}{\text{Fixed assets}}$$

$$= \frac{\$240,000,000}{\$35,800,000} = 6.70$$

ABC's sales are 6.70 times that of its average fixed assets.

What is the meaning of the sales-to-fixed-assets ratio?

While fixed assets in themselves do not produce sales, without them only limited sales can be made in a product-oriented company. This ratio can provide insight as to whether an organization has too much capacity or too little for a given sales volume.

Note: When comparing ratios of many organizations in the same industry, consider the age of the assets, price levels at the time of purchase, and the depreciation policies with their related effect on fixed asset valuation. For example, a low ratio could indicate an excessive valuation of the fixed assets without a comparable increase in sales.

What is stockholders' equity?

Stockholders' (shareholders' or owners') equity (or investors' capital)—a balance sheet entry—is equal to the difference between an organization's assets and its liabilities.

$$Equity = Assets - Liabilities$$

It is the third component of a balance sheet.

Example: In the following balance sheet, note that total assets are equal to total liabilities plus stockholders' equity.

ABC Co.
Balance Sheet
19X0 (in $000,000s)

	Amount
Current Assets	
Cash	$ 3.50
Marketable securities	3.30
Accounts receivable	28.70
Inventories	
Raw materials	26.80
Work in process	10.70
Finished goods	7.30
Subtotal	44.80
Prepaid expenses	0.25
Total current assets	$ 80.55
Property, Plant, and Equipment	
Land	$ 2.30
Buildings/improvement	20.00
Machinery/equipment	31.40
Subtotal	$ 53.70
Less: Accumulated depr'n.	17.90
Net fixed assets	$ 35.80
Deferred Charges	0.90
Total assets	**$117.25**
Current Liabilities	
Notes payable	$ 1.40
Current portion—LT debt	2.50
Accrued payroll	3.60
Accounts payable	20.85
Income tax payable	2.60
Total current liabilities	$ 30.95
Deferred Income Taxes	1.90
Long-Term Debt	26.70
Total liabilities	**$ 59.55**

Stockholders' Equity	
Common stock	$ 3.70
Paid-in capital	26.01
Retained earnings	27.99
Total equity capital	**$ 57.70**
Total liabilities/capital	**$117.25**

$$\text{Equity} = \text{Assets} - \text{Liabilities}$$
$$= \$117,250,000 - \$59,550,000$$
$$= \$57,700,000$$

What is the investors'-capital-to-sales ratio?

This ratio is the result of dividing stockholders' equity (investors' capital, a balance sheet entry) by sales.

$$\text{Investors'-capital-to-sales ratio} = \frac{\text{Stockholders' equity}}{\text{Sales}}$$

Example: With 19X0 sales of $240,000,000 (the "top line" of the income statement), ABC Co.'s equity was $57,700,000.

Stockholders' Equity	
Common stock	$ 3,700,000
Paid-in capital	26,010,000
Retained earnings	27,990,000
Total equity capital	**$57,700,000**

$$\text{Investors'-capital-to-sales ratio} = \frac{\text{Stockholders' equity}}{\text{Sales}}$$

$$= \frac{\$57,700,000}{\$240,000,000} = 0.2404, \text{ or } 24.0\%$$

Stockholders' equity (investors' capital) represents 24% of ABC's sales in 19X0.

What does the ratio of investors' capital to sales reflect?

This ratio reflects the percentage of sales financed by stockholders' equity. It answers the question as to whether investors are investing too much or too little for the sales volume being achieved. A high ratio indicates that sales are being fueled by capital. The lower the percentage, therefore, the more favorable the company's position.

What is the cash turnover ratio?

The cash turnover ratio relates sales (the "top line" on the income statement) to a company's cash balance (an entry in the current assets section of the balance sheet).

$$\text{Cash turnover} = \frac{\text{Sales}}{\text{Cash}}$$

Example: With sales of $240,000,000, ABC Co.'s current assets section is as follows:

	Amount
Current Assets	
Cash	**$ 3,500,000**
Marketable securities	3,300,000
Accounts receivable	28,700,000
Inventories	
Raw materials	26,800,000
Work in process	10,700,000
Finished goods	7,300,000
Subtotal	44,800,000
Prepaid expenses	250,000
Total current assets	$80,550,000

$$\text{Cash turnover} = \frac{\text{Sales}}{\text{Cash}} = \frac{\$240,000,000}{\$3,500,000} = 68.6$$

ABC Co. sales are over 68 times its cash balance.

What does the cash turnover indicate?

With this ratio, you can analyze and assess the effectiveness of an organization's use of its cash position to generate revenue. Generally, the higher the ratio, the more effective use management is making of cash.

Also, the turnover rate is helpful in determining preliminary cash balance forecasts based on sales projections.

Note: For best results an average cash position should be used.

Example: ABC Co. has ascertained that its cash position is historically 1/65 of its sales volume. Management projects a sales volume of $252,000,000 for the upcoming year.

$$\frac{1}{65} = \frac{\text{Sales}}{\text{Cash}} = \frac{\$252,000,000}{\text{Cash}}$$

Or:

$$\text{Cash} = \frac{252,000,000}{65} = \$3,876,923$$

ABC Co. can look for a cash position in the neighborhood of $3,800,000 or $3,900,000.

How is the total asset turnover computed?

The total asset turnover compares a company's sales (the income statement's "top line") to its total assets (from the balance sheet). It is usually expressed as a multiple.

$$\text{Total assets turnover ratio} = \frac{\text{Sales}}{\text{Total assets}}$$

Example: With annual sales of $240,000,000, part of ABC Co.'s balance is as follows:

	Amount
Current Assets	
Cash	$ 3,500,000
Marketable securities	3,300,000
Accounts receivable	28,700,000
Inventories	
Raw materials	26,800,000
Work in process	10,700,000
Finished goods	7,300,000
Subtotal	44,800,000
Prepaid expenses	250,000
Total current assets	$ 80,550,000
Property, Plant, and Equipment	
Land	$ 2,300,000
Buildings/improvement	20,000,000
Machinery/equipment	31,400,000
Subtotal	$ 53,700,000
Less: Accumulated depr'n.	17,900,000
Net fixed assets	$ 35,800,000
Deferred Charges	900,000
Total assets	**$117,250,000**

$$\text{Total asset turnover ratio} = \frac{\text{Sales}}{\text{Total assets}}$$

$$= \frac{240,000,000}{\$117,250,000} = 2.05$$

ABC's total assets generate a little over twice their value in sales volume.

Of what use is the asset turnover ratio?

This ratio gauges how well an organization is making use of its total assets. The higher the multiple, the more efficient the company.

Also, given a sales forecast, the organization can project its total assets position.

Example: ABC Co. knows from past experience that its sales run about twice the value of its total assets. For the upcoming year, the sales forecast is \$252,000,000.

$$\text{Total assets turnover ratio} = \frac{\text{Sales}}{\text{Total assets}}$$

Or:

$$\text{Total assets} = \frac{\text{Sales}}{\text{Total assets turnover ratio}}$$

$$= \frac{\$252,000,000}{2} = \$126,000,000$$

ABC Co. is looking for about \$126,000,000 in total assets in the coming year.

What is the operating leverage ratio?

The operating leverage ratio assesses the effect of fluctuating sales on operating profits.

$$\text{Operating leverage ratio} = \frac{\text{Sales} - \text{Variable expenses}}{\text{Sales} - \text{Total expenses}}$$

Since the operating income equals sales less the sum of variable and fixed expenses, then:

$$\text{Operating leverage ratio} = \frac{\text{Sales} - \text{Variable expenses}}{\text{Operating expenses}}$$

Example: With first-quarter sales at $300,000, MNO Corp. incurs variable costs of $234,000 and fixed expenses of $36,000.

$$\begin{aligned} \text{Operating} \atop \text{leverage ratio} &= \frac{\text{Sales} - \text{Variable expenses}}{\text{Sales} - \text{Fixed expenses}} \\[6pt] &= \frac{\$300,000 - \$234,000}{\$300,000 - (\$234,000 + \$36,000)} \\[6pt] &= \frac{\$300,000 - \$234,000}{\$300,000 - \$270,000} \\[6pt] &= \frac{\$66,000}{\$30,000} = 2.2 \end{aligned}$$

The first-quarter operating leverage factor is 2.2.

Why is the operating leverage factor important?

Operating leverage is the leverage a company gains from sales volume. High sales volumes give an organization income with which to operate. Decreased sales volumes creates situations in which operating income is spread thin, posing a threat to a company's operating ability. The operating leverage ratio enables management to evaluate this so-called "income risk." The operating leverage factor says that income from operations changes "so many times" the percentage change sales volume. Note in the following formula that the factor is inversely proportional to operating income (income from operations):

$$\text{Operating} \atop \text{leverage ratio} = \frac{\text{Sales} - \text{Variable expenses}}{\text{Operating expenses}}$$

Note: Income risk is distinguished from financial risk, which is posed by the heavy use of debt support by creditors.

Example: See the preceding example. An operating leverage factor of 2.2 means that operating income ($30,000 in the example) will change 2.2 times the percentage change in sales. If sales increase by 15%, then income from operations will increase by approximately 33%, or $9,900 (15% times 2.2): $30,000 times 0.33). For a decrease of 15% in sales, operating income would drop by $9,900.

Does the operating leverage factor change?

The operating leverage factor changes with fluctuations in sales volume and in expenses.

Example: In the second quarter of operation, MNO Corp. increases 15% to $345,000; in the third quarter, it drops by 15% to $255,000. Assume the rare occurrence that variable expenses remain at $234,000 and fixed expenses at $36,000.

For the increase in sales volume:

$$\text{Operating leverage ratio} = \frac{\text{Sales} - \text{Variable expenses}}{\text{Sales} - \text{Fixed expenses}}$$

$$= \frac{\$345,000 - \$234,000}{\$345,000 - (\$234,000 + \$36,000)}$$

$$= \frac{\$345,000 - \$234,000}{\$345,000 - \$270,000}$$

$$= \frac{\$111,000}{\$75,000} = +1.48$$

For the decrease in sales volume:

$$\text{Operating leverage ratio} = \frac{\text{Sales} - \text{Variable expenses}}{\text{Sales} - \text{Fixed expenses}}$$

$$= \frac{\$255,000 - \$234,000}{\$255,000 - (\$234,000 + \$36,000)}$$

$$= \frac{\$255,000 - \$234,000}{\$255,000 - \$270,000}$$

$$= \frac{\$21,000}{-\$15,000} = -1.40$$

When the sales volume changes (up or down), so did the operating leverage factor. At each of the revised sales levels, the operating factors change.

Gross Profit

What is gross profit?

Gross profit (gross margin) is equal to total sales less the cost of sales.

$$\text{Gross profit} = \text{Total sales} - \text{Cost of sales}$$

Example: Part of ABC Co.'s income statement is as follows:

Total sales	$240,000,000
Cost of sales	176,600,000
Gross profit	$ 63,400,000

ABC's gross profit, based on $240,000,000, is $63,400,000.

Can gross profit be expressed as a ratio of sales?

Yes. Gross profit is divided by total sales (less allowances for returns and bad debt).

Example: See preceding example.

$$\text{Gross-profit-to-sales ratio} = \frac{\text{Gross profit}}{\text{Sales}}$$

$$= \frac{\$63,400,000}{\$240,000,000} = 0.26, \text{ or } 26\%$$

ABC makes a 26% gross profit on sales. Expressed another way, for every dollar of sales made, ABC earns 26 cents in gross profit.

How does the gross-profit-to-sales ratio benefit management?

This ratio assists management in:

● Monitoring the cost of sales from one period to the next. A rise in this ratio leads to the question, is it costing the company more to fill orders? If so, why?

● Projecting cost of sales, given a sales estimate.

Example: In 19X0, ABC Co.'s sales were $240,000,000 and gross profit $63,400,000 (26%, see the preceding example). In 19X1, its estimated sales are $265,000,000, and its gross profit is typically 26% of sales.

$$\text{Gross-profit-to-sales ratio} = \frac{\text{Gross profit}}{\text{Sales}}$$

$$0.26 = \frac{\text{Gross profit}}{\$265,000,000}$$

Or:

$$\text{Gross profit} = 0.26 \times \$265,000,000 = \$68,900,000$$

ABC is looking for a little under $69,000,000 in gross profit in 19X1.

Let's assume that actual sales turn out to be $265,000,000 but that gross profit is actually only $58,600,000. That is a 22% ratio ($58,600,000 divided by $265,000,000)—lower than the historical average. Management's first question is why did the cost of sales rise?

Income from Operations (Operating Income)

What is income from operations?

Income from operations, or operating income, is equal to sales less all expenses—cost of sales, G&A, selling expenses, etc. It can also be defined as net income less G&A and selling expenses.

$$\text{Income from operations} = \text{Sales} - \left(\text{Cost of sales} + \text{G\&A} + \text{Selling expenses}\right)$$

which is the same as:

$$\text{Income from operations} = \text{Sales} - \left(\text{Cost of sales} + \text{Indirect expenses}\right)$$

Example: Part of ABC Co.'s income statement is as follows:

Total sales	$240,000,000
Cost of sales	176,600,000
Gross profit	$ 63,400,000
G&A expense	$ 13,900,000
Selling expense	11,300,000
Subtotal	$ 25,200,000
Income from operations	**$ 38,200,000**

$$\text{Income from operations} = \text{Sales} - \left(\text{Cost of sales} + \text{G\&A} + \text{Selling expenses}\right)$$

$$= \$240,000.000 - (\$176,600.000 + \$13.900.000 + \$11,300.000)$$

$$= \$240,000.000 - (\$201,800.000) = \$38,200,000$$

ABC's income from operations, based on $240,000,000, is $38,200,000.

Can income from operations be expressed as a ratio of sales?

Yes. Income from operations is divided by total sales (less allowances for returns and bad debt).

$$\text{Income-from-operations-to-sales ratio} = \frac{\text{Income from operations}}{\text{Sales}}$$

Example: Use the information from the preceding example.

$$\text{Income-from-operations-to-sales ratio} = \frac{\text{Income from operations}}{\text{Sales}}$$

$$= \frac{\$38,200,000}{\$240,000,000} = 0.159, \text{ or } 16\%$$

ABC makes a 16% income from operations on sales. Expressed another way, for every dollar of sales made, ABC earns 16 cents in operating income.

How does the income-from-operations-to-sales ratio benefit management?

This ratio assists management in:

- Monitoring operations from period to period. A drop in this ratio raises the question, are overall expenses increasing disproportionately to increases in sales?
- Indicating a company's ability to make a profit.

Example—monitoring operations: In 19X0, ABC Co.'s sales were $240,000,000 and operating income was $38,200,000 (16%, see the preceding example). In 19X1, its estimated sales are $265,000,000, and its operating income is typically 16% of sales.

$$\text{Income-from-operations-to sales ratio} = \frac{\text{Income from operations}}{\text{Sales}}$$

$$0.16 = \frac{\text{Income from operations}}{\$265,000,000}$$

Or:

$$\text{Income from operations} = 0.16 \times \$265,000,000$$
$$= \$42,400,000$$

ABC is looking for a little over $42,000,000 in operating income in 19X1.

Assume that actual sales turn out to be $265,000,000 and that operating income is actually only $46,300,000. That is a 17% ratio ($46,300,000 divided by $265,000,000)—higher than the historical average. The question is what caused the increase in overall expenses?

This ratio is also a good indicator of an organization's ability to make a profit. Period-to-period fluctuations can trigger investigations into the possibility of rising costs or decreased sales.

Example—indicating profit: Historically, XYZ Corp.'s operational-income-to-sales ratio has been 0.65, or 6.5%. In February, the following data is available:

(in $000,000s)

	Feb.	
Sales		
Direct labor	8.0	
Overhead	10.9	
Material and ODC	13.1	
Cost of sales		32.0
Indirect costs		2.1
Total all costs		34.1
Operational income		2.9

$$\text{Operational-income-to-sales ratio} = \frac{\text{Operational income (\$)}}{\text{Sales (\$)}}$$

$$= \frac{\$2,900,000}{\$37,000,000} = .078, \text{ or } 7.8\%$$

Operational income in May is 7.8% of sales revenue, quite high compared to the guideline of 6.5%. At this point, some of the relevant questions to ask are:

● Are sales down? How do May sales compare to the monthly average?

● Are expenses up? How do cost of sales, indirect costs, and individual elements of both compare to monthly averages?

● Is this variance a trend or is it due to unusual circumstances prevailing only in May?

Pretax Profit (Pretax Income, Pretax Earnings)

What is pretax profit?

Pretax profit is the profit left after deducting all expenses from operating and nonoperating income, but before providing for taxes. To obtain this value:

● Add other miscellaneous income (such as sales discounts, gain on sale of fixed assets, interest income, and the like) to operational income.

● Reduce this amount by other deductions (such as interest expense, project abandonments, deferred development, and loss on the sale of fixed assets).

$$\frac{\text{Pretax}}{\text{profit}} = \left(\begin{array}{c}\text{Operating} \\ \text{expenses}\end{array} + \begin{array}{c}\text{Nonoperating} \\ \text{expenses}\end{array}\right) - \left(\begin{array}{c}\text{All expenses} \\ \text{including interest} \\ \text{expense}\end{array}\right)$$

Note: Pretax profit is sometimes known as net income before taxes.

Example: Part of ABC Co.'s income statement looks like this:

Total sales	$ 240,000,000
Cost of sales	176,600,000
Gross profit	$ 63,400,000
G&A expense	$ 13,900,000
Selling expense	11,300,000
Subtotal	$ 25,200,000
Income from operations	$ 38,200,000
Other income	$ 48,000
Interest expense	72,000
Subtotal	$ (24,000)
Pretax profit	**$ 37,960,000**

ABC's pretax profit is $37,960,000.

How is the ratio of pretax profit to sales computed?

An organization's pretax profit (net income before taxes) is divided by total sales.

$$\frac{\text{Pretax-profit-to-}}{\text{sales ratio}} = \frac{\text{Pretax profit}}{\text{Sales}}$$

Example: ABC's pretax profit is $37,960,000, based on sales of $240,000,000,

$$\begin{aligned}\frac{\text{Pretax-profit-to-}}{\text{sales ratio}} &= \frac{\text{Pretax profit}}{\text{Sales}} \\ &= \frac{\$37,960,000}{\$240,000,000} = 0.158, \text{ or } 15.8\%\end{aligned}$$

ABC's pretax profit is a little under 16% of its sales.

Net Income (The Bottom Line)

What is net income?

Net income is the amount left after adding income from other (nonoperational) sources and deducting all expenses and taxes from total sales.

Net income = (Sales + Other income) − (All expenses + Taxes)

Example: ABC Co.'s income statement is as follows:

Total sales	$ 240,000,000
Cost of sales	176,600,000
Gross profit	$ 63,400,000
G&A expense	$ 13,900,000
Selling expense	11,300,000
Subtotal	$ 25,200,000
Income from operations	$ 38,200,000
Other income	$ 48,000
Interest expense	72,000
Subtotal	$ (24,000)
Pretax profit	$ 37,960,000
Taxes (at 50%)	18,980,000
Net income	**$ 18,980,000**

ABC's net income is $18,980,000.

Why are net income ratios important?

Inasmuch as net income represents the "bottom line" of operational success, these ratios are used to assess profitability.

How do you calculate the ratio of net income to sales?

Divide net income by net sales (that is, total sales less allowances for returns and bad debt).

$$\text{Net-income-to-sales ratio} = \frac{\text{Net income}}{\text{Net sales}}$$

Example: ABC Co.'s net income was $18,980,000, which was derived from $240,000,000 in net sales.

$$\text{Net-income-to-sales ratio} = \frac{\text{Net income}}{\text{Net sales}}$$

$$= \frac{\$18,980,000}{\$240,000,000} = 0.08, \text{ or } 8\%$$

ABC Co. earns net income that is equal to 8% of net sales. Put another way, for every dollar of net sales made, ABC earns 8 cents in net income.

Of what use is the net-income-to-sales ratio?

This ratio, if proven valid, enables management to project net income based on sales estimates, as well as to compare actual results against performance in past periods.

Example: ABC Co. projects $265,000,000 in net sales for the upcoming year. In the past, it has earned an average of 8% of sales in net income.

$$\text{Net-income-to-sales ratio} = \frac{\text{Net income (projected)}}{\text{Net sales (estimated)}}$$

$$0.08 = \frac{\text{Net income (projected)}}{\$265,000,000}$$

Or:

$$\text{Net income (projected)} = 0.08 \times \$265,000,000$$
$$= \$21,200,000$$

ABC may reasonably expect a little over $21,200,000 in net income in the coming year.

What is equity?

Equity is a balance sheet entry that is equal the difference between total assets and total liabilities. Also known as shareholders', stockholders', or owners' equity, it includes retained earnings and represents the investors' ownership interest in the company. On the balance sheet equity is the sum of preferred stock, common stock, and retained earnings.

Example: Part of ABC Co.'s balance sheet is as follows:

Corporate bonds (long-term, funded debt)	$ 3,700,000
Common stock and retained earnings	26,010,000
Preferred stock	27,990,000
Total capitalization	$57,700,000

Owners' equity is $57,700,000.

What is the ratio of net income to equity?

This ratio is derived by dividing net income (from the income statement) by stockholders' equity (from the balance sheet).

$$\text{Net-income-to-capital ratio} = \frac{\text{Net income}}{\text{Stockholders' equity}}$$

Example: ABC Co. earned $18,980,000 in net income for 19X0 (income statement).

Pretax profit	$37,960,000	15.8
Taxes (at 50%)	18,980,000	7.9
Net income	$18,980,000	7.9

In the same year, its stockholders' equity (capital) was $57,700,000 (balance sheet).

Stockholders' Equity	
Common stock	$ 3,700,000
Paid-in capital	26,010,000
Retained earnings	27,990,000
Total equity capital	**$57,700,000**

$$\text{Net-income-to-capital ratio} = \frac{\text{Net income}}{\text{Stockholders' equity}}$$

$$= \frac{\$18,980,000}{\$57,700,000} = 0.329, \text{ or } 32.9\%$$

The ratio of net income to stockholders' equity is 32.9%.

Are preferred stock dividends included when calculating the ratio of net income to capital?

It may be. If a corporation has issued preferred stock, then the dividends must be deducted from net income and the par value subtracted from capital (or net worth).

$$\text{Net-income-to-capital ratio} = \frac{\text{Net income} - \text{Preferred dividends}}{\text{Capital} - \text{Preferred stock par value}}$$

Example: ABC Co. earned $18,980,000 in net income for 19X0 (income statement). It must pay a $2.25 dividend on each of 6,000 shares of preferred stock (for a total of $13,500), whose par value is $600,000. In the same year, its stockholders' equity (capital) was $57,700,000 (balance sheet).

Stockholders' Equity	
Common stock	$ 3,700,000
Paid-in capital	26,010,000
Retained earnings	27,990,000
Total equity capital	**$57,700,000**

$$\text{Net-income-to-capital ratio} = \frac{\text{Net income} - \text{Preferred dividends}}{\text{Capital} - \text{Preferred stock par value}}$$

$$= \frac{\$18,980,000 - \$13,500}{\$57,700,000 - \$600,000}$$

$$= \frac{\$18,966,500}{\$57,100,000} = 0.332, \text{ or } 33.2\%$$

The ratio of net income (less preferred dividends) to capital (less preferred stock) is 33.2%.

What does the ratio of net income to equity tell management?

This ratio reflects the return on equity in terms of free-and-clear earnings. Since net income represents profit after all expenses and taxes are paid, this ratio demonstrates how well management is using stockholders' equity to produce profits. The higher the percentage, the better management is "leveraging" equity to produce profits.

What is meant by earnings per common share?

Earnings per common share are equal to net income divided by the number of common shares issued and outstanding. Shares that have been "issued and outstanding" are those that are held by investors. They are to be distinguished from two other types of shares:

● Authorized shares are those that have been authorized by the corporation's state charter, but not issued for public sale. These shares do not enter into the earnings per share computation.

● Treasury stock consists of shares that were authorized, issued for public sale, and then bought back by the corporation. These shares do not enter into the earnings per share calculation. Only issued and outstanding shares are included in the calculation.

$$\text{Earnings per common share} = \frac{\text{Net income}}{\text{Issued and outstanding shares}}$$

Note: The number of shares issued and outstanding varies constantly. The value used for computation is therefore an average figure.

Example: ABC Co. has net income of $18,980,000 and 3,432,188 shares of common stock issued and outstanding.

$$\text{Earnings per common share} = \frac{\text{Net income}}{\text{Issued and outstanding shares}}$$

$$= \frac{\$18,980,000}{3,432,188 \text{ shares}} = \$5.53 \text{ per share}$$

ABC's earnings per common share are $5.53.

Do preferred stock dividends affect earnings per common share?

Yes. If the corporation has an obligation to pay dividends on preferred stock, the amount of dividends must be deducted from net income.

$$\text{Earnings per common share} = \frac{\text{Net income} - \text{Preferred stock dividends}}{\text{Issued and outstanding shares}}$$

Note: The number of shares issued and outstanding varies constantly. The value used for computation is therefore an average figure.

Example: ABC Co. has net income of $18,980,000 and 3,432,188 shares of common stock issued and outstanding. It must also pay a dividend of $1.75 per share of preferred stock, with 500,000 shares of preferred issued and outstanding.

Preferred shares outstanding	500,000
Dividend per share	× $1.75
Total dividends	$875,000

$$\text{Earnings per common share} = \frac{\text{Net income} - \text{Preferred stock dividends}}{\text{Issued and outstanding shares}}$$

$$= \frac{\$18,980,000 - \$875,000}{3,432,188 \text{ shares}}$$

$$= \frac{\$18,105,000}{3,432,188} = \$5.27$$

With preferred stock dividends subtracted from net income, ABC's earnings per common share are $5.27. Compare this amount with the earnings per share in the preceding example.

Who is interested in earnings per share?

Investors are primarily interested in earnings per share, because it reflects the profit flowing to stockholders for each
share held.

Can earnings per share be computed for preferred stock?

Yes. The calculation is the same as for common stock.

$$\frac{\text{Earnings per}}{\text{preferred share}} = \frac{\text{Net income}}{\text{Preferred shares issued and outstanding}}$$

Example: MNO Corp. has $175,000 net income, with 5,000
preferred shares issued and outstanding.

$$\frac{\text{Earnings per}}{\text{preferred share}} = \frac{\text{Net income}}{\text{Preferred shares issued and outstanding}}$$

$$= \frac{\$175,000}{5,000} = \$35 \text{ per share}$$

Earnings per preferred share of MNO Corp. are $35.

HOW MUCH IS THE PRODUCT COSTING THE COMPANY?
COST OF SALES (DIRECT EXPENSES)

What is the cost of sales?

Sometime known as the cost of goods sold, the cost of sales
consists of the expenses that can be directly attributed to the
making of the company's product or the rendering of its
service. Examples of such "direct" costs are assembly line
workers, raw materials that go into the product, equipment
used to produce goods, and so on.

How is the cost of sales compared to sales?

The total cost of sales is divided by the "top line," sales or
revenues.

$$\text{Cost-of-sale-to-sale ratio} = \frac{\text{Cost of sales}}{\text{Sales}}$$

Example: The following monthly data is available for XYZ
Corp.

(in $000,000s)

	Jan
Sales	$44.0
Direct labor	9.6
Overhead	13.0
Material & ODC	15.8
Cost of sales	$38.4
Gross profit	5.6
G&A/selling expenses	2.7
Income from operations	$ 2.9

$$\text{Cost-of-sales-to-sale ratio} = \frac{\text{Cost of sales}}{\text{Sales}}$$

$$= \frac{\$38,400,000}{\$44,000,000} = 0.8727, \text{ or } 87.3\%$$

How is this ratio used?

The ratio is useful in two ways: First, if the organization has established an average ratio of cost of sales (or cost of goods sold, COGS) to sales, it confirms whether an actual cost of sales figure is above or below the historical average. Second, a validated average ratio provides a fairly reliable planning statistic to "ballpark" a total cost of sales value based on a projected sales volume.

How is this sales ratio used to evaluate actual data?

With actual data on hand and a valid historical ratio, an organization can compare them to determine whether the actual figure is above or below average.

Example: XYZ Corp. uses an historically validated cost-of-sales-to-sales ratio of 88.1%. That is, on average, its cost of sales runs 88.1% of total sales volume. For the month of January, XYZ's cost-of-sales-to-sales ratio is 87.3% (see preceding example). This is 0.8% less than the average (88.1% less 87.3%).

How would the cost-of-sales-to-sales ratio assist planners in making projections?

Planners can apply the organization's historically average ratio to the projected sales volume for a given upcoming period, to arrive at an estimated cost of sales.

Example: XYZ Corp.'s sales management projects $36,500,000 in sales for the month of February. The company's average cost-of-sales-to-sales ratio is 88.1%

$$\text{Cost-of-sale-to-sale ratio} = \frac{\text{Cost of sales}}{\text{Sales}}$$

$$0.881 = \frac{\text{Cost of Sales}}{\$36,500,000}$$

Or:

$$\text{Cost of sales} = 0.881 \times \$36,500,000 = \$32,156,500$$

For the month of February, XYZ can expect cost of sales in the neighborhood of $32,156,500.

Can types of costs of sales be evaluated like the overall cost of sales?

Yes. In fact, in many cases it is generally more useful to compare individual types of costs to sales, rather than the overall cost of sales. For each category, however, the formula is the same. Cost of sales consists of several categories:

- Direct labor (personnel)
- Overhead (factory overhead)
- Material and other direct costs (ODC)

$$\text{Cost-of-sales-to-sale ratio} = \frac{\text{Cost of sales}}{\text{Sales}}$$

Example: The following monthly data is available for XYZ Corp.:

(in $000,000s)

	Jan
Sales	$44.0
Direct labor	9.6
Overhead	13.0
Material & ODC	15.8
Cost of sales	$38.4
Gross profit	5.6
G&A/selling expenses	2.7
Income from operations	$ 2.9

$$\text{Cost-of-sales-to-sale ratio} = \frac{\text{Cost of labor}}{\text{Sales}}$$
$$= \frac{\$9,600,000}{\$44,000,000} = 0.2181, \text{ or } 21.8\%$$

$$\text{Cost-of-sales-to-sale ratio} = \frac{\text{Cost of overhead}}{\text{Sales}}$$
$$= \frac{\$13,000,000}{\$44,000,000} = 0.2954, \text{ or } 29.6\%$$

$$\text{Cost-of-sales-} \atop \text{to-sale ratio} = \frac{\text{Cost of material \& ODC}}{\text{Sales}}$$

$$= \frac{\$15,800,000}{\$44,000,000} = 0.3590, \text{ or } 35.9\%$$

Any of the individual cost elements may be used to check the reasonableness of sales projections and/or to estimate costs for upcoming periods.

SELLING, GENERAL, AND ADMINISTRATIVE (G&A) EXPENSES

What are selling, general, and administrative (G&A) expenses?

General and administrative costs are those associated with operating the business such as controller's staffs or procurement. Selling expenses are those related to marketing and administering contracts. Selling, general, and administrative expenses are listed as operating expenses (along with cost of goods sold and depreciation) on the income statement. In many companies, they are itemized as part and parcel of the overall expense reporting format.

Example: XYZ Corp.'s overall cost reporting format for 19X1 is as follows:

(in $000,000s)

Expense	$	‰ of Total Expense*
Indirect labor	27.0	47.4
Misc. labor benefits	3.7	6.5
Retirement plan	1.3	2.3
Management incentive	**0.7**	**1.2**
Supplies	5.4	9.5
Taxes & insurance	2.7	0.6
Depreciation	0.8	1.4
Equipment rentals	2.2	3.9
Utilities	0.8	1.4
Telephone & telegraph	2.7	4.7
Travel	1.4	2.5
Professional/outside services	2.0	3.5
Entertainment	0.6	1.0
Dues and donations	0.5	0.9
Miscellaneous	0.6	1.1
Advertising/promotion	**3.0**	**5.3**
Sales commissions	**1.2**	**2.1**
Total expenses	**$56.60**	**95.30**

*Individual expenses are calculated as ratios of overall expenses; such as executives' compensation.

In the preceding listing. "Management incentive" is a G&A expense, while "advertising/promotion" and "Sales commissions" are selling expenses. The company chooses to isolate other G&A expenses, such as executives compensation.

Can selling/G&A expenses be compared to gross profit?

Yes. The sum of selling, general, and administrative costs is divided by the company's gross profit for the period. The result is a ratio, which may be expressed as a decimal or percentage.

$$\text{Selling-G\&A-to-gross-profit ratio} = \frac{\text{Selling, G\&A (\$)}}{\text{Gross profit}}$$

Example: In 19X1, XYZ Corp. incurred G&A expenses of $1,200,000 and selling expenses of $4,200,000. Its gross profit for the year was $155,000,000.

$$\begin{aligned}
\text{Selling-G\&A-to-gross-profit ratio} &= \frac{\text{Selling, G\&A (\$)}}{\text{Gross profit}} \\
&= \frac{\$4,200,000 + \$1,200,000}{\$155,000,000} \\
&= \frac{\$5,400,000}{\$155,000,000} = 0.0348, \text{ or } 3.5\%
\end{aligned}$$

Does this ratio benefit management?

Yes. If the ratio of selling, general, and administrative costs to gross profit proves to be valid over time, you may apply it to the profit for preliminary values until actual or better data is on hand.

Example: XYZ Corp. projects a gross profit of $169,000,000. Over the years, selling, general, and administrative expenses have come to an average of 3.5% of gross profit.

$$\begin{aligned}
\text{Selling-G\&A-to-gross-profit ratio} &= \frac{\text{Selling, G\&A (\$)}}{\text{Gross profit}} \\
0.035 &= \frac{\text{Selling, G\&A (\$)}}{\$169,000,000}
\end{aligned}$$

Or:

Selling, G&A ($) = $0.035 \times \$169,000,000 = \$5,915,000$

XYZ Corp. may reasonably expect to incur about $5,900,000 in selling, general, and administrative expenses in the coming year.

Can selling/G&A expenses be related to total sales?

Yes. The sum of these expenses is divided by total sales, to produce a ratio that can be expressed as a decimal or percentage.

$$\text{Selling-G\&A-to-total-sales ratio} = \frac{\text{Selling, G\&A (\$)}}{\text{Total sales}}$$

Example: In 19X1, XYZ Corp. incurred G&A expenses of $1,200,000 and selling expenses of $4,200,000. Its total sales for the year were $1,100,000,000.

$$\begin{aligned}
\text{Selling-G\&A-to-total-sales ratio} &= \frac{\text{Selling, G\&A (\$)}}{\text{Total sales}} \\
&= \frac{\$4,200,000 + \$1,200,000}{\$1,100,000,000} \\
&= \frac{\$5,400,000}{\$1,100,000,000} = 0.0049, \text{ or } 0.49\%
\end{aligned}$$

Does this ratio benefit management?

Yes. If the ratio of selling, general, and administrative costs to total sales proves to be valid over time, you may apply it to the profit for preliminary values until actual or better data is on hand.

Example: XYZ Corp. projects total sales of $1,210,000,000. Over the years, selling, general, and administrative expenses have come to an average of 0.49%.

$$\begin{aligned}
\text{Selling-G\&A-to-total-sales ratio} &= \frac{\text{Selling, G\&A (\$)}}{\text{Total sales}} \\
0.0049 &= \frac{\text{Selling, G\&A (\$)}}{\$1,210,000,000}
\end{aligned}$$

Or:

$$\text{Selling, G\&A (\$)} = 0.0049 \times \$1,210,000,000 = \$5,929,000$$

XYZ Corp. may reasonably expect to incur about $5,900,000 in selling, general, and administrative expenses in the coming year.

Note: Compare this estimate with that of the preceding example.

Can selling/G&A expenses be compared to net income?

Yes. The sum of these expenses is divided by net income, to produce a ratio that can be expressed as a decimal or percentage.

$$\text{Selling-G\&A-to-net-income ratio} = \frac{\text{Selling, G\&A (\$)}}{\text{Net income}}$$

Example: In 19X1, XYZ Corp. incurred G&A expenses of $1,200,000 and selling expenses of $4,200,000. Its net income for the year was $49,025,000.

$$\text{Selling-G\&A-to-net-income ratio} = \frac{\text{Selling, G\&A (\$)}}{\text{Net income}}$$

$$= \frac{\$4,200,000 + \$1,200,000}{\$49,025,000}$$

$$= \frac{\$5,400,000}{\$49,025,000} = 0.11, \text{ or } 11\%$$

Selling/G&A expenses are running about 11% of net income.

Does this ratio benefit management?

Yes. If the ratio of selling, general, and administrative costs to net income proves to be valid over time, you may apply it to the profit for preliminary values until actual or better data is on hand.

Example: XYZ Corp. projects next year's net income $53,900,000. Over the years, selling, general, and administrative expenses have come to an average of 11%.

$$\text{Selling-G\&A-to-net-income ratio} = \frac{\text{Selling, G\&A (\$)}}{\text{Net income}}$$

$$0.11 = \frac{\text{Selling, G\&A (\$)}}{\$53,900,000}$$

Or:

$$\text{Selling, G\&A (\$)} = 0.11 \times \$53,900,000 = \$5,929,000$$

XYZ Corp. may reasonably expect to incur about $5,900,000 in selling, general, and administrative expenses in the coming year.

Note: Compare this estimate with those of the preceding two examples.

Can selling/G&A expenses be compared individually to total sales, gross profit, or net income?

Either type of expense can be compared to total sales, gross profit, or net income. In any of these cases, the individual expense is divided by total sales, gross profit, or net income. (Only one formula and example are shown.)

$$\text{Selling-expenses-to-total-sales ratio} = \frac{\text{Selling expenses}}{\text{Total sales}}$$

Example: The following data is available for XYZ Corp.:

Total sales	$1,100,000,000
Net income	49,025,000
Selling expenses:	
Advertising & promotion	$3,000,000
Selling commissions	1,200,000
Total selling expenses	4,200,000

$$\text{Selling-expenses-to-total-sales ratio} = \frac{\text{Selling expenses}}{\text{Total sales}}$$

$$= \frac{\$4,200,000}{\$1,100,000,000} = 0.00382, \text{ or } 0.38\%$$

XYZ's selling expenses come to about 0.38% of total sales.

By applying the preceding general formula, an array of ratios can be developed and trend analysis applied.

Example: XYZ Corp. has put together the following data for the years 19X0 and 19X1:

(in $000s)

	19X1	19X0	Variance ($)	Variance (%)
Total sales	$1,100,000	$995,000	$105,000	+ 10.6
Net income	49,025	38,350	10,675	+ 27.8
Selling expenses:				
Adv. & promo.	3,000	2,800	200	+ 7.1
Commissions	1,200	1,400	(200)	− 14.3
Total	4,200	4,200		
Ratios to Total Sales				
Adv. & promotion	.27%	.28%	−0.01%	− 3.6%
Commisions	.11%	.14%	−0.03%	−21.4%
Ratios to Net Income				
Adv. & promotion	6.1%	7.3%	−1.2%	−16.4%
Commissions	2.4%	3.7%	−1.3%	−35.1%

Ratio to sales:

● The decline in advertising and promotion of 3.6% may have resulted from a greater proportional increase in sales.

● The decrease in commission expense ratio is accounted for by the increase in total sales, which was greater than the increase in commission dollars.

Ratio to net income:

● The ratio of commissions to net income went down primarily because the 27.8% rise in net income more than offset the 7.1% increase in commissions.

- The 35.1% decrease in sales commissions is due to the 27.8% increase in net income versus a 14.3% decline in commissions.

Assuming these expense ratios are consistent from one period to another, their analysis enables management to:

- Assess trends in the relationships between selling expenses and sales volume and/or net income.
- Establish expense limitations and controls.
- Use guidelines based on historical experience for expense surveillance and for planning a realistic selling expense budget.

HOW IS THE COMPANY MANAGING ITS CASH FLOW?

What is cash flow?

Cash flow is the net amount when disbursements are deducted from cash receipts.

$$\text{Cash flow} = \text{Cash receipts} - \text{Cash disbursements}$$

Note: If disbursements are greater than receipts for period, cash flow can be negative.

Example: First-quarter cash receipts for MNO Corp. are $136,900, and its cash disbursements are $144,200.

$$\begin{aligned} \text{Cash flow} &= \text{Cash receipts} - \text{Cash disbursements} \\ &= \$136,900 - \$144,200 = -\$7,300 \end{aligned}$$

In the first quarter, MNO had a negative cash flow of $7,300; that is, it paid out $7,300 more cash than it received.

Which items are considered cash receipts?

Cash receipts include any source, operational or other not, that results in a cash inflow for the organization. In addition to billed sales, receipts can be progress payments, customer advances, investment income, interest on loans, rents on company-owned properties, and so on.

Example: MNO Corp.'s cash receipts for the first quarter are:

Billed sales	$ 58,500
Progress payments	47,300
Customer advances	9,100
Investment income	2,000
Interest on loan	20,000
Total cash receipts	$136,900

What are cash disbursements?

Cash disbursements are any items that result in the flow of cash out of the organization: accounts payable, payroll, federal income taxes, other taxes, deferred compensation fund payments, loan payments, interest payments, lease payments, insurance premium instalments, and so on.

Example: MNO Corp.'s cash disbursement for the first quarter are as follows:

Accounts payable	$ 85,100
Gross payroll	51,000
Income and other taxes	3,400
Retirement fund	3,500
Interest payment	1,100
Total cash disbursements	$144,100

How are cash flow ratios calculated?

Cash flow ratios are comparisons between individual receipt or disbursement items and their related totals.

$$\text{Cash flow ratio} = \frac{\text{Individual receipt item}}{\text{Total receipt}}$$

$$\text{Cash flow ratio} = \frac{\text{Individual disbursement item}}{\text{Total disbursements}}$$

Example: MNO Corp.'s cash receipts for the first quarter are:

Billed sales	$ 58,500
Progress payments	47,300
Customer advances	9,100
Investment income	2,000
Interest on loan	20,000
Total cash receipts	$136,900

Each item of cash receipt can be expressed as a percentage or decimal portion of total receipts. For billed sales:

$$\text{Cash flow ratio} = \frac{\text{Individual receipt item}}{\text{Total receipt}}$$

$$= \frac{\$58,500}{\$136,900} = 0.427, \text{ or } 42.7\%$$

Billed sales represent 42.7% of MNO's first-quarter cash receipts. Each item of receipt can be expressed as a ratio and displayed as a cash receipt schedule:

	$	%
Billed sales	$ 58,500	42.7
Progress payments	47,300	34.6
Customer advances	9,100	6.6
Investment income	2,000	1.5
Interest on loan	20,000	14.6
Total cash receipts	$136,900	100.0

The same can be done for disbursements (using the formula above):

	$	%
Accounts payable	$ 85,100	59.0
Gross payroll	51,000	35.5
Income and other taxes	3,400	2.3
Retirement fund	3,500	2.4
Interest payment	1,100	0.8
Total cash disbursements	$144,100	100.0

What is a cash flow statement?

A cash flow statement consists of two breakdowns: cash receipts and disbursements, with a summary for the organization's net cash position.

Example: On the last day of the prior year's last quarter, MNO Corp. had a cash balance of $8,900. This is the beginning cash balance for this year's first quarter. The company's cash flow statement for the first quarter is as follows:

	$	%
Billed sales	$ 58,500	42.7
Progress payments	47,300	34.6
Customer advances	9,100	6.6
Investment income	2,000	1.5
Interest on loan	20,000	14.6
Total cash receipts	$ 136,900	100.0
Accounts payable	$ 85,100	59.0
Gross payroll	51,000	35.5
Income and other taxes	3,400	2.3
Retirement fund	3,500	2.4
Interest payment	1,100	0.8
Total cash disbursements	$ 144,100	100.0
Net cash increase (decrease)	$ (7,300)	
Beginning balance	8,900	
Ending balance	$ 1,600	

MNO Corp. had a first-quarter net cash position of $1,600. This becomes the beginning balance for the second quarter.

What do cash ratios do for management?

Cash ratios enable management to determine the sources of greatest cash inflow and outflow, and possibly to take steps to improve the organization's overall cash position.

Example: Given MNO Corp.'s cash flow statement (see preceding example), several observations can be made:

- The company came dangerously close to a negative net cash position in the first quarter.

- Billed sales and progress payments represent the major portion (approximately 88%) of receipts. Remedial measures are probably best focused on these areas, as opposed to areas with lesser contributions to a positive cash position. Steps must be taken to increase billings and/or collections in the next quarter.

- Measures might also be considered that will limit or defer second-quarter disbursements.

- Borrowed funds to meet short-term cash needs are a possibility too.

How are cash flow ratios analyzed for reasonableness?

Cash ratios may be compared to industry standards or to the organization's annual figures. The rational is that, the year being statistically a larger "sample" of historical data than a month or a quarter, it may act as a norm for shorter periods.

Example: Part of MNO Corp.'s annual cash flow statement is as follows:

	First Quarter		Annual	
	$	%	$	%
Billed sales	$ 58,500	42.7	$318,000	50.1
Progress payments	47,300	34.6	240,700	37.8
Customer advances	9,100	6.6	44,800	7.0
Investment income	2,000	1.5	7,900	1.2
Interest on loan	20,000	14.6	25,000	3.9
Total cash receipts	$ 136,900	100.0	$636,400	100.0
Accounts payable	$ 85,100	59.0	$367,600	60.8
Gross payroll	51,000	35.5	213,100	35.3
Income and other taxes	3,400	2.3	6,400	1.1
Retirement fund	3,500	2.4	10,700	1.8
Interest payment	1,100	0.8	6,500	1.1
Total cash disbursements	$ 144,100	100.0	$604,300	100.0

Net cash increase			
(decrease)	$ (7,300)	$ 3,080	
Beginning balance	8,900	8,900	
Ending balance	$ 1,600	$ 11,980	

- Year-end billed sales collections (50.1%) are 7.4% greater than those of the first quarter (42.7%).

- Year-end progress payment collections (37.8%) also lead first-quarter receipts (34.6%).

- The annual accounts payable and gross payroll ratios (60.8% and 35.3%) are lower than the first quarter levels (59.0% and 35.5%).
  All-in-all, MNO Corp. had a weak first quarter, compared to the company's annual figures.

Are there other ways to analyze a company's cash position?

There are significant relationships among an organization's billed sales, cash receipts, and accounts receivable. Management can learn much by monitoring the relevant ratios, which are:

- Cash receipts to billed sales and progress payments
- Ending accounts receivable to billed sales and progress payments
- Ending accounts receivable to the sum of billed sales, progress payments, and the beginning cash balance
- Ending accounts receivable to cash receipts
- Cash receipts to ending accounts receivable

Any of these cash flow ratios may be used, if proven valid over time, to assist in projecting cash positions in upcoming periods.

What is the ratio of cash receipts to billed sales and progress payments?

To arrive at this ratio for a given period, divide cash receipts by the sum of billed sales and progress payments.

$$\text{Cash-receipts-to-billed-sales-plus-progress-payments ratio} = \frac{\text{Cash receipts}}{\text{Billed sales} + \text{Progress payments}}$$

Example: MNO Corp.'s annual billed sales and progress payments are $560,000; its cash receipt, $558,200.

$$\begin{aligned}\text{Cash-receipts-to-billed-}\\\text{sales-plus-progress-}\\\text{payments ratio}\end{aligned} &= \frac{\text{Cash receipts}}{\begin{aligned}\text{Billed sales +}\\\text{Progress payments}\end{aligned}}$$

$$= \frac{\$558,200}{\$560,000} = 0.997, \text{ or } 99.7\%$$

Cash receipts represent over 99% of billed sales and progress payments.

How do you compute the ratio between the ending accounts receivable balance and the sum of billed sales and progress payments?

To calculate this ratio for a non-annual period, divide the end-of-period accounts receivable balance by the sum of billed sales and progress payments.

$$\begin{aligned}\text{Ending-receivables-}\\\text{to-billed-sales-plus-}\\\text{progress-payments}\\\text{ratio}\end{aligned} = \frac{\text{Ending accounts receivable}}{\begin{aligned}\text{Billed}\\\text{sales}\end{aligned} + \begin{aligned}\text{Progress}\\\text{payments}\end{aligned}}$$

For an annual period, the billed sales and progress payments have to be converted to an average quarterly figure, that is, divided by 4. The annual total represents the sum of 4 quarters' worth of cash inflow, while the ending accounts receivable balance is the same as the fourth-quarter ending balance.

$$\begin{aligned}\text{Ending-receivables-}\\\text{to-billed-sales-}\\\text{plus-progress-}\\\text{payments ratio}\end{aligned} = \frac{\text{Ending accounts receivable}}{\left(\begin{aligned}\text{Billed}\\\text{sales}\end{aligned} + \begin{aligned}\text{Progress}\\\text{payments}\end{aligned}\right)/4}$$

Example: MNO Corp.'s annual billed sales and progress payments are $560,000; its end-of-year accounts receivable balance, $34,400.

$$\begin{aligned}\text{Ending-receivables-}\\\text{to-billed-sales-}\\\text{plus-progress-}\\\text{payments ratio}\end{aligned} = \frac{\text{Ending accounts receivable}}{\left(\begin{aligned}\text{Billed}\\\text{sales}\end{aligned} + \begin{aligned}\text{Progress}\\\text{payments}\end{aligned}\right)/4}$$

$$= \frac{\$34,400}{\$560,000 \,/4}$$

$$= \frac{\$34,400}{\$140,000} = 0.246, \text{ or } 24.6\%$$

The end-of-year accounts receivable balance represents almost 25% of the average quarterly sales billings and progress payments.

How do you compute the ratio between the ending accounts receivable balance and the sum of billed sales, progress payments, and beginning balance?

To calculate this ratio for a nonannual period, divide the end-of-period accounts receivable balance by the sum of billed sales, progress payments, and the beginning cash balance.

$$\text{Ending-receivables-to-billed-sales,-progress-payments,-and-beginning-balance ratio} = \frac{\text{Ending accounts receivable}}{\text{Billed sales} + \text{Progress payments} + \text{Beginning cash balance}}$$

For an annual period, the total of billed sales and progress payments has to be converted to an average quarterly figure, that is, divided by 4. The annual total represents the sum of 4 quarters' worth of cash inflow, while the ending accounts receivable balance is the same as the fourth-quarter ending balance. The annual beginning cash balance is the same as the first quarter's.

$$= \frac{\text{Ending accounts receivable}}{\left(\text{Billed sales} + \text{Progress payments}\right)/4 + \text{Beginning cash balance}}$$

Example: MNO Corp.'s annual billed sales and progress payments are $560,000, its end-of-year accounts receivable balance $34,400, and the first-quarter beginning cash balance $32,600.

$$= \frac{\text{Ending accounts receivable}}{\left(\text{Billed sales} + \text{Progress payments}\right)/4 = \text{Beginning cash balance}}$$

$$= \frac{\$34,400}{\$560,000/4 + \$32,600}$$

$$= \frac{\$34,400}{\$140,000 + \$32,600}$$

$$= \frac{\$34,400}{\$172,600} = 0.199, \text{ or } 19.9\%$$

The end-of-year accounts receivable balance represents almost 20% of the sum of the average quarterly sales billings and progress payments plus the beginning cash balance.

What is the ratio of the ending receivable balance to cash receipts?

To compute this ratio, divide cash receipt total by the given period's ending accounts receivable balance.

$$\text{Cash-receipts-to-ending-receivables ratio} = \frac{\text{Cash receipts}}{\text{Ending receivables}}$$

For the annual ratio, the cash receipts total must be divided by 4, so as to convert it to an average quarterly figure. (The ending receivables balance is the fourth-quarter's ending balance.)

$$\text{Cash-receipts-to-ending-receivables ratio} = \frac{\text{Cash receipts}/4}{\text{Ending receivables}}$$

Example: MNO Corp.'s end-of-year cash receipts total is $558,200, and its fourth-quarter ending accounts receivables balance, $34,400.

$$\text{Cash-receipts-to-ending-receivables ratio} = \frac{\text{Cash receipts}/4}{\text{Ending receivables}}$$

$$= \frac{\$558,200/4}{\$34,400}$$

$$= \frac{\$139,550}{\$34,400} = 4.057, \text{ or } 405.7\%$$

CHAPTER 2

THE ORGANIZATION'S FINANCIAL STATUS: ANALYZING THE BALANCE SHEET

WORDS TO KNOW

Accounting equation. The equation reflected in the balance sheet: assets − liabilities = stockholders' equity.

Accounts payable. Cash amounts that the corporation owes to others.

Accounts receivable. Cash amounts that are owed to the corporation as the result of sales.

Accumulated depreciation. The total of all depreciation taken on a fixed asset since the year it was purchased through the current year.

Asset. Something of value that is owned by or owed to the corporation.

Balance sheet. A financial statement that contains the three primary elements of a business enterprise: assets, liabilities, and stockholders' (shareholders', owners') equity. The three elements must "balance" out according to the so-called accounting equation: Assets = Liabilities + Equity.

Capital. *See* Stockholders' equity.

Capitalization. *See* Stockholders' equity.

Capitalization structure. *See* Capital structure.

Capital structure. How a company's capital is derived, such as from investors or from lenders (e.g., bondholders).

Credit sales. *See* Total credit sales.

Common stock. Shares reflecting ownership in a corporation that are bought and sold in the open market by investors.

The common stock entry on the balance sheet reflects the par value only.

Cost of goods sold. *See* Cost of sales.

Cost of sales (cost of goods sold). The cost of making or buying a product sold, or of providing a service rendered, consisting of direct personnel, direct materials (and other direct costs), and factory overhead.

Current asset. An asset whose useful life is less than one year, such as cash, securities, accounts receivable.

Deferred charges. An expense that has been incurred but whose payment, for whatever reasons, has been put off until some time in the future.

Depreciation. Distribution of the original cost of a fixed asset, such as a building or fleet of cars, over the number of years in the asset's useful life.

Direct material. An element of cost of sales, the cost of materials used in making a product or in rendering a service.

Direct personnel (labor). The portion of cost of sales attributable to paying employees who are directly involved in the production of goods.

Equity capital. *See* Stockholders' equity.

Factory overhead. An element of cost of sales, the part of factory overhead directly attributable to making a product. (Some fixed factory costs may be regarded as indirect costs.)

Finished goods. Product that has been completed and is awaiting shipment.

Fixed asset. An asset whose useful life is greater than one year, such as a manufacturing plant, an office building, or heavy equipment.

Gross profit. The difference between sales and cost of sales.Indirect personnel (labor).

Inventory. Goods owned by the corporation, in the form of raw materials, work in process, or finished goods.

Investors' capital. *See* Stockholders' equity.

Liability. A debt or obligation of the corporation.

Long-term Debt. Debt whose term is greater than one year, such as a ten-year bank loan or a thirty-year corporate bond issue.

Marketable security. A security that is easily traded, such as a stock or bond.

Net fixed assets. Fixed assets less accumulate depreciation.

Owners' equity. *See* Stockholders' equity.

Paid-in Capital. Money taken in by the corporation for the sale of stock.

Preferred stock. Shares reflecting ownership in a corporation that pay fixed dividends.

Prepaid expenses. An asset in the form of an expense, such as rent or insurance premiums, that has been paid in advance.

Raw materials. Materials used in the making of finished goods.

Retained earnings. The earnings that a corporation accumulates since its startup—profits that are "kept," as opposed to being distributed as dividends.

Sales. *See* Total credit sales.

Shareholders' equity. *See* Stockholders' equity.

Stockholders' (shareholders', owners') equity (equity capital, investors' capital, capital, capitalization). The difference between total assets and total liabilities. It represents the investors' ownership interest in the company.

Vertical analysis. Each balance sheet entry within a total (such as cash or notes payable) is divided by the total itself (such as total assets or total current liabilities). The resulting ratio is then placed next to the dollar amount of the entry in the balance sheet.

Work in process (progress). Product that is not yet completed, such as automobiles partly through the assembly line.

FAMILIARIZING WITH THE BALANCE SHEET

What is the balance sheet?

The balance sheet is a financial statement that contains the three primary elements of a business enterprise: assets, liabilities, and stockholders' (shareholders', owners') equity. The three elements must "balance" out according to the so-called accounting equation:

$$\text{Assets} = \text{Liabilities} + \text{Equity}$$

Note: Since the balance sheet is a "snapshot" of a company's financial condition, it is sometimes called the statement of financial position.

Example: Note in the following balance sheet how total assets equals the sum of total liabilities and stockholders' equity.

ABC Co.
Balance Sheet
19X0 (in $000,000s)

	Amount	
Current Assets		
Cash	$ 3.50	
Marketable securities	3.30	
Accounts receivable	28.70	
Inventories		
Raw materials	26.80	
Work in process	10.70	
Finished goods	7.30	
Subtotal	44.80	
Prepaid expenses	0.25	
Total current assets	$80.55	
Property, Plant, and Equipment		
Land	$ 2.30	
Buildings/improvement	20.00	
Machinery/equipment	31.40	
Subtotal	$53.70	
Less: Accumulated depr'n.	17.90	
Net fixed assets	$35.80	
Deferred Charges	0.90	
Total assets		**$117.25**
Current Liabilities		
Notes payable	$ 1.40	
Current portion—LT debt	2.50	
Accrued payroll	3.60	
Accounts payable	20.85	
Income tax payable	2.60	
Total current liabilities	$30.95	
Deferred Income Taxes	1.90	
Long-Term Debt	26.70	
Total liabilities		**$ 59.55**
Stockholders' Equity		
Common stock	$ 3.70	
Paid-in capital	26.01	
Retained earnings	27.99	
Total equity capital		**$ 57.70**
Total liabilities/capital		**$117.25**

What is vertical analysis?

The vertical approach to balance sheet analysis, each entry within a total (such as cash or notes payable) is divided by the total itself (such as total assets or total current liabilities). The resulting ratio is then placed next to the dollar amount of the entry in the balance sheet.

$$\text{Vertical analysis ratio} = \frac{\text{Individual entry}}{\text{Total}}$$

Example: Part of ABC Co.'s balance sheet is as follows:

ABC Co.
Balance Sheet
19X0 (in $000,000s)

	Amount
Current Assets	
Cash	$ 3.50
Marketable securities	3.30
Accounts receivable	28.70
Inventories	
Raw materials	26.80
Work in process	10.70
Finished goods	7.30
Subtotal	44.80
Prepaid expenses	0.25
Total current assets	$ 80.55
Property, Plant, and Equipment	
Land	$ 2.30
Buildings/improvement	20.00
Machinery/equipment	31.40
Subtotal	$ 53.70
Less: Accumulated depr'n.	17.90
Net fixed assets	$ 35.80
Deferred Charges	0.90
Total assets	$117.25

To do a vertical analysis of ABC's current assets, each entry under current assets is divided by total assets. Use cash as an example.

$$\begin{aligned} \text{Vertical analysis ratio} &= \frac{\text{Individual entry}}{\text{Total}} \\ &= \frac{\text{Cash}}{\text{Total assets}} \\ &= \frac{\$3,500,000}{\$117,250,000} = 0.0299, \text{ or } 3.0\% \end{aligned}$$

Cash represents 3.0% of ABC's total assets. A ratio can be calculated for each of the other entries in the assets section of the ABC balance sheet.

ABC Co.
Balance Sheet
19X0 (in $000,000s)

	Amount	Ratio
Current Assets		
Cash	$ 3.50	3.0
Marketable securities	3.30	2.8
Accounts receivable	28.70	24.5
Inventories		
Raw materials	26.80	22.9
Work in process	10.70	9.1
Finished goods	7.30	6.2
Subtotal	44.80	38.2
Prepaid expenses	0.25	0.2
Total current assets	$ 80.55	68.7
Property, Plant, and Equipment		
Land	$ 2.30	2.0
Buildings/improvement	20.00	17.1
Machinery/equipment	31.40	26.7
Subtotal	$ 53.70	45.8
Less: Accumulated depr'n.	17.90	15.3
Net fixed assets	$ 35.80	30.5
Deferred Charges	0.90	0.8
Total assets	$117.25	100.0

Can vertical analysis be applied to the balance sheet as a whole?

Yes. Within each of the three components of the balance sheet (assets, liabilities, owners'/stockholders' equity), individual entries can be compared to the totals. The same formula applies throughout the statement.

$$\text{Vertical analysis ratio} = \frac{\text{Individual entry}}{\text{Total}}$$

Example: ABC's 19X0 balance sheet can be analyzed as follows:

ABC Co.
Balance Sheet
19X0 (in $000,000s)

	Amount	Ratio
Current Assets		
Cash	$ 3.50	3.0
Marketable securities	3.30	2.8
Accounts receivable	28.70	24.5
Inventories		
Raw materials	26.80	22.9
Work in process	10.70	9.1
Finished goods	7.30	6.2
Subtotal	44.80	38.2
Prepaid expenses	0.25	0.2
Total current assets	$ 80.55	68.7
Property, Plant, and Equipment		
Land	$ 2.30	2.0
Buildings/improvement	20.00	17.1
Machinery/equipment	31.40	26.7
Subtotal	$ 53.70	45.8
Less: Accumulated depr'n.	17.90	15.3
Net fixed assets	$ 35.80	30.5
Deferred Charges	0.90	0.8
Total assets	$117.25	100.0
Current Liabilities		
Notes payable	$ 1.40	1.2
Current portion—LT debt	2.50	2.1
Accrued payroll	3.60	3.1
Accounts payable	20.85	17.8
Income tax payable	2.60	2.2
Total current liabilities	$ 30.95	26.4
Deferred Income Taxes	1.90	1.6
Long-Term Debt	26.70	22.8
Total liabilities	$ 59.55	50.8
Stockholders' Equity		
Common stock	$ 3.70	3.1
Paid-in capital	26.01	22.2
Retained earnings	27.99	23.9
Total equity capital	$ 57.70	49.2
Total liabilities/capital	$117.25	100.0

Of what benefit is vertical analysis?

Vertical analysis provides management with a snapshot of
the composition of assets, liabilities, and equity. If the proportion of an individual entry changes from one period to the

next, management can monitor the change and take the appropriate action. Also, the ratios can be compared to industry standards, to determine whether the organization is within the norms.

Note: When developing ratios for guidelines or for comparisons with industry norms, you generally obtain more reliable results by using averaged balance sheet data, not just data from one period.

Example: In the following portion of ABC Co.'s 19X0 balance sheet, accounts receivable ($28,700,000) and inventories ($44,800,000) represent the major elements in current assets.

(in $000,000s)

	Amount	Ratio
Current Assets		
Cash	$ 3.50	3.0
Marketable securities	3.30	2.8
Accounts receivable	**28.70**	**24.5**
Inventories		
Raw materials	**26.80**	**22.9**
Work in process	**10.70**	**9.1**
Finished goods	**7.30**	**6.2**
Subtotal	**44.80**	**38.2**
Prepaid expenses	0.25	0.2
Total current assets	$ 80.55	68.7
Property, Plant, and Equipment		
Land	$ 2.30	2.0
Buildings/improvement	20.00	17.1
Machinery/equipment	31.40	26.7
Subtotal	$ 53.70	45.8
Less: Accumulated depr'n.	17.90	15.3
Net fixed assets	$ 35.80	30.5
Deferred Charges	0.90	0.8
Total assets	$117.25	100.0

In 19X1, the ratio of accounts receivable to total assets rises to 27.9%, and the ratio of inventories drops slightly to 38.0%. While the effect on total assets is negligible (and, in fact, total assets increase), management must investigate the changes in the ratios of the individual entries. One possible explanation is that, given a rise in sales, ABC has been filling orders at a greater pace than it did last year. This might explain why receivables are up and inventories down.

ASSETS

Fixed Assets

Can fixed assets be compared to total assets?

The ratio of fixed to total assets (both balance sheet entries) is a useful one.

$$\text{Fixed-assets-to-total-assets ratio} = \frac{\text{Fixed assets}}{\text{Total assets}}$$

Example: The assets part of the ABC Co. balance is as follows:

	Amount
Current Assets	
Cash	$ 3,500,000
Marketable securities	3,300,000
Accounts receivable	28,700,000
Inventories	
Raw materials	26,800,000
Work in process	10,700,000
Finished goods	7,300,000
Subtotal	44,800,000
Prepaid expenses	250,000
Total current assets	$ 80,550,000
Property, Plant, and Equipment	
Land	$ 2,300,000
Buildings/improvement	20,000,000
Machinery/equipment	31,400,000
Subtotal	$ 53,700,000
Less: Accumulated depr'n.	17,900,000
Net fixed assets	**$ 35,800,000**
Deferred Charges	900,000
Total assets	**$117,250,000**

$$\text{Fixed-assets-to-total-assets ratio} = \frac{\text{Fixed assets}}{\text{Total assets}}$$

$$= \frac{\$35,800,000}{\$117,250,000} = 0.305, \text{ or } 30.5\%$$

ABC's fixed assets represent 30.5% of its total assets.

How does the fixed-to-total-assets ratio serve management?

This ratio helps in two ways:

- As a guideline in estimating fixed assets expenditures given total assets.
- As a tool in measuring fixed asset growth in proportion to total assets.

Example: ABC Co. has determined that fixed assets have maintained a steady level at 30% of total assets. In 19X1, total assets are $124,500,000 and fixed assets $41,200,000.

$$\text{Fixed-assets-to-total-assets ratio} = \frac{\text{Fixed assets}}{\text{Total assets}}$$

$$= \frac{\$41,200,000}{\$124,500,000} = 0.331, \text{ or } 33.1\%$$

This is slightly higher than ABC's guideline of 30%.

Can fixed assets be compared to stockholders' equity?

Yes. Fixed assets are divided by stockholders' (shareholders', owners') equity (both balance sheet entries).

$$\text{Fixed-assets-to-stockholders'-equity ratio} = \frac{\text{Stockholders' equity}}{\text{Fixed assets}}$$

Note: Average values should be used for fixed assets and equity.

Example: The relevant portions of ABC Co. balance sheet are as follows:

Property, Plant, and Equipment	
Land	$ 2,300,000
Buildings/improvement	20,000,000
Machinery/equipment	31,400,000
Subtotal	$53,700,000
Less: Accumulated depr'n.	17,900,000
Net fixed assets	**$35,800,000**
• • •	
Stockholders' Equity	
Common stock	$ 3,700,000
Paid-in capital	26,010,000
Retained earnings	27,990,000
Total equity capital	**$57,700,000**

$$\text{Fixed-assets-to-stockholders'-equity ratio} = \frac{\text{Fixed assets}}{\text{Stockholders' equity}}$$

$$= \frac{\$35,800,000}{\$57,700,000} = 0.620, \text{ or } 62.0\%$$

Fixed assets represent 62% of ABC's equity.

What does the fixed-asset-to-equity ratio mean?

This ratio indicates the percentage of an organization's fixed assets that financed with the owners' equity (capital). Large fixed asset investments mean two things:

- They lead to greater fixed costs (depreciation, taxes, maintenance, and so on), with its related higher breakeven point. If sales volume drops, profit margins suffer immediately.

- They detract funds from working capital, which means lower accounts receivables, inventory, and cash. A company in such a situation may not have enough working capital to meet the requirements of increased sales volumes. In the absence of an overriding reason for such large fixed asset commitments, this condition usually reflects an inefficient use of capital.

Arriving at a "reasonable" ratio depends the nature and needs of the individual business.

What is the fixed asset turnover?

The fixed asset turnover is a comparison of annualized sales (the "top line" of the income statement) to the average value of fixed assets (a balance sheet item).

$$\frac{\text{Fixed asset}}{\text{turnover}} = \frac{\text{Sales}}{\text{Fixed assets}}$$

Example: With annual sales of $240,000,000, ABC Co. has fixed assets of $35,800,000.

Property, Plant, and Equipment	
Land	$ 2,300,000
Buildings/improvement	20,000,000
Machinery/equipment	31,400,000
Subtotal	$53,700,000
Less: Accumulated depr'n.	17,900,000
Net fixed assets	**$35,800,000**

$$\begin{align} \text{Fixed asset} \atop \text{turnover} &= \frac{\text{Sales}}{\text{Fixed assets}} \\ &= \frac{\$240,000,000}{\$35,800,000} = 6.70 \end{align}$$

ABC enjoys a sales volume that is 6.70 times the value of its fixed assets.

What does the fixed asset turnover reflect?

This ratio may be used to assess performance, but with caution. For example, comparing the turnover ratios of two or more organizations may be misleading if some rent buildings while others own them. Heavy depreciation will increase fixed assets and lower the turnover ratio, while lease payments will lead to a higher ratio.

The ratio is also useful as a planning guideline. It can uncover too much or too little capacity, that is, either too much or too little plant and equipment to support a given sales volume.

How may sales be related to fixed assets?

Sales (from the income statement) may be expressed as a multiple of the average value of fixed assets (a balance sheet entry).

$$\text{Fixed-assets-to} \atop \text{sales ratio} = \frac{\text{Sales}}{\text{Fixed assets}}$$

Example: With annual sales of $240,000,000, ABC Co. has fixed assets of $35,800,000.

Property, Plant, and Equipment	
Land	$ 2,300,000
Buildings/improvement	20,000,000
Machinery/equipment	31,400,000
Subtotal	$53,700,000
Less: Accumulated depr'n.	17,900,000
Net fixed assets	**$35,800,000**

$$\begin{align} \text{Fixed-assets-to} \atop \text{sales ratio} &= \frac{\text{Sales}}{\text{Fixed assets}} \\ &= \frac{\$240,000,000}{\$35,800,000} = 6.70 \end{align}$$

ABC's sales are 6.70 times that of its average fixed assets.

What is the meaning of the sales-to-fixed-assets ratio?

While fixed assets in themselves do not produce sales, without them only limited sales can be made in a product-oriented company. This ratio can provide insight as to whether an organization has too much capacity or too little for a given sales volume.

Note: When comparing ratios of many organizations in the same industry, consider the age of the assets, price levels at the time of purchase, and the depreciation policies with their related effect on fixed asset valuation. For example, a low ratio could indicate an excessive valuation of the fixed assets without a comparable increase in sales.

LIABILITIES

Is there reason to compare total liabilities to total assets?

Yes. The average value of total liabilities (total debt) can be divided by the average total assets.

$$\text{Total-debt-to-total-assets ratio} = \frac{\text{Total debt (liabilities)}}{\text{Total assets}}$$

Example: ABC Co.'s balance sheet, in part, looks like this:

	Amount
Current Assets	
Cash	$ 3,500,000
Marketable securities	3,300,000
Accounts receivable	28,700,000
Inventories	
Raw materials	26,800,000
Work in process	10,700,000
Finished goods	7,300,000
Subtotal	44,800,000
Prepaid expenses	250,000
Total current assets	$ 80,550,000
Property, Plant, and Equipment	
Land	$ 2,300,000
Buildings/improvement	20,000,000
Machinery/equipment	31,400,000
Subtotal	$ 53,700,000
Less: Accumulated depr'n.	17,900,000
Net fixed assets	$ 35,800,000
Deferred Charges	900,000
Total assets	**$117,250,000**

Current Liabilities	
Notes payable	$ 1,400,000
Current portion—LT debt	2,500,000
Accrued payroll	3,600,000
Accounts payable	20,850,000
Income tax payable	2,600,000
Total current liabilities	$ 30,950,000
Deferred Income Taxes	1,900,000
Long-Term Debt	26,700,000
Total liabilities	**$ 59,550,000**

$$\text{Total-debt-to-total-assets ratio} = \frac{\text{Total debt (liabilities)}}{\text{Total assets}}$$

$$= \frac{\$59,550,000}{\$117,250,000} = 0.508, \text{ or } 50.8\%$$

ABC's total debt represents about 50% of its total assets.

What can you tell from the ratio of total debt to total assets?

This ratio is a gauge of how much total debt an organization can incur and still cope without financial difficulty. While a universal ratio is not possible, certainly a ratio over 50% is subject to question: More than half of the company's total assets would be financed on a short-term basis by vendors and creditors.

How are fixed assets compared to long-term debt?

Fixed assets (property, plant, and equipment) can divided by long-term (funded) debt, both balance sheet items.

$$\text{Fixed-assets-to-long-term-debt ratio} = \frac{\text{Fixed assets}}{\text{Long-term debt}}$$

Example: ABC's balance sheet, in part, looks like this:

Property, Plant, and Equipment	
Land	$ 2,300,000
Buildings/improvement	20,000,000
Machinery/equipment	31,400,000
Subtotal	$ 53,700,000
Less: Accumulated depr'n.	17,900,000
Net fixed assets	$ 35,800,000
Deferred Charges	900,000
Total assets	**$117,250,000**

Current Liabilities
  Notes payable $ 1,400,000
  Current portion—LT debt   2,500,000
  Accrued payroll   3,600,000
  Accounts payable   20,850,000
  Income tax payable   2,600,000
    Total current liabilities $ 30,950,000

Deferred Income Taxes   1,900,000

Long-Term Debt   **26,700,000**

    Total liabilities $ 59,550,000

$$\text{Fixed-assets-to-long-term-debt ratio} = \frac{\text{Fixed assets}}{\text{Long-term debt}}$$

$$= \frac{\$117,250,000}{\$26,700,000} = 4.39$$

ABC's fixed assets are worth 4.39 times its long-term debt.

What does the ratio of fixed assets to long-term debt mean to analysts?

This comparison reflects the general degree of protection for the bondholders' investment, providing the bondholders have priority claims on the assets. The adequacy of an individual ratio can be determined only by experience from period to period or by comparison with industry norms.

How are total assets compared to long-term debt?

Total assets are divided by the amount of long-term debt (both balance sheet entries), to arrive at the asset coverage ratio.

$$\text{Asset coverage ratio} = \frac{\text{Total assets}}{\text{Long-term debt}}$$

Example: ABC Co.'s balance sheet, in part, looks like this:

	Amount
Current Assets	
Cash	$ 3,500,000
Marketable securities	3,300,000
Accounts receivable	28,700,000

Inventories	
Raw materials	26,800,000
Work in process	10,700,000
Finished goods	7,300,000
Subtotal	44,800,000
Prepaid expenses	250,000
Total current assets	$ 80,550,000
Property, Plant, and Equipment	
Land	$ 2,300,000
Buildings/improvement	20,000,000
Machinery/equipment	31,400,000
Subtotal	$ 53,700,000
Less: Accumulated depr'n.	17,900,000
Net fixed assets	$ 35,800,000
Deferred Charges	900,000
Total assets	**$117,250,000**
Current Liabilities	
Notes payable	$ 1,400,000
Current portion—LT debt	2,500,000
Accrued payroll	3,600,000
Accounts payable	20,850,000
Income tax payable	2,600,000
Total current liabilities	$ 30,950,000
Deferred Income Taxes	1,900,000
Long-Term Debt	**26,700,000**
Total liabilities	$ 59,550,000

$$\text{Asset coverage ratio} = \frac{\text{Total assets}}{\text{Long-term debt}}$$

$$= \frac{\$117,250,000}{\$59,550,000} = 1.97$$

ABC Co. has its long-term debt covered nearly two times over by the value of its total assets.

What is the significance of the asset coverage ratio?

This ratio indicates the safety of the lender's capital. The greater the ratio, the greater the security.

STOCKHOLDERS' EQUITY

What is stockholders' equity?

Stockholders' (shareholders' or owners') equity—sometimes known as investors' capital, or just capital—is equal to the difference between an organization's assets and its liabilities.

$$\text{Equity} = \text{Assets} - \text{Liabilities}$$

It is the third component of a balance sheet.

Example: In the following balance sheet, note that total assets are equal to total liabilities plus stockholders' equity.

ABC Co.
Balance Sheet
19X0 (in $000,000s)

	Amount
Current Assets	
Cash	$ 3.50
Marketable securities	3.30
Accounts receivable	28.70
Inventories	
Raw materials	26.80
Work in process	10.70
Finished goods	7.30
Subtotal	44.80
Prepaid expenses	0.25
Total current assets	$ 80.55
Property, Plant, and Equipment	
Land	$ 2.30
Buildings/improvement	20.00
Machinery/equipment	31.40
Subtotal	$ 53.70
Less: Accumulated depr'n.	17.90
Net fixed assets	$ 35.80
Deferred Charges	0.90
Total assets	**$117.25**
Current Liabilities	
Notes payable	$ 1.40
Current portion—LT debt	2.50
Accrued payroll	3.60
Accounts payable	20.85
Income tax payable	2.60
Total current liabilities	$ 30.95

Deferred Income Taxes	1.90
Long-Term Debt	26.70
Total liabilities	**$ 59.55**
Stockholders' Equity	
Common stock	$ 3.70
Paid-in capital	26.01
Retained earnings	27.99
Total equity capital	**$ 57.70**
Total liabilities/capital	**$117.25**

$$\text{Equity} = \text{Assets} - \text{Liabilities}$$
$$= \$117,250,000 - \$59,550,000$$
$$= \$57,700,000$$

What makes stockholders' equity change?

Stockholders' equity (or capital) increases if assets increase and/or if liabilities decrease. Equity declines if the value of assets drops or if liabilities rise.

$$\text{Equity} = \text{Assets} - \text{Liabilities}$$

Example: ABC Co.'s total assets, total liabilities, and stockholders' equity were as follows for 19X0:

$$\text{Equity} = \text{Assets} - \text{Liabilities}$$
$$\$57,700,000 = \$117,250,000 - \$59,550,000$$

In 19X1, total assets rise to $117,300,000, but total liabilities rose to $61,100,000. With the rise in liabilities more than offsetting the increase in assets, stockholders' equity must drop.

$$\text{Equity} = \text{Assets} - \text{Liabilities}$$
$$= \$117,300,000 - \$61,100,000 = \$56,200,000$$

ABC's equity in 19X1 is $56,200,000, compared to $59,550,000 in 19X0.

How is stockholders' equity analyzed?

Stockholders' equity (or capital) is analyzed by means of a number of ratios:

- Capital structure ratio
- Investors' capital to sales

- Net income to capital (or net worth, equity)
- Retained earnings to capital
- Capital to total liabilities
- Capital to noncurrent assets
- Capital employed
- Rate of return on capital employed (sometimes known as net income to total assets)
- Current debt to stockholders' equity

What is capital structure?

The phrase capital structure has different meanings to various people. Organizational accountants and analysts use the term capital to identify the organization's equity, that is, the funds invested in the company by investors. Investment analysts, concerned with the broader aspect of the capital structure, include not only owners' equity but also long-term creditors' loans. This long-term (funded) debt may take the form of bond issues or notes to financial institutions. In some instances, even current liabilities may be included as part of capital.

In the broadest sense, then, capital may include:

- Preferred stock, entered either at par value or market value
- Common stock at par value
- Paid-in capital
- Retained earnings (earnings surplus)
- Long-term debt
- Short-term debt

What is paid-in capital?

Paid-in (surplus or excess) is the amount received by a corporation for its stock in excess of the stock's par value.

$$\text{Paid-in capital} = \text{Sale price} - \text{Par value}$$

Example: ABC Co. conducted an initial public offering of 1,480,000 shares of common stock with a par value of $2.50 per share ($3,700,000). Interest in its stock was very high among the investing public, to the extent that, when all proceeds from the offering were in, they amounted to $29,710,000.

$$\text{Paid-in capital} = \text{Sale price} - \text{Par value}$$
$$= \$29,710,000 - \$3,700,000 = \$26,010,000$$

On the balance sheet, these amounts are reported as follows:

Stockholders' Equity	
Common stock	$ 3,700,000 (par value)
Paid-in capital	26,010,000

• • •

What are retained earnings?

Retained earnings, or earned surplus, reflect the portion of stockholders' equity that comes from operational profits, as opposed to investments and loans. These earnings are what is left over after all such obligations, including dividends, are met.

Example: Part of ABC Co.'s balance sheet consists of the following entries:

Stockholders' Equity	
Common stock	$ 3,700,000
Paid-in capital	26,010,000
Retained earnings	**27,990,000**
Total equity capital	$57,700,000

ABC's retained earnings reflect profits from operations.

Notes: Retained earnings may be listed in the same entry as common stock: for example, "Common stock and retained earnings."

Also, if ABC had corporate bonds outstanding, the proceeds of that issuance would be listed in this section of the balance sheet, separately from retained earnings.

What are capital structure ratios?

Capital structure ratios, expressed as a decimal or percentage, relate a particular portion of a corporation's capitalization to its total capitalization. Commonly, only the equity and debt portions of a company's capital structure are calculated. In each case, the formula is the same.

$$\text{Capital structure ratio} = \frac{\text{Preferred stock } or \text{ Common stock } or \text{ Long-term debt}}{\text{Total capital}}$$

Example: XYZ Corp. has the following capital structure:

Preferred stock (at par value)	$ 600,000
Common stock and retained earnings	1,600,000
Long-term loans (bond issue)	400,000
Total capital	$2,600,000

$$\begin{array}{c} \text{Capital} \\ \text{structure} \\ \text{ratio} \end{array} = \dfrac{\begin{array}{c}\text{Preferred} \\ \text{stock}\end{array}}{\text{Total capital}}$$

$$= \dfrac{\$600,000}{\$2,600,000} = 0.231, \text{ or } 23.1\%$$

Preferred stock, listed at par value, represents 23.1% of XYZ Corp.'s total capital structure. The other two ratios are calculated in the same way.

Preferred stock (at par value)	$ 600,000	23.1
Common stock and retained earnings	1,600,000	61.5
Long-term loans (bond issue)	400,000	15.4
Total capital	$2,600,000	100.0

Note: Preferred stock may also be listed at market value.

Is long-term debt always included as part of a corporation's capital structure?

Both long-term debt and equity are always considered part of a company's capitalization, but they may be reported distinctly on the balance sheet. Long-term debt (such as corporate bonds) may be listed in the balance sheet as a liability; it is a loan that has to be repaid at some time in the future. Equity represents an investment in the company by investors, who are owners; hence its position in the equity part of the balance sheet.

$$\begin{array}{c}\text{Capital} \\ \text{structure ratio}\end{array} = \dfrac{\text{Long-term debt}}{\text{Owners' equity } + \text{ Long-term debt}}$$

Or:

$$\begin{array}{c}\text{Capital} \\ \text{structure ratio}\end{array} = \dfrac{\text{Long-term debt}}{\text{Total capitalization}}$$

Example: Portions of ABC Co.'s balance sheet are as follows:

Current Liabilities	
Notes payable	$ 1,400,000
Current portion—LT debt	2,500,000
Accrued payroll	3,600,000
Accounts payable	20,850,000
Income tax payable	2,600,000
Total current liabilities	$ 30,950,000

Deferred Income Taxes	1,900,000
Long-Term Debt	**26,700,000**
Total liabilities	$ 59,550,000

Stockholders' Equity	
Common stock	$ 3,700,000
Paid-in capital	26,010,000
Retained earnings	27,990,000
Total equity capital	**$57,700,000**

$$\text{Capital structure ratio} = \frac{\text{Long-term debt}}{\text{Owners' equity + Long-term debt}}$$

$$= \frac{\$26,700,000}{\$57,700,000 + \$26,700,000}$$

Or:

$$\text{Capital structure ratio} = \frac{\text{Long-term debt}}{\text{Total capitalization}}$$

$$= \frac{\$26,700,000}{\$84,400,000} = 0.316, \text{ or } 31.6\%$$

Long-term debt represents a little over 30% of ABC's capitalization.

What does the long-term debt ratio say about an organization?

This ratio gauges how much a corporation depends on borrowed capital, as opposed to investors' equity. Excessive dependence on debt not only makes a company vulnerable to changes in interest rates, but also makes it less investment-worthy. Generally, when long-term debt exceeds 25% of total capital, the structure may become unsatisfactory, or even detrimental to the company's success.

What is the investors'-capital-to-sales ratio?

This ratio is the result of dividing stockholders' equity by sales.

$$\text{Investors'-capital-to-sales ratio} = \frac{\text{Stockholders' equity}}{\text{Sales}}$$

Example: With 19X0 sales of $240,000,000 (the "top line" of the income statement), ABC Co.'s equity was $57,700,000.

Stockholders' Equity	
Common stock	$ 3,700,000
Paid-in capital	26,010,000
Retained earnings	27,990,000
Total equity capital	**$57,700,000**

$$\text{Investors'-capital-to-sales ratio} = \frac{\text{Stockholders' equity}}{\text{Sales}}$$

$$= \frac{\$57,700,000}{\$240,000,000} = 0.2404, \text{ or } 24.0\%$$

Stockholders' equity (investors' capital) represents 24% of ABC's sales in 19X0.

What does the ratio of investors' capital to sales indicate?

This ratio reflects the percentage of sales financed by stockholders' equity. It answers the question as to whether investors are investing too much or too little for the sales volume being achieved. A high ratio indicates that sales are being fueled by capital. The lower the percentage, therefore, the more favorable the company's position.

What is the ratio of net income to capital?

This ratio is derived by dividing net income (from the income statement) by stockholders' equity (from the balance sheet).

$$\text{Net-income-to-capital ratio} = \frac{\text{Net income}}{\text{Stockholders' equity}}$$

Example: ABC Co. earned $18,980,000 in net income for 19X0 (income statement).

Pretax profit	$37,960,000	15.8
Taxes (at 50%)	18,980,000	7.9
Net income	$18,980,000	7.9

In the same year, its stockholders' equity (capital) was $57,700,000 (balance sheet).

Stockholders' Equity	
Common stock	$ 3,700,000
Paid-in capital	26,010,000
Retained earnings	27,990,000
Total equity capital	**$57,700,000**

$$\text{Net-income-to-capital ratio} = \frac{\text{Net income}}{\text{Stockholders' equity}}$$

$$= \frac{\$18,980,000}{\$57,700,000} = 0.329, \text{ or } 32.9\%$$

The ratio of net income to stockholders' equity is 32.9%.

Is preferred stock included when calculating the ratio of net income to capital?

It may be. If a corporation has issued preferred stock, then the dividends must be deducted from net income and the par value subtracted from capital (or net worth).

$$\text{Net-income-to-capital ratio} = \frac{\text{Net income} - \text{Preferred dividends}}{\text{Capital} - \text{Preferred stock par value}}$$

Example: ABC Co. earned $18,980,000 in net income for 19X0 (income statement). It must pay a $2.25 dividend on each of 6,000 shares of preferred stock (for a total of $13,500), whose par value is $600,000. In the same year, its stockholders' equity (capital) was $57,700,000 (balance sheet).

Stockholders' Equity	
Common stock	$ 3,700,000
Paid-in capital	26,010,000
Retained earnings	27,990,000
Total equity capital	**$57,700,000**

$$\text{Net-income-to-capital ratio} = \frac{\text{Net income} - \text{Preferred dividends}}{\text{Capital} - \text{Preferred stock par value}}$$

$$= \frac{\$18,980,000 - \$13,500}{\$57,700,000 - \$600,000}$$

$$= \frac{\$18,966,500}{\$57,100,000} = 0.332, \text{ or } 33.2\%$$

The ratio of net income (less preferred dividends) to capital (less preferred stock) is 33.2%.

What does the ratio of net income to capital tell management?

This ratio reflects the return on capital in terms of free-and-clear earnings. Since net income represents profit after all expenses and taxes are paid, this ratio demonstrates the how well management is using stockholders' equity to produce profits. The higher the percentage, the better management is doing.

What is the ratio of retained earnings to capital?

To compute this ratio, divide retained earnings by total stockholders' equity. (Both amounts come from the balance sheet.)

$$\text{Retained-earnings-to-capital ratio} = \frac{\text{Retained earnings}}{\text{Stockholder's equity}}$$

Example: ABC Co.'s balance sheet shows the following information:

Stockholders' Equity	
Common stock	$ 3,700,000
Paid-in capital	26,010,000
Retained earnings	**27,990,000**
Total equity capital	**$57,700,000**

$$\text{Retained-earnings-to-capital ratio} = \frac{\text{Retained earnings}}{\text{Stockholder's equity}}$$
$$= \frac{\$27,990,000}{\$57,700,000} = 0.485, \text{ or } 48.5\%$$

Nearly half ABC's equity consists of retained earnings; that is, it comes from operational profits.

What does the ratio of retained earnings to capital indicate?

The higher the percentage, the more a company's capital is derived from profits. High percentages mean that management is generating profitability through its efforts, not relying on heavy capitalization. Start-up companies, for example, may have very low or nonexistent retained earnings because they lean heavily on venture capital; they are not in a position to generate profits. Going concerns have higher percentages of retained earnings because their products or services are generating sales and, depending on management, profits.

How is the capital-to-total-liabilities ratio computed?

To calculate this ratio, divide stockholders' equity by total liabilities (both balance sheet items).

$$\text{Capital-to-total-liabilities ratio} = \frac{\text{Capital}}{\text{Total liabilities}}$$

Note: Average figures should be used for capital (equity) and total liabilities.

Example: Part of ABC Co.'s balance sheet is as follows:

Current Liabilities	
Notes payable	$ 1,400,000
Current portion—LT debt	2,500,000
Accrued payroll	3,600,000
Accounts payable	20,850,000
Income tax payable	2,600,000
Total current liabilities	$ 30,950,000
Deferred Income Taxes	1,900,000
Long-Term Debt	26,700,000
Total liabilities	**$ 59,550,000**
Stockholders' Equity	
Common stock	$ 3,700,000
Paid-in capital	26,010,000
Retained earnings	27,990,000
Total equity capital	**$57,700,000**

$$\text{Capital-to-total-liabilities ratio} = \frac{\text{Capital}}{\text{Total liabilities}}$$

$$= \frac{\$57,700,000}{\$59,550,000} = 0.969, \text{ or } 96.9\%$$

Nearly all (96.9%) of ABC's liabilities are offset by capital.

What is the significance of the ratio of capital to total liabilities?

This ratio tells creditors how well an organization is able to contract and meet its debt obligations. The higher this percentage, the better the company's ability to meet its obligations.

Can total liabilities be compared to equity?

Average total liabilities (total debt) can be divided by average equity (capital), both balance sheet entries.

$$\text{Total-liabilities-to-equity ratio} = \frac{\text{Total liabilities}}{\text{Equity}}$$

Example: ABC Co.'s balance sheet, in part, looks like this:

Current Liabilities	
Notes payable	$ 1,400,000
Current portion—LT debt	2,500,000
Accrued payroll	3,600,000
Accounts payable	20,850,000
Income tax payable	2,600,000
Total current liabilities	$ 30,950,000
Deferred Income Taxes	1,900,000
Long-Term Debt	26,700,000
Total liabilities	**$ 59,550,000**
Stockholders' Equity	
Common stock	$ 3,700,000
Paid-in capital	26,010,000
Retained earnings	27,990,000
Total equity capital	**$57,700,000**

$$\text{Total-liabilities-to-equity ratio} = \frac{\text{Total liabilities}}{\text{Equity}}$$

$$= \frac{\$59,550,000}{\$57,700,000} = 1.03$$

What does the ratio of total liabilities to equity mean to the analyst?

A low ratio indicates that the organization can meet its overall debt obligations only with difficulty. The higher the ratio, the better these obligations are "covered."

What is the capital-to-noncurrent-assets ratio?

To obtain this ratio, divide the capital by noncurrent assets (both balance sheet items). Noncurrent assets are the sum of fixed assets and deferred charges.

$$\text{Capital-to-noncurrent-assets ratio} = \frac{\text{Capital}}{\text{Noncurrent assets}}$$

Example: Portions of ABC Co.'s balance sheet are as follows:

Property, Plant, and Equipment	
Land	$ 2,300,000
Buildings/improvement	20,000,000
Machinery/equipment	31,400,000
Subtotal	$53,700,000
Less: Accumulated depr'n.	17,900,000
Net fixed assets	$35,800,000

Deferred Charges	900,000

• • •

Stockholders' Equity	
Common stock	$ 3,700,000
Paid-in capital	26,010,000
Retained earnings	27,990,000
Total equity capital	**$57,700,000**

Noncurrent assets are the sum of:

Net fixed assets	$35,800,000
Deferred charges	900,000
Noncurrent assets	$36,700,000

$$\text{Capital-to-noncurrent-assets ratio} = \frac{\text{Capital}}{\text{Noncurrent assets}}$$

$$= \frac{\$57,700,000}{\$36,700,000} = 1.572, \text{ or } 1.57\%$$

How important is the ratio of capital to noncurrent assets?

This ratio is important to creditors. It indicates how well stockholders' equity (capital) supports the noncurrent assets of the company, with surplus available for current asset operating requirements. The more the ratio exceeds 100%, the more favorable the organization's ability to meet creditor commitments and debts.

What is the ratio of capital employed?

To compute this ratio:

• Adjust capital (stockholders' equity) by deducting the value of assets that do not contribute to operating income, such as marketable securities or other forms of investment. (These are all balance sheet entries.)

• Divide the adjusted capital value into sales (the "top line" on the income statment).

$$\text{Capital-employed ratio} = \frac{\text{Sales}}{\text{Capital} - \text{Nonoperational assets}}$$

Note: To compare periods, use end-of-period figures.

Example: ABC Co.'s sales are $240,000,000. Portions of ABC Co.'s balance sheet are as follows:

	Amount
Current Assets	
Cash	$ 3,500,000
Marketable securities	**3,300,000**
Accounts receivable	28,700,000
Inventories	
Raw materials	26,800,000
Work in process	10,700,000
Finished goods	7,300,000
Subtotal	44,800,000
Prepaid expenses	250,000
Total current assets	$ 80,550,000
Property, Plant, and Equipment	
Land	$ 2,300,000
Buildings/improvement	20,000,000
Machinery/equipment	31,400,000
Subtotal	$ 53,700,000
Less: Accumulated depr'n.	17,900,000
Net fixed assets	$ 35,800,000
Deferred Charges	900,000
Total assets	**$117,250,000**
	• • •
Stockholders' Equity	
Common stock	$ 3,700,000
Paid-in capital	26,010,000
Retained earnings	27,990,000
Total equity capital	**$ 57,700,000**

*Adjust total capital by deducting the value of marketable securities:

Total equity capital	$ 57,700,000
Less: Marketable securities	3,300,000
Adjusted capital	$ 54,400,000

$$\text{Capital-employed ratio} = \frac{\text{Sales}}{\text{Capital} - \text{Nonoperational assets}}$$

$$= \frac{\$240,000,000}{\$54,400,000} = 4.41$$

Sales amounted to 4.4 times the value of assets (or capital) employed.

What does the capital-employed ratio say about an organization?

This ratio reflects how well capital (adjusted to exclude nonoperational assets) is being used to produce revenue (sales). The higher the rate, the more effectively capital is being utilized.

How is the rate of return on capital computed?

The profit rate of return on sales may be computed by dividing either net income or income from operations (operating income) by sales.

$$\text{Profit return on sales} = \frac{\text{Net income or Operating income}}{\text{Sales}}$$

Example: ABC Co.'s sales are $240,000,000, with net income of $18,980,000.

$$\text{Profit return on sales} = \frac{\text{Net income or Operating income}}{\text{Sales}}$$

$$= \frac{\$18,980,000}{\$240,000,000} = 0.0791, \text{ or } 7.9\%$$

ABC earned a net-income profit return of 7.9% on sales. The same formula applies to operating income.

To determine this rate, multiply the capital-employed ratio by the profit rate on sales. If

$$\text{Rate of return on capital} = \text{Capital-employed ratio} \times \text{Profit return on sales}$$

Then

$$\text{Rate of return on capital} = \text{Capital-employed ratio} \times \frac{\text{Net income or Operating income}}{\text{Sales}}$$

Example: See the preceding example for the calculation of ABC Co.'s capital-employed ratio (4.41). ABC's income statement is as follows:

	Amount
Total sales	**$ 240,000,000**
Cost of sales	176,600,000
Gross profit	$ 63,400,000
G&A expense	$ 13,900,000
Selling expense	11,300,000
Subtotal	$ 25,200,000
Income from operations	**$ 38,200,000**

Other income	$ 48,000
Interest expense	72,000
Subtotal	$ (24,000)
Pretax profit	$ 37,960,000
Taxes (at 50%)	18,980,000
Net income	**$ 18,980,000**

Using operating income for profit on sales:

$$\begin{matrix} \text{Rate of} \\ \text{return} \\ \text{on capital} \end{matrix} = \begin{matrix} \text{Capital-} \\ \text{employed} \\ \text{ratio} \end{matrix} \times \begin{matrix} \text{Net income or} \\ \dfrac{\text{Operating income}}{\text{Sales}} \end{matrix}$$

$$= 4.41 \times 7.9\% = 34.8\%$$

The rate of return on ABC capital is 34.8%.

Note: The rate of return on capital using operating income is 70.2%.

What does the rate of return on capital employed tell management?

Obviously, higher rates of return are favorable: A high rate of capital employed (sometimes called turnover) usually means that capital is being used efficiently. Also:

- An improved capital-employed ratio generally means an increase in the rate of return on capital employed.
- An organization selling higher-priced items (such as automobiles or business computer systems) has a lower rate of return than one selling lower-priced products. Lower-priced items must have a higher profit margin to achieve a favorable return on the capital assets employed.

How is current debt compared to owners' equity?

Current (short-term) debt (liabilities) may be divided by owners' equity (both balance sheet entries), to arrive at ratio indicating the proportion of capital furnished by short-term creditors.

$$\begin{matrix} \text{Current-debt-to-} \\ \text{equity ratio} \end{matrix} = \dfrac{\text{Current debt (liabilities)}}{\text{Equity}}$$

Note: If the current portion of long-term debt is listed among current liabilities on the balance sheet, it must be deducted before making this computation.

Example: Portions of ABC Co.'s balance sheet look like this:

Current Liabilities	
Notes payable	$ 1,400,000
Current portion—LT debt	2,500,000
Accrued payroll	3,600,000
Accounts payable	20,850,000
Income tax payable	2,600,000
Total current liabilities	**$30,950,000**

• • •

Stockholders' Equity	
Common stock	$ 3,700,000
Paid-in capital	26,010,000
Retained earnings	27,990,000
Total equity capital	**$57,700,000**

Long-term debt must be deducted from the total of current liabilities:

Total current liabilities	$30,950,000
Less: Current portion of long-term debt	2,500,000
Current debt (liabilities)	$28,450,000

$$\text{Current-debt-to-equity ratio} = \frac{\text{Current debt (liabilities)}}{\text{Equity}}$$

$$= \frac{\$28,450,000}{\$57,700,000} = 0.493, \text{ or } 49.3\%$$

Current debt is about 49% of ABC's equity.

What is a favorable current-debt-to-equity ratio?

Determining a favorable ratio is difficult because it depends on a number of factors, such as how quickly receivables and inventory turn over, the operational environment, the working capital position, and the average ratios of other organizations in the same industry.

WORKING CAPITAL

What is working capital?

Working capital, sometimes known as net working capital or net current assets, is equal to the difference between current assets and current liabilities, both balance sheet entries.

Working capital = Current assets − Current liabilities

Example: Portions of ABC Co.'s balance sheet are as follows:

	Amount
Current Assets	
Cash	$ 3,500,000
Marketable securities	3,300,000
Accounts receivable	28,700,000
Inventories	
Raw materials	26,800,000
Work in process	10,700,000
Finished goods	7,300,000
Subtotal	44,800,000
Prepaid expenses	250,000
Total current assets	**$80,550,000**
• • •	
Current Liabilities	
Notes payable	$ 1,400,000
Current portion—LT debt	2,500,000
Accrued payroll	3,600,000
Accounts payable	20,850,000
Income tax payable	2,600,000
Total current liabilities	**$30,950,000**

Working capital = Current assets − Current liabilities
= $80,550,000 − $30,950,000 = $49,600,000

ABC Co. has working capital of $49,600,000.

What does working capital reflect?

The more working capital a company has, the greater is its liquidity.

How is average working capital computed?

Average working capital is computed by adding the working capital values at the beginning and end of an accounting period and dividing by 2.

$$\text{Average working capital} = \frac{\text{Beginning working capital} + \text{End working capital}}{2}$$

Example: ABC Co.'s working capital at the beginning of 19X0 was $48,100,000. It was $49,600,000 at the end of the year.

$$\begin{aligned} \text{Average} \\ \text{working} \\ \text{capital} \end{aligned} = \frac{\begin{aligned}\text{Beginning working} \\ \text{capital}\end{aligned} + \begin{aligned}\text{End working} \\ \text{capital}\end{aligned}}{2}$$

$$= \frac{\$48,100,000 + \$49,600,00}{2}$$

$$= \frac{\$97,700,000}{2} = \$48,850,000$$

ABC's average working capital for 19X0 is $48,850,000.

What is the working capital turnover?

Working capital turnover is a ratio of sales to average working capital.

$$\begin{aligned}\text{Working-capital} \\ \text{ratio}\end{aligned} = \frac{\text{Sales}}{\text{Working capital}}$$

Example: ABC Co. has sales of $240,000,000 and average working capital of $48,850,000 (see preceding example).

$$\begin{aligned}\text{Working-capital} \\ \text{ratio}\end{aligned} = \frac{\text{Sales}}{\text{Working capital}}$$

$$= \frac{\$240,000,000}{\$48,850,000} = 4.91$$

ABC's working capital turnover is 4.91; that is, it generates almost sales equal to about 5 times the amount of its working capital.

What does the working capital turnover represent?

This turnover indicates how well management is using working capital to generate revenues—how many "times" it is turning working capital over into sales revenues. The higher the ratio, the better management looks. There is, however, no normal ratio for each industry. The "right" ratio depends on the nature of the business, along with its requirements, asset turnover, and sales demands.

Can working capital be compared to sales?

Yes. The average working capital figure can be divided by sales (usually annualized).

$$\begin{aligned}\text{Working-capital-} \\ \text{to-sales ratio}\end{aligned} = \frac{\text{Working capital}}{\text{Sales}}$$

Example: ABC Co. has sales of $240,000,000 and average working capital of $48,850,000 (see page 70).

$$\begin{aligned}\text{Working-capital-} \atop \text{to-sales ratio} &= \frac{\text{Working capital}}{\text{Sales}} \\ &= \frac{\$48,850,000}{\$240,000,000} = 0.204, \text{ or } 20.4\%\end{aligned}$$

ABC's working capital represents 20.4% of sales.

Of what use is the working-capital-to-sales ratio?

The primary use of this ratio is using it to arrive at working capital needs, given a sales projection.

Example: ABC Co.'s working capital historically runs at a level that is about 20% of sales. For the upcoming year, management forecasts sales of $252,000,000.

$$\begin{aligned}\text{Working-capital-} \atop \text{to-sales ratio} &= \frac{\text{Working capital}}{\text{Sales}} \\ 0.20 &= \frac{\text{Working capital}}{\$252,000,000}\end{aligned}$$

Or:

Working capital = 0.20 × $252,000,000 = $50,400,000

For 19X1, ABC needs a little over $50,000,000 in working capital to meet its sales projection.

Can current assets and/or current liabilities (both balance sheet items) be compared to working capital?

Yes. Changes in the relative proportion of either current assets or current liabilities has a direct effect on the amount of working capital.

$$\text{Current-assets-to-} \atop \text{working-capital ratio} = \frac{\text{Current assets}}{\text{Working capital}}$$

Or:

$$\text{Current-liabilities-to-} \atop \text{working-capital ratio} = \frac{\text{Current liabilities}}{\text{Working capital}}$$

Example: ABC Co.'s working capital is $49,600,000. (See page 69 for computation of working capital.) Portions of ABC's balance sheet are as follows:

	Amount
Current Assets	
Cash	$ 3,500,000
Marketable securities	3,300,000
Accounts receivable	28,700,000
Inventories	
Raw materials	26,800,000
Work in process	10,700,000
Finished goods	7,300,000
Subtotal	44,800,000
Prepaid expenses	250,000
Total current assets	**$80,550,000**
• • •	
Current Liabilities	
Notes payable	$ 1,400,000
Current portion—LT debt	2,500,000
Accrued payroll	3,600,000
Accounts payable	20,850,000
Income tax payable	2,600,000
Total current liabilities	**$30,950,000**

$$\text{Current-assets-to-working-capital ratio} = \frac{\text{Current assets}}{\text{Working capital}}$$

$$= \frac{\$80,550,000}{\$49,600,000} = 1.62$$

$$\text{Current-liabilities-to-working-capital ratio} = \frac{\text{Current liabilities}}{\text{Working capital}}$$

$$= \frac{\$30,950,000}{\$49,600,000} = 0.623, \text{ or } 62.3\%$$

Is it helpful to compare current assets or liabilities to working capital?

Yes. Since the amount of working capital is directly dependent on current assets and liabilities, assessing their ratios is critical to understanding the source of an organization's working capital.

Note: Average figures should be used for working capital, current assets, and current liabilities.

Example: See the preceding example. In 19X0, ABC Co.'s ratio of current assets to working capital is 1.62, that of current liabilities 0.62. In 19X1, working capital is $50,000,000 (a slight increase over the previous year), with $37,500,000 in current liabilities and $87,500,000 in current assets. If ABC's current assets have traditionally been 1.62 times its working capital, then its working capital should have been $54,012,345.

$$\frac{\text{Current-assets-to-}}{\text{working-capital ratio}} = \frac{\text{Current assets}}{\text{Working capital}}$$

$$1.62 = \frac{\$87,500,000}{\text{Working capital}}$$

Or:

$$\text{Working capital} = \frac{\$87,500,00}{1.62} = \$54,012,345$$

But the actual ratio is different:

$$\frac{\text{Current-assets-to-}}{\text{working-capital ratio}} = \frac{\text{Current assets}}{\text{Working capital}}$$

$$= \frac{\$87,500,000}{\$50,000,000} = 1.75$$

This type of situation should be investigated by management.

Can working capital be compared to current assets or current liabilities?

It is helpful to relate working capital to either of its components, current assets or current liabilities.

$$\frac{\text{Working-capital-to-}}{\text{current-assets ratio}} = \frac{\text{Working capital}}{\text{Current assets}}$$

Or:

$$\frac{\text{Working-capital-to-}}{\text{current-liabilities ratio}} = \frac{\text{Working capital}}{\text{Current liabilities}}$$

Note: Average figures should be used for working capital, current assets, and current liabilities.

Example: ABC Co. has working capital of $49,600,000. (See page 69 for the computation of working capital.) Parts of the ABC balance sheet are as follows:

	Amount
Current Assets	
Cash	$ 3,500,000
Marketable securities	3,300,000
Accounts receivable	28,700,000

	Amount
Inventories	
Raw materials	26,800,000
Work in process	10,700,000
Finished goods	7,300,000
Subtotal	44,800,000
Prepaid expenses	250,000
Total current assets	**$80,550,000**

• • •

	Amount
Current Liabilities	
Notes payable	$ 1,400,000
Current portion—LT debt	2,500,000
Accrued payroll	3,600,000
Accounts payable	20,850,000
Income tax payable	2,600,000
Total current liabilities	**$30,950,000**

$$\text{Working-capital-to-current-assets ratio} = \frac{\text{Working capital}}{\text{Current assets}}$$

$$= \frac{\$49,600,000}{\$80,550,000} = 0.616, \text{ or } 61.6\%$$

$$\text{Working-capital-to-current-liabilities ratio} = \frac{\text{Working capital}}{\text{Current liabilities}}$$

$$= \frac{\$49,600,000}{\$30,950,000} = 1.60, \text{ or } 160\%$$

Working capital represents 61.6% of ABC's current assets and 160% of current liabilities.

How does comparing working capital to current assets or current liabilities help management?

These comparisons, if proven historically valid, can assist in projecting working capital, given current assets and/or liabilities forecasts. They also act as a backup means of checking estimates arrived at by other means.

What is the inventory-to-working-capital ratio?

This comparison relates the average inventory value (a balance sheet item) to average working capital.

$$\text{Inventory-to-Working-capital ratio} = \frac{\text{Inventory}}{\text{Working capital}}$$

Example: ABC Co.'s working capital is $49,600,000. The current assets part of the company's balance sheet is as follows:

	Amount
Current Assets	
Cash	$ 3,500,000
Marketable securities	3,300,000
Accounts receivable	28,700,000
Inventories	
Raw materials	**26,800,000**
Work in process	**10,700,000**
Finished goods	**7,300,000**
Subtotal	**44,800,000**
Prepaid expenses	250,000
Total current assets	**$80,550,000**

$$\text{Inventory-to-working-capital ratio} = \frac{\text{Inventory}}{\text{Working capital}}$$

$$= \frac{\$44,800,000}{\$49,600,000} = 0.903, \text{ or } 90.3\%$$

ABC's inventory represents about 90% of its working capital.

What is the significance of the inventory-to-working-capital ratio?

This ratio, by showing the percentage of working capital invested in inventory, demonstrates the part of current assets that are the least liquid. Inventories that greatly exceed working capital indicate that current liabilities exceed liquid current assets (cash and cash equivalents). The company might want to consider decreasing the proportion of its inventory.

How is working capital related to funded debt?

Average working capital is divided by the average value of funded (or long-term) debt (a balance sheet entry).

$$\text{Working-capital-to-funded-debt ratio} = \frac{\text{Working capital}}{\text{Funded debt}}$$

Example: ABC Co. has average working capital of $49,600,000. (See page 69 for the calculation of working capital.)

Current Liabilities	
Notes payable	$ 1,400,000
Current portion—LT debt	2,500,000
Accrued payroll	3,600,000
Accounts payable	20,850,000
Income tax payable	2,600,000
Total current liabilities	$30,950,000
Deferred Income Taxes	1,900,000
Long-Term Debt	**26,700,000**
Total liabilities	$59,550,000

$$\text{Working-capital-to-funded-debt ratio} = \frac{\text{Working capital}}{\text{Funded debt}}$$

$$= \frac{\$49,600,000}{\$26,700,000} = 1.86$$

Working capital represents 1.86 times the value of ABC's funded debt.

Why compute the ratio of working capital to funded debt?

This ratio answers the question as to whether an organization could liquidate its long-term debt from working capital. If the ratio is greater than 1, the answer is yes; if less than 1, no.

Caution: Even given an adequate ratio, a company may not be able to meet its funded debt obligation if it has not reserved enough of its working capital in cash or cash-equivalent form.

LIQUIDITY RATIOS

What is a liquidity ratio?

The liquidity of a business is its capability to meet current debt obligations. A reasonably sound liquidity position enables an organization to obtain the financing to take advantage of investment opportunities and respond to operational emergencies. Liquidity ratios measure how well a corporation is able to meet its obligations. The common liquidity ratios are:

- Current (working capital) ratio
- Acid test ratio
- Cash ratio
- Cash turnover ratio

- Accounts receivable turnover
- Total asset turnover ratio

See the "Working Capital" section of this chapter for other liquidity ratios:

- Working capital to sales
- Working capital to current assets
- Working capital to current liabilities
- Inventory to working capital

See Chapter 4 for inventory turnover ratios, also considered liquidity ratios.

What is the current ratio?

Sometimes known as the working capital ratio, the current ratio compares current assets to current liabilities.

$$\frac{\text{Current}}{\text{ratio}} = \frac{\text{Current assets}}{\text{Current liabilities}}$$

Note: The current ratio is expressed as a multiple.

Example: Parts of ABC's balance sheet are as follows:

	Amount
Current Assets	
Cash	$ 3,500,000
Marketable securities	3,300,000
Accounts receivable	28,700,000
Inventories	
Raw materials	26,800,000
Work in process	10,700,000
Finished goods	7,300,000
Subtotal	44,800,000
Prepaid expenses	250,000
Total current assets	**$80,550,000**
Current Liabilities	
Notes payable	$ 1,400,000
Current portion—LT debt	2,500,000
Accrued payroll	3,600,000
Accounts payable	20,850,000
Income tax payable	2,600,000
Total current liabilities	**$30,950,000**

$$\frac{\text{Current}}{\text{ratio}} = \frac{\text{Current assets}}{\text{Current liabilities}}$$

$$= \frac{\$80,550,000}{\$30,950,000} = 2.60$$

ABC's current ratio is 2.60; that is, its assets are worth 2.60 times its liabilities.

What is the significance of the current ratio?

The current ratio indicates the number of times current assets will pay off current liabilities. Historically, a 2:1 ratio has been considered the ideal minimum. Of course, there are exceptions. Some corporations with a 2:1 ratio or more may have hidden financial problems.

How is the acid test ratio calculated?

This ratio compares the company's current liabilities with its quick assets—cash, marketable securities, and accounts receivable. These assets are considered "quick" because they either are cash or can be converted to cash virtually overnight. Other types of assets, such as inventory, work in process, and the like, take much longer to convert to cash and are therefore excluded from this calculation.

$$\text{Acid test ratio} = \frac{\text{Cash + Marketable securities + Accounts receivable}}{\text{Current liabilities}}$$

Or:

$$\text{Acid test ratio} = \frac{\text{Quick assets}}{\text{Current liabilities}}$$

Note: The acid test ratio is expressed as a multiple.

Example: Portions of ABC Co.'s balance sheet are as follows:

	Amount
Current Assets	
Cash	**$ 3,500,000**
Marketable securities	**3,300,000**
Accounts receivable	**28,700,000**
Inventories	
Raw materials	26,800,000
Work in process	10,700,000
Finished goods	7,300,000
Subtotal	44,800,000
Prepaid expenses	250,000
Total current assets	$80,550,000

• • •

	Amount
Current Liabilities	
Notes payable	$ 1,400,000
Current portion—LT debt	2,500,000
Accrued payroll	3,600,000
Accounts payable	20,850,000
Income tax payable	2,600,000
Total current liabilities	**$30,950,000**

$$\text{Acid test ratio} = \frac{\$3,500,000 + \$3,300,000 + \$28,700,000}{\$30,950,000}$$

Or:

$$\text{Acid test ratio} = \frac{\$35,500,000}{\$30,950,000} = 1.15$$

ABC Co. can cover its current liabilities 1.15 times over within a few days' notice.

What does the acid test ratio say about an organization?

The acid test determines how well a corporation can meet its current obligations immediately—within days. It tells management and analysts whether the company could, in the worst case, pay all its current obligations. Normally, the ratio should be no less than 1.

How does the cash ratio differ from the acid test?

The cash ratio includes even fewer assets than the acid test; it leaves out accounts receivable. The only two types of assets figured in are cash and marketable securities, on the assumption that cash is on hand and securities can be liquidated with a phone call. (Marketably securities are considered "cash equivalents.")

$$\text{Cash ratio} = \frac{\text{Cash} + \text{Marketable securities}}{\text{Current liabilities}}$$

Note: The cash ratio is usually expressed as decimal or percentage.

Example: Portions of ABC Co.'s balance sheet are as follows:

	Amount
Current Assets	
Cash	**$ 3,500,000**
Marketable securities	**3,300,000**
Accounts receivable	28,700,000
Inventories	
Raw materials	26,800,000
Work in process	10,700,000
Finished goods	7,300,000
Subtotal	44,800,000
Prepaid expenses	250,000
Total current assets	$80,550,000
Current Liabilities	
Notes payable	$ 1,400,000
Current portion—LT debt	2,500,000
Accrued payroll	3,600,000
Accounts payable	20,850,000
Income tax payable	2,600,000
Total current liabilities	**$30,950,000**

$$\text{Cash ratio} = \frac{\text{Cash} + \text{Marketable securities}}{\text{Current liabilities}}$$

$$= \frac{\$3,500,000 + \$3,300,000}{\$30,950,000}$$

$$= 0.2197, \text{ or } 22\%$$

ABC Co.'s cash and cash equivalents can meet 22% of its current obligations.

Is there a "good" cash ratio?

There is no "normal" cash ratio applicable to all companies in all industries. Management must evaluate its company's own ratio in light of corporate objectives and policies, as well as industry norms.

What is the cash turnover ratio?

The cash turnover ratio relates sales (the "top line" on the income statement) to a company's cash balance (an entry in the current assets section of the balance sheet).

$$\text{Cash turnover} = \frac{\text{Sales}}{\text{Cash}}$$

Example: With sales of $240,000,000, ABC Co.'s current assets section is as follows:

	Amount
Current Assets	
Cash	**$ 3,500,000**
Marketable securities	3,300,000
Accounts receivable	28,700,000
Inventories	
Raw materials	26,800,000
Work in process	10,700,000
Finished goods	7,300,000
Subtotal	44,800,000
Prepaid expenses	250,000
Total current assets	$80,550,000

$$\text{Cash turnover} = \frac{\text{Sales}}{\text{Cash}} = \frac{\$240,000,000}{\$3,500,000} = 68.6$$

ABC Co. sales are over 68 times its cash balance.

What does the cash turnover indicate?

With this ratio, you can analyze and assess the effectiveness of an organization's use of its cash position to generate revenue. Generally, the higher the ratio, the more effective use management is making of cash.

Also, the turnover rate is helpful in determining preliminary cash balance forecasts based on sales projections.

Note: For best results an average cash position should be used.

Example: ABC Co. has ascertained that its cash position is historically $\frac{1}{65}$ of its sales volume. Management projects a sales volume of $252,000,000 for the upcoming year.

$$\frac{1}{65} = \frac{\text{Sales}}{\text{Cash}} = \frac{\$252,000,000}{\text{Cash}}$$

Or:

$$\text{Cash} = \frac{252,000,000}{65} = \$3,876,923$$

ABC Co. can look for a cash position in the neighborhood of $3,800,000 or $3,900,000.

What is the (accounts) receivable turnover?

The receivables turnover is the ratio of total credit sales to receivables. (It is also known as the sales-to-receivables ratio.)

$$\text{Receivables turnover} = \frac{\text{Total credit sales}}{\text{Receivables balance}}$$

Example: XYZ Corp.'s sales for the first quarter of 19X1 were $252,800,000, and its receivables balance $110,400,000. XYZ's receivables turnover is:

$$\text{Receivables turnover} = \frac{\text{Total credit sales}}{\text{Receivables balance}}$$
$$= \frac{\$252,800,000}{\$110,400,000} = 2.29, \text{ or } 229\%$$

Note: The receivables turnover is normally expressed as an annual figure, not quarterly.

How is the receivables turnover converted to an annual figure?

There are two methods. First, the more precise procedure is to start with annualized sales and an average receivables balance.

Example: XYZ Corp.'s annual sales are $1,077,000,000, and its average receivables for the year are $107,300,000. Its annual receivables turnover is:

$$\text{Receivables turnover} = \frac{\text{Total credit sales}}{\text{Receivables balance}}$$
$$= \frac{\$1,077,000,000}{\$107,300,000} = 10.04, \text{ or } 1,004\%$$

Second, quarterly figures may be used and projected for the year by multiplying the resultant ratio by 4.

$$\begin{array}{c}\text{Annual receivables} \\ \text{turnover}\end{array} = \begin{array}{c}\text{Quarterly} \\ \text{receivables turnover}\end{array} \times 4$$

Example: XYZ Corp.'s sales for the first quarter of 19X1 were $252,800,000, and its receivables balance $110,400,400. XYZ's receivables turnover (or turnover) is:

$$\text{Receivables turnover} = \frac{\text{Total credit sales}}{\text{Receivables balance}}$$

$$= \frac{\$252,800,000}{\$110,400,000} = 2.29, \text{ or } 229\%$$

$$\begin{matrix}\text{Annual receivables} \\ \text{turnover}\end{matrix} = \begin{matrix}\text{Quarterly} \\ \text{receivables turnover}\end{matrix} \times 4$$

$$= 2.29, \text{ or } 229\%, \times 4 = 9.16, \text{ or } 916\%$$

How is the receivables turnover best analyzed?

Receivables turnover is compared to the trends in sales and receivables over a number of time periods. Although annual periods are preferable, quarters can be compared too. One period is established as the baseline, and the sales and receivables amounts are assigned a "baseline" value of 100%.

Example: The following quarterly data is for XYZ Corp. The first quarter is the baseline period. Both the sales and the receivables turnover trends for that quarter are assigned the value of 100%.

(in $000,000s)

Qtr	Sales	% of Trend	Receivables	% of Trend	Receivables-to-Sales Ratio
1	$252.8	100%	$110.4	100%	229%
2	$274.9	109%	$111.5	101%	247%
3	$276.2	109%	$102.3	93%	270%
4	$273.1	108%	$105.1	95%	260%

The sales trend clearly indicates increases in the last three quarters of 19X1. Receivables decreased in the last two quarters but slightly increased in the second quarter (101%). The receivables turnover trend is favorable because increases in sales did not result in higher receivables, which would have necessitated a greater capital investment in outstanding customer accounts.

Note: In ascertaining why sales and receivables values vary, the two main factors are price and sales volume.

How is the total asset turnover computed?

The total asset turnover compares a company's sales (the income statement's "top line") to its total assets (from the balance sheet). It is usually expressed as a multiple.

$$\text{Total assets turnover ratio} = \frac{\text{Sales}}{\text{Total assets}}$$

Example: With annual sales of $240,000,000, part of ABC Co.'s balance is as follows:

	Amount
Current Assets	
Cash	$ 3,500,000
Marketable securities	3,300,000
Accounts receivable	28,700,000
Inventories	
Raw materials	26,800,000
Work in process	10,700,000
Finished goods	7,300,000
Subtotal	44,800,000
Prepaid expenses	250,000
Total current assets	$ 80,550,000
Property, Plant, and Equipment	
Land	$ 2,300,000
Buildings/improvement	20,000,000
Machinery/equipment	31,400,000
Subtotal	$ 53,700,000
Less: Accumulated depr'n.	17,900,000
Net fixed assets	$ 35,800,000
Deferred Charges	900,000
Total assets	**$117,250,000**

$$\text{Total assets turnover ratio} = \frac{\text{Sales}}{\text{Total assets}}$$

$$= \frac{\$240,000,000}{\$117,250,000} = 2.05$$

ABC's total assets generate a little over twice their value in sales volume.

Of what use is the asset turnover ratio?

This ratio gauges how well an organization is making use of its total assets. The higher the multiple, the more efficient the company.

Also, given a sales forecast, the organization can project its total assets position.

Example: ABC Co. knows from past experience that its sales run about twice the value of its total assets. For the upcoming year, the sales forecast is $252,000,000.

$$\text{Total assets turnover ratio} = \frac{\text{Sales}}{\text{Total assets}}$$

Or:

$$\text{Total assets} = \frac{\text{Sales}}{\text{Total assets turnover ratio}}$$
$$= \frac{\$252,000,000}{2} = \$126,000,000$$

ABC Co. is looking for about $126,000,000 in total assets in the coming year.

PROFITABILITY RATIOS

What is meant by earnings per common share?

Earnings per common share are equal to net income divided by the number of common shares issued and outstanding. Shares that have been "issued and outstanding" are those that are held by investors. They are to be distinguished from two other types of shares:

- Authorized shares are those that have been authorized by the corporation's state charter, but not issued for public sale. These shares do not enter into the earnings per share computation.

- Treasury stock consists of shares that were authorized, issued for public sale, and then bought back by the corporation. These shares do not enter into the earnings per share calculation. Only issued and outstanding shares are included in the calculation.

$$\frac{\text{Earnings per}}{\text{common share}} = \frac{\text{Net income}}{\text{Issued and outstanding shares}}$$

Note: The number of shares issued and outstanding varies constantly. The value used for computation is therefore an average figure.

Example: ABC Co. has net income of $18,980,000 and 3,432,188 shares of common stock issued and outstanding.

$$\frac{\text{Earnings per}}{\text{common share}} = \frac{\text{Net income}}{\text{Issued and outstanding shares}}$$
$$= \frac{\$18,980,000}{3,432,188 \text{ shares}} = \$5.53 \text{ per share}$$

ABC's earnings per common share are $5.53.

Do preferred stock dividends affect earnings per common share?

Yes. If the corporation has an obligation to pay dividends on preferred stock, the amount of dividends must be deducted from net income.

$$\frac{\text{Earnings per}}{\text{common share}} = \frac{\text{Net income} - \text{Preferred stock dividends}}{\text{Issued and outstanding shares}}$$

Note: The number of shares issued and outstanding varies constantly. The value used for computation is therefore an average figure.

Example: ABC Co. has net income of $18,980,000 and 3,432,188 shares of common stock issued and outstanding. It must also pay a dividend of $1.75 per share of preferred stock, with 500,000 shares of preferred issued and outstanding.

Preferred shares outstanding	500,000
Dividend per share	× $1.75
Total dividends	$875,000

$$\frac{\text{Earnings per}}{\text{common share}} = \frac{\text{Net income} - \text{Preferred stock dividends}}{\text{Issued and outstanding shares}}$$

$$= \frac{\$18,980,000 - \$875,000}{3,432,188 \text{ shares}}$$

$$= \frac{\$18,105,000}{3,432,188} = \$5.27$$

With preferred stock dividends subtrated from net income, ABC's earnings per common share are $5.27. Compare this amount with the earnings per share in the preceding example.

Who is interested in earnings per share?

Investors are primarily interested in earnings per share, because it reflects the profit flowing to stockholders for each share held.

Can earnings per share be computed for preferred stock?

Yes. The calculation is the same as for common stock.

$$\text{Earnings per preferred share} = \frac{\text{Net income}}{\text{Preferred shares issued and outstanding}}$$

Example: MNO Corp. has $175,000 net income, with 5,000 preferred shares issued and outstanding.

$$\text{Earnings per preferred share} = \frac{\text{Net income}}{\text{Preferred shares issued and outstanding}}$$

$$= \frac{\$175,000}{5,000} = \$35 \text{ per share}$$

Earnings per preferred share of MNO Corp. are $35.

What is the price-earnings (PE) ratio?

As a value assigned to stock based on a computation, the earnings per common share is rarely the same as the price investors are willing to pay for the stock in the marketplace— the market price. The price-earnings (PE) ratio describes the relationship between the (market) price and earnings per share.

$$\text{Price-earnings ratio} = \frac{\text{Market price per share}}{\text{Earnings per share}}$$

Note: Generally, the market price is a multiple of earnings per share. Hence the PE ratio is also known as the price multiple.

Example: ABC Co. common stock is trading for $16 a share. Its earnings per share is $5.53.

$$\text{Price-earnings ratio} = \frac{\text{Market price per share}}{\text{Earnings per share}}$$

$$= \frac{\$16}{\$5.53} = 2.89$$

ABC common stock enjoys a PE ratio of 2.89.

Is a high PE ratio favorable for investors?

Generally, yes. The PE ratio reflects investors' expectations of a company. The expectation that a corporation will be very profitable in the future is part of the market price, which is driven up by a surplus of buyers. Such a corporation will have a ratio that is higher than the averaged market PE or the industrial norm.

Troubled corporations, theoretically, should always have low PE ratios, to account for lack of investor interest. But they can sometimes have high ratios, not because they are profitable, but rather because the earnings per share is falling at a faster rate than the market price. For a while, the low earnings per share yields a high PE.

What is the capitalization rate?

The capitalization rate is the converse of the price-earnings (PE) ratio.

$$\text{Capitalization rate} = \frac{\text{Earnings per share}}{\text{Market price per share}}$$

Example: ABC Co. common stock is trading for $16 a share. Its earnings per share is $5.53.

$$\text{Capitalization rate} = \frac{\text{Earnings per share}}{\text{Market price per share}}$$

$$= \frac{\$5.53}{\$16} = 0.35, \text{ or } 35\%$$

ABC common stock has a capitalization rate of 35%.

Of what significance is the capitalization rate?

This rate shows how much investors, by means of buying and selling in the stock market, are capitalizing the value of the company's earnings.

What is book value?

Book value is the value of a stock based only on the issuing corporation's equity.

$$\text{Book value} = \frac{\text{Stockholders' equity}}{\text{Common shares issued and outstanding}}$$

Example: With 3,432,188 common shares issued and outstanding, ABC Corp.'s stockholders' equity is $57,700,000.

• • •

Stockholders' Equity	
Common stock	$ 3,700,000
Paid-in capital	26,010,000
Retained earnings	27,990,000
Total equity capital	**$57,700,000**

$$\text{Book value} = \frac{\text{Stockholders' equity}}{\text{Common shares issued and outstanding}}$$

$$= \frac{\$57,700,000}{3,432,188 \text{ shares}} = \$16.81$$

The book value of ABC common stock is $16.81.

What does book value mean?

Book value tells an investor what the common stock would be worth if the company were to liquidate all its assets, pay off all its liabilities, and go out of business. Sometimes known as net asset value, this figure is a gauge of the value of the company's assets per share. It is called "net" becasue liabilities are deducted.

How is the dividend-return ratio calculated?

The dividend-return ratio is a yield, computed by dividing the common stock dividend by its market value.

$$\text{Dividend-return ratio} = \frac{\text{Dividend}}{\text{Market value}}$$

Note: Market value is defined as the price at which the stock is bought, not the current market value.

Example: With ABC Co. common stock trading at $25 per share, the company's Board declares a dividend of $2 per share.

$$\text{Dividend-return ratio} = \frac{\text{Dividend}}{\text{Market value}}$$

$$= \frac{\$2}{\$25} = .08, \text{ or } 8\%$$

The dividend yield on ABC common stock is 8%.

How valuable is the common stock dividend yield?

It is a good indicator of yield to investors seeking income—dividend payments, and it can be used to compare dividend yields of various common stocks. The dividend yield does not, however, account for increases or declines in the underlying value of the stock. If a stock appreciates in value during an investor's holding period, the heightened value is not reflected in this figure.

DEBT-PAYING CAPABILITY

What is the velocity method for calculating an organization's debt-paying capability?

Although the velocity method is used primarily for liquidation assessment, it can also be helpful in analyzing a company's ongoing debt-paying ability to its company's financial position. The term "velocity" is used because the method assesses how quickly the organization could pay off its debt if all its assets were liquidated. The rapidity of payment depends greatly on the maturity and aging of accounts receivable, payables, and inventory—how fast its own billings can be collected, when it has to make payments on bills, and how soon inventory can be converted to cash. The velocity method evaluates the timing of a company's cash inflow compared to its outflow.

The basic model is:

Current Assets:			
Cash		$_____	
Aged receivables (estimated) due in:			
30 days	$_____		_____
31-60 days	_____		_____
61-90 days	_____		_____
Total receivables		$_____	
Aged inventory (estimated), cash sales:			
30 days	$_____		_____
31-60 days	_____		_____
90-day credit sales	_____		_____
Total inventory		$_____	
Total all assets			$_____
Current Liabilities:			
Notes payable in 30 days		$_____	
Aged payables (estimated), due in:			
30 days	$_____		_____
31-60 days	_____		_____
61-90 days	_____		_____
Total payables		$_____	
Total all liabilities			$_____

Example: ABC Co. shows the following financial data:

(in $000s)

		%
Current Assets:		
Cash	$10,000	
Aged receivables (estimated) due in:		
30 days	$41,400	69.5
31-60 days	15,000	25.1
61-90 days	3,200	5.4
Total receivables	$59,600	
Aged inventory (estimated), cash sales:		
30 days	$11,500	15.5
31-60 days	9,000	12.2
90-day credit sales	53,600	72.3
Total inventory	$74,100	
Total all assets		$143,700
Current Liabilities:		
Notes payable in 30 days	$ 8,000	
Aged payables (estimated), due in:		
30 days	$28,000	58.1
31-60 days	14,700	30.5
61-90 days	5,500	11.4
Total payables	$48,200	
Total all liabilities		$56,200

ABC is in a favorable position to meet its immediate debt commitments.

● Accounts receivable represents 41.5% of the total current assets: $59,600 divided by $143,700 equals .4147, or 41.5%.

● The aged payable commitments represent 85.5% of the total current liabilities: $48,200 divided by $56,200.

● Most of the receivables (69.5%) are due to be collected within 30 days.

● Inventory will take longer to convert to cash, with credit sales representing the lion's share (72.3%).

● A little over half of accounts payable (58.1%) is due within 30 days, with the balance not due for 31 to 90 days.

● The current ratio (current assets divided by current liabilities; see page 000 for the calculation) is 2.6 ($143,700 divided by $56,200). This seems adequate in light of industry standards.

- The working capital ratio (working capital divided by liabilities; see page 000 for the calculation) is 1.6. This indicates that the owners' equity in the current assets is 1.6 times the creditors' current contribution to capital.

- However, the estimated cash receipts within 30 days plus cash balance after 30 days just about matches payables due within 30 days:

Cash	$10,000	
30-day receivables	41,400	
30-day inventory	11,500	
Total cash in 30 days		$62,900
Less:		
Notes payable in 30 days	$ 8,000	
Accounts payable in 30 days	28,000	
Total payable 30 days		$36,000
Cash balance		$26,900
Divided by total 30-day payables		$36,000
Ratio of 30-day cash balance to 30-day payables		74.7%

Note: This data does not represent a cash budget because it does not reflect estimated expenses, tax provisions, and miscellaneous commitments.

What is the calculation for the times-interest-earned ratio?

This ratio focuses on the number of times interest is covered by operating profits. The higher the ratio, the better off the company.

$$\text{Times-interest-earned ratio} = \frac{\text{Income from operations}}{\text{Interest expense}}$$

Example: In its first quarter of 19X1, ABC Co. had income from operations of $17,100,000 and paid $800,000 in interest on debt.

$$\text{Times-interest-earned ratio} = \frac{\text{Income from operations}}{\text{Interest expense}}$$

$$= \frac{\$17,100,000}{\$800,000} = 21.4$$

For the quarter, ABC had income from operations that was 21.4 times the amount of interest it owed.

Does the times-interest-earned ratio change with time?

Yes. The primary cause of fluctuations in the ratio is a change in income from operations.

Example: ABC shows the following data for 19X1:

(in $000s)					
		Quarter			*Annual*
	First	*Second*	*Third*	*Fourth*	*Period*
Income from operations	$17,100	$19,600	$16,500	$12,800	$66,000
Interest earned	$ 800	$ 800	$ 900	$ 900	$ 3,400
Times interest earned	21.4	24.5	18.3	14.2	19.4

Over the year, the time-interest-earned ratio fluctuated from 21.4 in the first quarter, through a high of 24.5 in the second, to 18.3 in the third quarter and 14.2 in the fourth, with an annual average of 19.4. Note that, while the level of interest remained for the most part constant, income from operations changed more dramatically.

What does the times-interest-earned ratio tell analysts?

This ratio answers the question, how adequately do earnings compare with the payment of bond interest? The higher the ratio, the better the organization is able to meet its interest payments.

Some organizations take a more conservative approach. They reduce the pretax income by the estimated federal income taxes before dividing the value by the bond interest.

What is the times-preferred-dividend ratio?

To calculate the times-preferred-dividend ratio, divide net income by the preferred stock dividend obligation.

$$\text{Times-preferred-dividend ratio} = \frac{\text{Net income}}{\text{Preferred dividend}}$$

Example: MNO Corp.'s stock dividend is $5 per share, with 5,000 shares issued and outstanding. The dividend requirement is therefore $25,000 (5,000 shares times $5 per share). Net income is $175,000.

$$\text{Times-preferred-dividend ratio} = \frac{\text{Net income}}{\text{Preferred dividend}}$$
$$= \frac{\$175,000}{\$25,000} = 7$$

The preferred dividend has been earned 7 times over.

What does the times-preferred-dividend ratio mean to the analyst?

Earnings per share (see page 000) does not consider the margin between earnings per share and the company's obligation to pay dividends on preferred stock. Dividends, however, may have a great effect on earnings per share. For preferred stockholders, the times-preferred-dividend ratio is a direct indication of how adequately the paying corporation can meet this obligation.

What is the ratio for interest plus funded debt?

This ratio assesses an organization's capacity to meet scheduled interest plus debt repayments. The portion of the long-term debt due for repayment within the current annual period is classified as a current liability on the balance sheet.

$$\text{Debt coverage} = \frac{\text{Pretax earnings}}{\text{Interest} + \dfrac{\text{Funded debt repayment}}{1 - \text{Tax rate}}}$$

A decline in the ratio over time is an unfavorable trend because, given stable interest expense and fixed funded debt repayments, the reason is usually declining pretax earnings. Such a decline serves as a warning to the organization (particularly if other debt-paying ratios are following the same pattern), that it may encounter problems in borrowing more money and in meeting schedule debt commitments. Trade vendors should also be concerned since trade payments may also be deferred.

Example: In addition to $800,000 in interest payments, ABC Corp. is schedule to make a funded debt repayment of $1,000,000 this quarter. Pretax earnings are $15,000,000, and the tax rate 52%.*

$$\begin{aligned}
\text{Debt coverage} &= \frac{\text{Pretax earnings}}{\text{Interest} + \dfrac{\text{Funded debt repayment}}{1 - \text{Tax rate}}} \\[2mm]
&= \frac{\$15,000,000}{\$800,000 + \dfrac{\$1,000,000}{1 - 0.52}} \\[2mm]
&= \frac{\$15,000,000}{\$800,000 + \dfrac{\$1,000,000}{0.48}} \\[2mm]
&= \frac{\$15,000,000}{\$800,000 + \$2,083,333} \\[2mm]
&= \frac{\$15,000,000}{\$2,883,333} = 5.2 \text{ times}
\end{aligned}$$

*Federal, state, and local corporate income taxes included. This figure is illustrative only; actual tax rates vary from state to state and from one corporation to another.

ABC Corp. has enough pretax earnings to cover its interest payments and debt repayments over 5 times.

LEVERAGE RATIOS

What is leverage?

Leverage is best explained by an example. An organization borrows funds at x% interest and invests the funds in assets that yield y%. If the y% yield is greater than the x% cost, then the difference represent pure gain to the equity stockholder. This is leverage—the use of certain fixed costs to enhance returns on investments or sales revenues. The purpose of leverage is that small changes in costs are associated with greater changes in return.

Example: A corporation may issue bonds to raise funds for new plant construction. The interest on the bonds and the depreciation on the plant become fixed assets, and the plant enables the company to fill a great many more orders and thereby increase sales.

What are leverage ratios?

Leverage ratios measure the degree to which a company makes use of leverage. Some basic leverage ratios are:

- Common stock leverage
- Net income to equity
- Interest paid to borrowed capital
- Leverage of borrowed capital to equity

What is common stock leverage?

This type of leverage is computed by dividing total equity by the value of common stock.

$$\frac{\text{Common stock}}{\text{leverage}} = \frac{\text{Total equity}}{\text{Common stock value}}$$

Example: MNO Corp. has the following capital structure:

Bonds	$3,000,000
Preferred stock	2,000,000
Common stock	2,800,000
Total capital	$7,800,000

$$\begin{aligned} \text{Common stock leverage} &= \frac{\text{Total equity}}{\text{Common stock value}} \\ &= \frac{\$7,800,000}{\$2,800,000} = 2.79 \end{aligned}$$

MNO Corp. has a common stock leverage factor of 2.79. For each dollar invested by the common stockholder, the bond creditors and preferred stockholders have invested $2.79.

What does the common stock leverage factor indicate?

Generally, if the leverage factor is above 2, the indications are that the bonds and preferred stock investments represent twice the common stock equity.

A low-leverage stock offers return advantages because interest and preferred dividend claims are so small—or non-existent—that most of the earnings are available for common stock dividends.

A high-leverage stock must be evaluated more carefully. For a conservative determination of the amount of net income available for common stock, you may include current liabilities when calculating leverage, that is, recognize current creditors' claims against assets. Generally, when leverage is high, changes in income before bond interest is deducted result in larger changes in the net income available (or earnings per share).

Note: Bond interest is an expense and is therefore deducted from pretax income. Dividends are not expenses and are subtracted from after-tax (net) income.

Example: With 400,000 shares of common stock issued and outstanding, the following data is available for MNO Corp.:

Income before bond interest	$1,000,000
Less: Bond interest ($3,000,000 worth of bonds at 8% interest)	240,000
Pretax income	760,000
Less: Provision for federal income taxes	380,000
Net income	380,000
Less: Preferred dividends ($2,000,000 worth of stock at 6% dividend rate)	120,000
Net income available for common stock	$ 260,000
Earnings per share (400,000 shares)	.65

Without the obligation to make interest and preferred stock dividend payments, the earnings per share are greatly increased.

Pretax income	$1,000,000
Less: Provision for federal income taxes	500,000
Net income available for common stock	$ 500,000
Earnings per share (400,000 shares)	1.25

MNO Corp. has $1.25 per share available, as opposed to 65 cents in its leveraged status.

What is the ratio of net income to equity?

To compare net income to equity, divide net income (from the income statement) by equity—not borrowed capital (from the balance sheet).

$$\text{Net-income-to-equity ratio} = \frac{\text{Net income}}{\text{Equity}}$$

Note: Equity excludes borrowed capital. On the balance sheet it would be the sum of preferred stock, common stock, and retained earnings.

Example: MNO Corp. has net income (pretax profit) of $228,000. Its capitalization structure is as follows:

Corporate bonds (long-term, funded debt)	$1,200,000
Common stock and retained earnings	1,400,000
Preferred stock	900,000
Total capitalization	$3,500,000

Owners' equity is $2,300,000 ($1,400,000 plus $900,000).

$$\text{Net-income-to-equity ratio} = \frac{\text{Net income}}{\text{Equity}}$$

$$= \frac{\$228,000}{\$2,300,000} = 0.099, \text{ or } 9.9\%$$

MNO's net-income-to-equity ratio is 9.9%.

What is indicated by the ratio of net income to equity?

This ratio reflects the return on investors' capital—how well management is using the capital to produce profits. The higher the ratio, the better.

What is the ratio of interest paid to borrowed capital?

This ratio compares the cost of borrowed capital, in dollars, to the amount of borrowed capital.

$$\text{Interest-paid-to-borrowed-capital ratio} = \frac{\text{Interest paid (\$)}}{\text{Borrowed capital}}$$

Note: Equity excludes borrowed capital. On the balance sheet it would be the sum of preferred stock, common stock, and retained earnings.

Example: MNO Corp. pays $110,000 a year on its borrowed capital of $1,200,000. Its capitalization structure is as follows:

Corporate bonds (long-term, funded debt)	$1,200,000
Common stock and retained earnings	1,400,000
Preferred stock	900,000
Total capitalization	$3,500,000

$$\text{Interest-paid-to-borrowed-capital ratio} = \frac{\text{Interest paid (\$)}}{\text{Borrowed capital}}$$

$$= \frac{\$110,000}{\$1,200,000} = 0.092, \text{ or } 9.2\%$$

The ratio of interest cost to borrowed capital is 9.2%.

Note: The interest-paid-to-borrowed-capital ratio is equivalent to the coupon rate of a bond issue.

How do you calculate the ratio of borrowed capital to equity?

Divide borrowed capital by all owners' equity—common stock, preferred, retained earnings, etc.

$$\text{Borrowed-capital-to-equity ratio} = \frac{\text{Borrowed capital}}{\text{Equity}}$$

Example: MNO Corp.'s capitalization structure is as follows:

Corporate bonds (long-term, funded debt)	$1,200,000
Common stock and retained earnings	1,400,000
Preferred stock	900,000
Total capitalization	$3,500,000

Borrowed capital is $1,200,000. Equity is $2,300,000 ($1,400,000 plus $900,000).

$$\text{Borrowed-capital-to-equity ratio} = \frac{\text{Borrowed capital}}{\text{Equity}}$$

$$= \frac{\$1,200,000}{\$2,300,000} = 0.522, \text{ or } 52.2\%$$

A little over half of MNO's capitalization is equity.

What is the funded capital ratio?

The funded capital ratio is computed by dividing fixed assets into the sum of long-term (funded) debt and owners' equity. (These amounts are all taken from the balance sheet.)

$$\text{Funded capital ratio} = \frac{\text{Long-term debt} + \text{Owners' equity}}{\text{Fixed assets}}$$

Example: With fixed assets of $760,000, MNO Corp.'s capitalization structure is as follows:

Corporate bonds (long-term, funded debt)	$1,200,000
Common stock and retained earnings	1,400,000
Preferred stock	900,000
Total capitalization	$3,500,000

Its long-term (funded) debt is $1,200,000, and its owners' equity is $2,300,000 ($1,400,000 plus $900,000).

$$\text{Funded capital ratio} = \frac{\text{Long-term debt} + \text{Owners' equity}}{\text{Fixed assets}}$$

$$= \frac{\$1,200,000 + \$2,300,000}{\$760,000}$$

$$= \frac{\$3,500,000}{\$760,000} = 4.61$$

MNO's fixed assets are financed 4.61 times by its total capitalization.

What is the importance of this ratio?

The funded capital ratio reflects how much of the borrowed and investors' capital goes toward the financing of fixed assets (plant, equipment, etc.).

CHAPTER 3

ANALYZING THE "TOP-LINE": SALES MANAGEMENT RATIOS

WORDS TO KNOW

Accounts receivable (receivables). Dollar amounts due to be paid to an organization.

Break-even point. The sales volume at which neither a profit nor a loss is made.

Capital. *See* Equity.

Credit sales. *See* Total credit sales.

COGS. *See* cost of sales.

Costs. *See* Expenses.

Cost of goods sold. *See* Cost of sales.

Cost of sales (cost of goods sold, direct costs). The cost of making or buying a product sold, or of providing a service rendered, consisting of direct personnel, direct materials (and other direct costs), and factory overhead.

Debt issue. A bond issued by a corporation. A bond represents monies loaned to the corporation by bondholders, unlike a share of stock which reflects ownership.

Direct expenses. *See* Cost of sales.

Direct labor (personnel). A direct cost for the labor needed to produce a company's product.

Direct material. An element of cost of sales, the cost of materials used in making a product or in rendering a service.

Direct personnel (labor). The portion of cost of sales attributable to paying employees who are directly involved in the production of goods.

Equity (capital, net worth). The difference between the value of a company's assets and the amount of its liabilities (both balance sheet totals). The interest of owners in a business.

Expenses. The costs of doing business. See Direct expenses, Indirect expenses.

Factory overhead. An element of cost of sales, the part of factory overhead directly attributable to making a product. (Some fixed factory costs may be regarded as indirect costs.)

G&A. *See* General and administrative expense.

General and administrative expense. An indirect cost associated with running a business, other than production or sales.

Gross profit. Sales less cost of sales.

Income from operations. *See* Operating income (also factory income).

Indirect expenses. A cost that cannot be directly attributed to production, such as selling expenses or general and administrative (G&A) costs.

Net credit sales. *See* Total credit sales.

Net income. All income (operating and nonoperating) less all expenses and taxes.

Net income before taxes. *See* Pretax profit.

Net sales. *See* Net credit sales.

Net worth. *See* Equity.

Operating expense. *See* indirect cost.

Operating income (income from operations). Sales less all expenses, fixed and variable.

Other direct costs (ODC). Overhead costs (costs other than labor and materials) that are directly attributable to the making of the company's product.

Other indirect costs (OIC). Overhead costs (costs other than selling expenses and G&A) that are not directly related to making the company's product but that are necessary for running a business.

Overhead. Cost of running a business, some of which may be considered direct and some indirect. See also Other direct costs, Other indirect costs.

Pretax earnings (income). Income left after deducting all expenses, but before allowing for taxes.

Receivables. *See* Accounts receivable.

Sales. *See* Total credit sales.

Selling expenses. An indirect cost associated with sales, selling expenses include the costs of marketing and contract administration.

Total credit sales. Total sales less allowances for returns and bad debt. Often used synonymously for "total sales" or "sales."

Variable expenses. Expenses that vary with the number of units of product made or with the amount of services rendered.

Vertical analysis. In an income statement, the expression of each entry as a ratio or percentage of sales.

Volume. The dollar amount of total credit sales.

HOW SALES CONTRIBUTE TO PROFIT AND INCOME: VERTICAL ANALYSIS OF THE INCOME STATEMENT

What is vertical analysis of the income statement?

In vertical analysis of the income statement, each income entry in the statement is expressed as a ratio or percentage of total sales. The income entries are:

- Gross profit
- Income from operations (or operating income)
- Pretax profit (or net income before taxes)
- Net income

Example: ABC Co.'s (nonitemized) income statement is as follows:

ABC Co.
Income Statement
19X0

	Amount	% Sales
Total sales	$ 240,000,000	100.00
Cost of sales	176,600,000	73.6
Gross profit	$ 63,400,000	26.4
G&A expense	$ 13,900,000	5.8
Selling expense	11,300,000	4.7
Subtotal	$ 25,200,000	10.5

	Amount	% Sales
Income from operations	$ 38,200,000	15.9
Other income	$ 48,000	0.2
Interest expense	72,000	0.3
Subtotal	$ (24,000)	(0.1)
Pretax profit	$ 37,960,000	15.8
Taxes (at 50%)	$ 18,980,000	7.9
Net income	$ 18,980,000	7.9

In each case, the income entry can be expressed as a percentage of sales. In this case, for instance, ABC's sales manager can see that the company is earning 7.9% in net income. That is, for every dollar of sales, ABC keeps a little under 8 cents in profit after taxes.

Gross Profit

What is gross profit?

Gross profit is equal to total sales less the cost of sales.

$$\text{Gross profit} = \text{Total sales} - \text{Cost of sales}$$

Example: Part of ABC Co.'s income statement is as follows:

Total sales	$240,000,000
Cost of sales	176,600,000
Gross profit	$ 63,400,000

ABC's gross profit, based on $240,000,000, is $63,400,000.

Can gross profit be expressed as a ratio of sales?

Yes. Gross profit is divided by total sales (less allowances for returns and bad debt).

$$\frac{\text{Gross-profit-}}{\text{to-sales ratio}} = \frac{\text{Gross profit}}{\text{Sales}}$$

Example: Use the information from the preceding example.

$$\frac{\text{Gross-profit-}}{\text{to-sales ratio}} = \frac{\text{Gross profit}}{\text{Sales}}$$

$$= \frac{\$63,400,000}{\$240,000,000} = 0.26, \text{ or } 26\%$$

ABC makes a 26% gross profit on sales. Expressed another way, for every dollar of sales made, ABC earns 26 cents in gross profit.

How does the gross-profit-to-sales ratio benefit the sales manager?

This ratio assists the sales manager in:

- Monitoring the cost of sales from one period to the next. A rise in this ratio leads to the question, is it costing the company more to fill orders? If so, why?
- Projecting cost of sales, given a sales estimate.

Example: In 19X0, ABC Co.'s sales were $240,000,000 and gross profit $63,400,000 (26%, see the preceding example). In 19X1, its estimated sales are $265,000,000, and its gross profit is typically 26% of sales.

$$\text{Gross-profit-to-sales ratio} = \frac{\text{Gross profit}}{\text{Sales}}$$

$$0.26 = \frac{\text{Gross profit}}{\$265,000,000}$$

Or:

$$\text{Gross profit} = 0.26 \times \$265,000,000 = \$68,900,000$$

ABC is looking for a little under $69,000,000 in gross profit in 19X1.

Let's assume that actual sales turn out to be $265,000,000 but that gross profit is actually only $58,600,000. That is a 22% ratio ($58,600,000 divided by $265,000,000)—lower than the historical average. Management's first question is why did the cost of sales rise?

Income from Operations

What is income from operations?

Income from operations, or operating income, is equal to sales (or revenues) less all direct and indirect expenses—cost of sales, G&A, selling expenses, overhead, etc. It can also be defined as net income less G&A and selling expenses.

$$\text{Income from operations} = \text{Sales} - \left(\text{Cost of sales} + \text{Indirect expenses} \right)$$

Example: Part of ABC Co.'s income statement is as follows:

Total sales	$240,000,000
Cost of sales	176,600,000
Gross profit	$ 63,400,000
G&A expense	$ 13,900,000
Selling expense	11,300,000
Subtotal	$ 25,200,000
Income from operations	**$ 38,200,000**

ABC's income from operations, based on $240,000,000, is $38,200,000.

Can income from operations be expressed as a ratio of sales?

Yes. Income from operations is divided by total sales (less allowances for returns and bad debt).

$$\text{Income-from-operations-to-sales ratio} = \frac{\text{Income from operations}}{\text{Sales}}$$

Example: Use the information from the preceding example.

$$\text{Income-from-operations-to-sales ratio} = \frac{\text{Income from operations}}{\text{Sales}}$$

$$= \frac{\$38,200,000}{\$240,000,000} = 0.159, \text{ or } 16\%$$

ABC makes a 16% income from operations on sales. Expressed another way, for every dollar of sales made, ABC earns 16 cents in operating income.

How does the income-from-operations-to-sales ratio benefit the sales manager?

This ratio assists the sales manager in:

● Monitoring operating from period to period. A drop in this ratio raises the question, are overall expenses increasing disproportionately to increases in sales?

● Projecting operating income, given a sales estimate.

Example: In 19X0, ABC Co.'s sales were $240,000,000 and operating income was $38,200,000 (16%, see the preceding example). In 19X1, its estimated sales are $265,000,000, and its operating income is typically 16% of sales.

$$\text{Income-from-operations-to-sales ratio} = \frac{\text{Income from operations}}{\text{Sales}}$$

$$0.16 = \frac{\text{Income from operations}}{\$265,000,000}$$

Or:

$$\text{Income from operations} = 0.16 \times \$265,000,000$$
$$= \$42,400,000$$

ABC is looking for a little over $42,000,000 in operating income in 19X1.

Assume that actual sales turn out to be $265,000,000 and that operating income is actually only $46,300,000. That is a 17% ratio ($46,300,000 divided by $265,000,000)—higher than the historical average. The question is what caused the increase in overall expenses?

This ratio is a good indicator of an organization's ability to make a profit. Period-to-period fluctuations can trigger investigations into the possibility of rising costs or decreased sales.

Example: Historically, XYZ Corp.'s operational-income-to-sales ratio has been 0.65, or 6.5%. In February, the following data is available:

(in $000,000s)	
	Feb.
Sales	37.0
Direct labor	8.0
Overhead	10.9
Material and ODC	13.1
Cost of sales	32.0
Indirect costs	2.1
Total all costs	34.1
Operational income	2.9

$$\text{Operational-income-to-sales ratio} = \frac{\text{Operational income (\$)}}{\text{Sales (\$)}}$$

$$= \frac{\$2,900,000}{\$37,000,000} = .078, \text{ or } 7.8\%$$

Operational income in May is 7.8% of sales revenue, quite high compared to the guideline of 6.5%. At this point, some of the relevant questions to ask are:

- Are sales down? How do May sales compare to the monthly average?
- Are expenses up? How do cost of sales, indirect costs, and individual elements of both compare to monthly averages?
- Is this variance a trend or is it due to unusual circumstances prevailing only in May?

Pretax Profit

What is pretax profit?

Pretax profit is the profit left after deducting all expenses from operating and nonoperating income, but before providing for taxes. To obtain this value:

- Add other miscellaneous income (such as sales discounts, gain on sale of fixed assets, interest income, and the like) to operational income.
- Reduce this amount by other deductions (such as interest expense, project abandonments, deferred development, and loss on the sale of fixed assets).

$$\begin{array}{c}\text{Pretax} \\ \text{profit}\end{array} = \left(\begin{array}{c}\text{Operating} \\ \text{income}\end{array} + \begin{array}{c}\text{Nonoperating} \\ \text{income}\end{array}\right) - \left(\begin{array}{c}\text{All expenses} \\ \text{including interest} \\ \text{expense}\end{array}\right)$$

Note: Pretax profit is sometimes known as net income before taxes.

Example: Part of ABC Co.'s income statement looks like this:

Total sales	$ 240,000,000
Cost of sales	176,600,000
Gross profit	$ 63,400,000
G&A expense	$ 13,900,000
Selling expense	11,300,000
Subtotal	$ 25,200,000
Income from operations	$ 38,200,000
Other income	$ 48,000
Interest expense	72,000
Subtotal	$ (24,000)
Pretax profit	**$ 37,960,000**

ABC's pretax profit is $37,960,000.

How is the ratio of pretax profit to sales computed?

An organization's pretax profit (net income before taxes) is divided by total sales.

$$\text{Pretax-profit-to-sales ratio} = \frac{\text{Pretax profit}}{\text{Sales}}$$

Example: ABC's pretax profit is $37,960,000, based on sales of $240,000,000,

$$\text{Pretax-profit-to-sales ratio} = \frac{\text{Pretax profit}}{\text{Sales}}$$

$$= \frac{\$37,960,000}{\$240,000,000} = 0.158, \text{ or } 15.8\%$$

ABC's pretax profit is a little under 16% of its sales.

Net Income

What is net income?

Net income is the amount left after adding income from other (nonoperational) sources and deducting all expenses and taxes from total sales.

$$\text{Net income} = (\text{Sales} + \text{Other income}) - (\text{All expenses} + \text{Taxes})$$

Example: ABC Co.'s income statement is as follows:

Total sales	$ 240,000,000
Cost of sales	176,600,000
Gross profit	$ 63,400,000
G&A expense	$ 13,900,000)
Selling expense	11,300,000
Subtotal	$ 25,200,000
Income from operations	$ 38,200,000
Other income	48,000
Interest expense	72,000
Subtotal	$ (24,000)
Pretax profit	$ 37,960,000
Taxes (at 50%)	18,980,000
Net income	$ 18,980,000

ABC's net income is $18,980,000.

Why are net income ratios important?

Inasmuch as net income represents the "bottom line" of operational success, these ratios are used to assess profitability.

How do you calculate the ratio of net income to sales?

Divide net income by net sales (that is, total sales less allowances for returns and bad debt).

$$\text{Net-income-to-sales ratio} = \frac{\text{Net income}}{\text{Net sales}}$$

Example: ABC Co.'s net income was $18,980,000, which was derived from $240,000,000 in net sales.

$$\text{Net-income-to-sales ratio} = \frac{\text{Net income}}{\text{Net sales}}$$

$$= \frac{\$18,980,000}{\$240,000,000} = 0.08, \text{ or } 8\%$$

ABC Co. earns net income that is equal to 8% of net sales. Put another way, for every dollar of net sales made, ABC earns 8 cents in net income.

Of what use is the net-income-to-sales ratio?

This ratio, if proven valid, enables the sales manager to project net income based on sales estimates, as well as to compare actual results against performance in past periods.

Example: ABC Co. projects $265,000,000 in net sales for the upcoming year. In the past, it has earned an average of 8% of sales in net income.

$$\text{Net-income-to-sales ratio} = \frac{\text{Net income (projected)}}{\text{Net sales (estimated)}}$$

$$0.08 = \frac{\text{Net income (projected)}}{\$265,000,000}$$

Or:

$$\text{Net income (projected)} = 0.08 \times \$265,000,000$$
$$= \$21,200,000$$

ABC may reasonably expect a little over $21,000,000 in net income in the coming year.

WHAT ARE SALES COSTING THE COMPANY?

Direct Costs (Cost-of-Sales)

What is cost of sales?

Sometimes known as cost of goods sold, cost of sales consists of the expenses that can be directly attributed to the making of the company's product or the rendering of its service. Examples of such "direct" costs are assembly line workers, raw materials that go into the product, equipment used to produce goods, and so on.

Example: Cost of sales (direct costs) are reflected on the income statement as follows:

(in $000,000s)

	Jan.
Sales	$44.0
Direct labor	9.6
Overhead	13.0
Material & ODC	15.8
Cost of sales	$38.4
Gross profit	5.6
G&A/selling expenses	2.7
Income from operations	$ 2.9

How is cost of sales compared to sales?

The total cost of sales is divided by the "top line," sales or revenues.

$$\text{Cost-of-sale-to-sale ratio} = \frac{\text{Cost of sales}}{\text{Sales}}$$

Example: The following monthly data is available for XYZ Corp.

(in $000,000s)

	Jan.
Sales	$44.0
Direct labor	9.6
Overhead	13.0
Material & ODC	15.8
Cost of sales	$38.4
Gross profit	5.6
G&A/selling expenses	2.7
Income from operations	$ 2.9

$$\text{Cost-of-sales-to-sale ratio} = \frac{\text{Cost of sales}}{\text{Sales}}$$

$$= \frac{\$38,400,000}{\$44,000,000} = 0.8727, \text{ or } 87.3\%$$

How is the cost-of-sales-to-sales ratio used?

The ratio is useful in two ways: First, if the organization has established an average ratio of cost of sales (or cost of goods sold, COGS) to sales, it confirms whether an actual cost of sales figure is above or below the historical average. Second, a validated average ratio provides a fairly reliable planning statistic to "ballpark" a total cost of sales value based on a projected sales volume.

How is the cost-of-sales-to-sales ratio used to evaluate actual data?

With actual data on hand and a valid historical ratio, an organization can compare them to determine whether the actual figure is above or below average.

Example: XYZ Corp. uses an historically validated cost-of-sales-to-sales ratio of 88.1%. That is, on average, its cost of sales runs 88.1% of total sales volume. For the month of January, XYZ's cost-of-sales-to-sales ratio is 87.3% (see preceding example). This is 0.8% less than the average (88.1% less 87.3%).

How would the cost-of-sales-to-sales ratio assist planners in making projections?

Planners can apply the organization's historically average ratio to the projected sales volume for a given upcoming period, to arrive at an estimated cost of sales.

Example: XYZ Corp.'s sales the sales manager projects $36,500,000 in sales for the month of February. The company's average cost-of-sales-to-sales ratio is 88.1%.

$$\text{Cost-of-sale-to-sale ratio} = \frac{\text{Cost of sales}}{\text{Sales}}$$

$$0.881 = \frac{\text{Cost of sales}}{\$36,500,000}$$

Or:

$$\text{Cost of sales} = 0.881 \times \$36,500,000 = \$32,156,500$$

For the month of February, XYZ can expect cost of sales in the neighborhood of $32,156,500.

Can individual types of costs of sales be evaluated in terms of sales?

Yes. In fact, in many cases it is generally more useful to compare individual types of costs to sales, rather than the overall cost of sales. For each category, however, the formula is the same. Cost of sales consists of several categories:

- Direct labor (personnel)
- Overhead (factory overhead)
- Material and other direct costs (ODC)

$$\text{Cost-of-sales-to-sale ratio} = \frac{\text{Cost of sales}}{\text{Sales}}$$

Example: The following monthly data is available for XYZ Corp.:

(in $000,000s)

	Jan.
Sales	$44.0
Direct labor	9.6
Overhead	13.0
Material & ODC	15.8
Cost of sales	$38.4
Gross profit	5.6
G&A/selling expenses	2.7
Income from operations	$ 2.9

$$\text{Cost-of-sales-to-sale ratio} = \frac{\text{Cost of labor}}{\text{Sales}}$$

$$= \frac{\$9,600,000}{\$44,000,000} = 0.2181, \text{ or } 21.8\%$$

$$\text{Cost-of-sales-to-sale ratio} = \frac{\text{Cost of overhead}}{\text{Sales}}$$

$$= \frac{\$13,000,000}{\$44,000,000} = 0.2954, \text{ or } 29.5\%$$

$$\text{Cost-of-sales-to-sale ratio} = \frac{\text{Cost of material \& ODC}}{\text{Sales}}$$

$$= \frac{\$15,800,000}{\$44,000,000} = 0.3590, \text{ or } 35.9\%$$

Any of the individual cost elements may be used to check the reasonableness of sales projections and/or to estimate costs for upcoming periods.

Can an individual type of cost be expressed as a percentage of overall COS?

Yes. To monitor cost elements, each type of expense may be expressed as a percentage of overall cost of sales.

$$\text{Direct-cost-to-cost-of-sales ratio} = \frac{\text{Individual direct cost}}{\text{Cost of sales}}$$

Example: XYZ Corp. shows the following monthly data:

(in $000,000s)

	Jan.
Sales	44.0
Direct labor	9.6
Overhead	13.0
Material & ODC	15.8
Cost of sales	$38.4

$$\text{Direct-cost-to-cost-of-sales ratio} = \frac{\text{Direct labor}}{\text{Cost of sales}}$$
$$= \frac{\$9,600,000}{\$38,400,000} = .250, \text{ or } 25\%$$

$$\text{Direct-cost-to-cost-of-sales ratio} = \frac{\text{Overhead expenses}}{\text{Cost of sales}}$$
$$= \frac{\$13,000,000}{\$38,400,000} = .338, \text{ or } 33.8\%$$

$$\text{Direct-cost-to-cost-of-sales ratio} = \frac{\text{Material \& ODC}}{\text{Cost of sales}}$$
$$= \frac{\$15,800,000}{\$38,400,000} = .411, \text{ or } 41.1\%$$

What use is it to monitor individual cost-of-sale elements?

While the overall ratio of cost of sales to sales may remain in line with the historical average, an individual cost element may be increasing disproportionately.

Example: XYZ Corp. shows the following monthly and six-month data:

(in $000,000s)

	Jan.	Jan. Ratios*	Six-Month Average
Sales	44.0	—	225.3
Direct labor	9.6	0.25	59.0
Overhead	13.0	0.34	51.0
Material & ODC	15.8	0.41	86.9
Cost of sales	$38.4		$196.9
Cost-of-sales-to-sales ratio	0.87		

*See preceding example for calculations.

The six-month ratios for cost-of-sale elements are calculated and compared to January's:

$$\text{Direct-cost-to-cost-of-sales ratio} = \frac{\text{Direct labor}}{\text{Cost of sales}}$$

$$= \frac{\$59,000,000}{\$196,900,000} = 0.299, \text{ or } 30\%$$

$$\text{Direct-cost-to-cost-of-sales ratio} = \frac{\text{Overhead expenses}}{\text{Cost of sales}}$$

$$= \frac{\$51,000,000}{\$196,900,000} = 0.259, \text{ or } 26\%$$

$$\text{Direct-cost-to-cost-of-sales ratio} = \frac{\text{Material \& ODC}}{\text{Cost of sales}}$$

$$= \frac{\$86,900,000}{\$196,900,000} = .441, \text{ or } 44\%$$

Note: Individual cost rates add up to 100% (30 plus 26 plus 44).

(in $000,000s)

	Jan.	Jan. Ratios*	Six-Month Average	Six-Month Ratios
Sales	44.0		225.3	
Direct labor	9.6	0.25	59.0	0.30
Overhead	13.0	0.34	51.0	0.26
Material & ODC	15.8	0.41	86.9	0.44
Cost of sales	$38.4		$196.9	
Cost-of-sales-to-sales ratio	0.87			

*See preceding example for calculations.

While direct labor and materials for January (0.25 and 0.41) were lower than the six-month ratios (0.30 and 0.44), overhead showed an 8-point jump (0.34 in January compared to 0.26 for the half-year).

This increase in overhead would not be detected if only the cost-of-sales-to-sales ratio were computed:

$$\text{Cost-of-sale-to-sale ratio} = \frac{\text{Cost of sales}}{\text{Sales}}$$

$$= \frac{\$196,900,000}{\$225,300,000} = 0.874, \text{ or } 87\%$$

The January ratio (0.87) matches the six-month ratio exactly, leading one to believe that cost of sales is well in hand.

Direct Personnel Costs

What is the sales-to-direct-personnel relationship?

Preliminary sales projections can be made, or sales projections arrived at by other means may be cross-checked, by means of the relationship between sales and direct personnel. Sales is divided by the number of direct personnel employed, the result being a per-capita distribution of the sales volume.

$$\text{Sales per direct personnel} = \frac{\text{Sales volume}}{\text{Number of direct personnel}}$$

Example: ABC Corp.'s sales the sales manager projects next quarter's sales volume at $252,800,000, and it will employ 34,737 direct laborers. Historically, the sales per direct personnel average has been $7,750. How reasonable does the sale projection seem?

$$\text{Sales per direct personnel} = \frac{\text{Sales volume}}{\text{Number of direct personnel}}$$

$$= \frac{\$252,800,000}{34,737 \text{ workers}} = \$7,278 \text{ per worker}$$

Compared to the historical average of $7,750, $7,278 is a little low but not dramatically so. The lower-than-average projection may be the effect of below-average sales projections.

What is the relationship of sales to total personnel?

Total personnel includes direct and indirect workers. Some organizations may relate sales volume to total employees.

However, for organizations that are top-heavy with indirect personnel (high overhead), due to either inadequate controls or the nature of the business, the results may be skewed. They may not be able to make use of this ratio.

$$\text{Sales per total personnel} = \frac{\text{Sales volume}}{\text{Number of total personnel}}$$

Example: ABC Corp.'s sales the sales manager projects next quarter's sales volume at $252,800,000, and it will employ 46,780 people altogether. Historically, the sales per direct personnel average has been $5,250. How reasonable does the sales projection seem?

$$\text{Sales per total personnel} = \frac{\text{Sales volume}}{\text{Number of total personnel}}$$

$$= \frac{\$252,800,000}{46,780 \text{ workers}} = \$5,404 \text{ per worker}$$

Compared to the historical average of $5,250, $5,404 is slightly above average. The sales projection seems reasonable.

Indirect Expenses

What are indirect expenses?

Usually, indirect expenses consist of:

- General and administrative (G&A) costs, such as the cost of payroll computer systems, the wages of bookkeepers, or retainers for corporate attorneys.
- Selling expenses, such as general advertising, a salesperson's company car, or commissions.
- Other indirect costs (OIC), which cannot be attributed to the making of a specific product. Examples are depreciation on a plant in which many products are made, utility and heating expenses, or delivery fleet lease payments and maintenance costs.

$$\text{Indirect expenses} = \text{G\&A} + \text{selling expenses} + \text{OIC}$$

Example: Hudson Co.'s annual selling expenses are $5,400,000, and its G&A costs $4,900,000. It also incurs depreciation and other types of expenses that cannot be attributed to specific products to the tune of $2,300.000.

$$\text{Indirect expenses} = \text{G\&A} + \text{selling expenses} + \text{OIC}$$
$$= \$4,900,000 + \$5,400,000 + \$2,300,000$$
$$= \$12,600,000$$

Selling, General, Administrative (G&A) Expenses

What are selling, general, and administrative expenses?

General and administrative costs are those associated with nonproduction functions, such as controller's staffs or procurement. Selling expenses are those related to marketing and administering contracts. Selling, general, and administrative expenses are listed as operating expenses (along with cost of goods sold and depreciation) on the income statement. In many companies, they are itemized as part and parcel of the overall expense reporting format.

Example: XYZ Corp.'s overall cost reporting format for 19X1 is as follows:

(in $000,000s)

Expense	$	% of Total Expense*
Indirect labor	$27.0	47.4
Misc. labor benefits	3.7	6.5
Retirement plan	1.3	2.3
Management incentive	**0.7**	**1.2**
Supplies	5.4	9.5
Taxes & insurance	2.7	0.6
Depreciation	0.8	1.4
Equipment rentals	2.2	3.9
Utilities	0.8	1.4
Telephone & telegraph	2.7	4.7
Travel	1.4	2.5
Professional/outside services	2.0	3.5
Entertainment	0.6	1.0
Dues and donations	0.5	0.9
Miscellaneous	0.6	1.1
Advertising/promotion	**3.0**	**5.3**
Sales commissions	**1.2**	**2.1**
Total expenses	$56.60	95.3

*Individual expenses are calculated as ratios of overall expenses; percentages do not total to 100% due to rounding.

In the preceding listing, "Management incentive" is a G&A expense, while "advertising/promotion" and "Sales commissions" are selling expenses. The company choose to isolate other G&A expenses, such as executives' compensation.

Can selling/G&A expenses be related to total sales?

Yes. The sum of these expenses is divided by total sales, to produce a ratio that can be expressed as a decimal or percentage.

$$\text{Selling-G\&A-to-total-sales ratio} = \frac{\text{Selling, G\&A (\$)}}{\text{Total sales}}$$

Example: In 19X1, XYZ Corp. incurred G&A expenses of $1,200,000 and selling expenses of $4,200,000. Its total sales for the year were $1,100,000,000.

$$\begin{aligned} \text{Selling-G\&A-to-total-sales ratio} &= \frac{\text{Selling, G\&A (\$)}}{\text{Total sales}} \\ &= \frac{\$4,200,000 + \$1,200,000}{\$1,100,000,000} \\ &= \frac{\$5,400,000}{\$1,100,000,000} = 0.0049, \text{ or } 0.049\% \end{aligned}$$

Does this ratio benefit the sales manager?

Yes. If the ratio of selling, general, and administrative costs to total sales proves to be valid over time, you may apply it to the profit for preliminary values until actual or better data is on hand.

Example: XYZ Corp. projects total sales of $1,210,000,000. Over the years, selling, general, and administrative expenses have come to an average of 0.049%.

$$\begin{aligned} \text{Selling-G\&A-to-total-sales ratio} &= \frac{\text{Selling, G\&A (\$)}}{\text{Total sales}} \\ 0.0049 &= \frac{\text{Selling, G\&A (\$)}}{\$1,210,000,000} \end{aligned}$$

Or:

$$\begin{aligned} \text{Selling, G\&A (\$)} &= 0.0049 \times \$1,210,000,000 \\ &= \$5,929,000 \end{aligned}$$

XYZ Corp. may reasonably expect to incur about $5,900,000 in selling, general, and administrative expenses in the coming year.

Note: Compare this estimate with that of the preceding example.

Can selling/G&A expenses be compared to gross profit?

Yes. The sum of selling, general, and administrative costs is divided by the company's gross profit for the period. The result is a ratio, which may be expressed as a decimal or percentage.

$$\text{Selling-G\&A-to-gross-profit ratio} = \frac{\text{Selling, G\&A (\$)}}{\text{Gross profit}}$$

Example: In 19X1, XYZ Corp. incurred G&A expenses of $1,200,000 and selling expenses of $4,200,000. Its gross profit for the year was $155,000,000.

$$\begin{aligned}
\text{Selling-G\&A-to-gross-profit ratio} &= \frac{\text{Selling, G\&A (\$)}}{\text{Gross profit}} \\[2mm]
&= \frac{\$4,200,000 + \$1,200,000}{\$155,000,000} \\[2mm]
&= \frac{\$5,400,000}{\$155,000,000} = 0.0348, \text{ or } 3.5\%
\end{aligned}$$

Does this ratio benefit the sales manager?

Yes. If the ratio of selling, general, and administrative costs to gross profit proves to be valid over time, you may apply it to the profit for preliminary values until actual or better data is on hand.

Example: XYZ Corp. projects a gross profit of $169,000,000. Over the years, selling, general, and administrative expenses have come to an average of 3.5% of gross profit.

$$\begin{aligned}
\text{Selling-G\&A-to-gross-profit ratio} &= \frac{\text{Selling, G\&A (\$)}}{\text{Gross profit}} \\[2mm]
0.035 &= \frac{\text{Selling, G\&A (\$)}}{\$169,000,000}
\end{aligned}$$

Or:

$$\text{Selling, G\&A (\$)} = 0.035 \times \$169,000,000 = \$5,915,000$$

XYZ Corp. may reasonably expect to incur about $5,900,000 in selling, general, and administrative expenses in the coming year.

Can selling/G&A expenses be compared to net income?

Yes. The sum of these expenses is divided by net income, to produce a ratio that can be expressed as a decimal or percentage.

$$\text{Selling-G\&A-to-net-income ratio} = \frac{\text{Selling, G\&A (\$)}}{\text{Net income}}$$

Example: In 19X1, XYZ Corp. incurred G&A expenses of $1,200,000 and selling expenses of $4,200,000. Its net income for the year was $49,025,000.

$$\text{Selling-G\&A-to-net-income ratio} = \frac{\text{Selling, G\&A (\$)}}{\text{Net income}}$$

$$= \frac{\$4,200,000 + \$1,200,000}{\$49,025,000}$$

$$= \frac{\$5,400,000}{\$49,025,000} \quad 0.11, \text{ or } 11\%$$

Selling, general, and administrative expenses are running about 11% of net income.

Does this ratio benefit the sales manager?

Yes. If the ratio of selling, general, and administrative costs to net income proves to be valid over time, you may apply it to the profit for preliminary values until actual or better data is on hand.

Example: XYZ Corp. projects next year's net income $53,900,000. Over the years, selling, general, and administrative expenses have come to an average of 11%.

$$\text{Selling-G\&A-to-net-income ratio} = \frac{\text{Selling, G\&A (\$)}}{\text{Net income}}$$

$$0.11 = \frac{\text{Selling, G\&A (\$)}}{\$53,900,000}$$

Or:

$$\text{Selling, G\&A (\$)} = 0.11 \times \$53,900,000 = \$5,929,000$$

XYZ Corp. may reasonably expect to incur about $5,900,000 in selling, general, and administrative expenses in the coming year.

Note: Compare this estimate with those of the preceding two examples.

Can selling expenses/G&A expenses be compared individually to total sales, gross profit, or net income?

Either type of expense can be compared to total sales, gross profit, or net income. In any of these cases, the individual expense is divided by total sales, gross profit, or net income. (Only one formula and example are shown.)

$$\text{Selling-expenses-to-total-sales ratio} = \frac{\text{Selling expenses}}{\text{Total sales}}$$

Example: The following data is available for XYZ Corp.:

Total sales		$1,100,000,000
Net income		49,025,000
Selling expenses:		
Advertising & promotion	$3,000,000	
Selling commissions	1,200,000	
Total selling expenses		4,200,000

$$\text{Selling-expenses-to-total-sales ratio} = \frac{\text{Selling expenses}}{\text{Total sales}}$$
$$= \frac{\$4,200,000}{\$1,100,000,000} = 0.00382, \text{ or } 0.38\%$$

XYZ's selling expenses come to about 0.38% of total sales.

By applying the preceding general formula, an array of ratios can be developed and trend analysis applied.

Example: XYZ Corp. has put together the following data for the years 19X0 and 19X1:

(in $000s)

	19X1	19X0	Variance ($)	Variance (%)
Total sales	$1,100,000	$995,000	$105,000	+10.6
Net income	49,025	38,350	10,675	+27.8
Selling expenses:				
Adv. & promo.	3,000	2,800	200	+ 7.1
Commissions	1,200	1,400	(200)	−14.3
Total	4,200	4,200		
Ratios to Total Sales				
Adv. & promotion	.27%	.28%	−0.01%	− 3.6%
Commisions	.11%	.14%	−0.03%	−21.4%
Ratios to Net Income				
Adv. & promotion	6.1%	7.3%	−1.2%	−16.4%
Commissions	2.4%	3.7%	−1.3%	−35.1%

Ratio to sales:

- The decline in advertising and promotion of 3.6% may have resulted from a greater proportional increase in sales.

- The decrease in commission expense ratio is accounted for

by the increase in total sales, which was greater than the increase in commission dollars.

Ratio to net income:

- The ratio of commissions to net income went down primarily becauyse the 27.8% rise in net income more than offset the 7.1% increase in commissions.

- The 35.1% decrease in sales commissions is due to the 27.8% increase in net income versus a 14.3% decline in commissions.

Assuming these these expense ratios are consistent from one period to another, their analysis enables the sales manager to:

- Assess trends in the relationships between selling expenses and sales volume and/or net income.

- Establish expense limitations and controls.

- Use guidelines based on historical experience for expense surveillance and for planning a realistic selling expense budget.

How is the rate of selling expenses and G&A per direct labor hour computed?

The sum of selling, general, and administrative expenses is divided by the total number of direct labor hours performed within the period. The result is a rate, expressed as dollars per direct labor hour.

$$\text{Selling-G\&A-per-direct-labor-hour rate} = \frac{\text{Selling, G\&A expenses}}{\text{Direct labor hours}}$$

Example: In 19X1, XYZ Corp. incurred G&A expenses of $1,200,000 and selling expenses of $4,200,000. During the year, it paid for 39,400,000 direct labor hours.

$$\text{Selling-G\&A-per-direct-labor-hour rate} = \frac{\text{Selling, G\&A expenses}}{\text{Direct labor hours}}$$

$$= \frac{\$4,200,000 + \$1,200,000}{39,400,000}$$

$$= \frac{\$5,400,000}{39,400,000} = 0.137, \text{ or } \$0.14/\text{hour}$$

For every direct labor hour performed, XYZ Corp. spends 14 cents on selling, general, and administrative expenses.

Of what benefit is the rate of selling/G&A expenses per direct labor hour?

As direct labor hours and sales activity increase, they affect G&A and selling expenses. If a combined G&A and selling expense "rate" can be historically validated, it can expresses what these expenses "should" be as a dollar rate per direct labor hour. Companies can use this rate per hour or the ratio of selling/G&A to direct labor *dollars* (see next section). But the comparison to direct labor *hours* is more commonly used because an increase in hourly labor rate does not act as a "hidden" source of higher labor costs.

Can selling, general, and administrative expenses be compared to direct labor dollars?

Yes. The sum of selling and G&A costs can be divided by the total direct labor dollars spent in a period. The result is a ratio, expressed as a decimal or percentage.

$$\text{Selling-G\&A-to-direct-labor-dollars ratio} = \frac{\text{Selling, G\&A (\$)}}{\text{Direct labor dollars}}$$

Example: In 19X1, XYZ Corp. incurred G&A expenses of $1,200,000 and selling expenses of $4,200,000. During the year, it paid $198,000,000 in direct labor costs.

$$
\begin{aligned}
\text{Selling-G\&A-per-direct-labor-dollar rate} &= \frac{\text{Selling, G\&A (\$)}}{\text{Direct labor dollars}} \\
&= \frac{\$4,200,000 + \$1,200,000}{\$198,000,000} \\
&= \frac{\$5,400,000}{\$198,000,000} \\
&= 0.027, \text{ or } 2.7\%
\end{aligned}
$$

The ratio of selling, general, and administrative expenses to direct labor dollars is 2.7%. Expressed another way: For every direct labor dollar spent, XYZ Corp. spends 2.7% (or 2.7 cents) on selling, general, and administrative expenses.

What purpose is served by the ratio of selling/G&A to direct labor dollars?

If the ratio can be accepted as a guideline, it enables the sales manager to insert an estimated dollar figure in expense projections.

Example: XYZ Corp. estimates that it will spend $205,000,000 on direct labor dollars in the coming year.

Also, the ratio of selling, general, and administrative costs to direct labor dollars has been, on average, 2.7%.

$$\begin{array}{c} \text{Selling-G\&A-to-direct-} \\ \text{labor-dollars ratio} \end{array} = \frac{\text{Selling, G\&A (\$)}}{\text{Direct labor dollars}}$$

$$0.027 = \frac{\text{Selling, G\&A (\$)}}{\$205{,}000{,}000}$$

Or:

Selling, G&A ($) = 0.027 × $205,000,000 = $5,535,000

XYZ can reasonably expect to pay $5,535,000 in selling, general, and administrative expenses in the year to come.

Overhead

What is overhead?

Overhead is an indirect expense relating to service and support activities in a company, other than selling or G&A. These expenses are not directly related to the manufacturing of the company product. The term overhead is often used as a synonym for all indirect expenses, including selling and G&A.

Can indirect costs be compared to total costs?

Yes. Rising "overhead," if not detected, can erode profit margins. Comparing indirect with direct costs is one way of monitoring this outflow of funds.

$$\begin{array}{c} \text{Indirect-to-direct-} \\ \text{cost ratio} \end{array} = \frac{\text{Indirect costs}}{\begin{array}{c}\text{Direct costs + Indirect costs} \\ \text{(cost of sales)}\end{array}}$$

Example: In July, XYZ Corp.'s total cost of sales is $33,000,000, its indirect costs $2,200,000. Over the previous half-year, its six-month cost of sales was $225,500,000, indirect costs $13,800,000.

The six-month ratio:

$$\begin{array}{c} \text{Indirect-to-direct-} \\ \text{cost ratio} \end{array} = \frac{\text{Indirect costs}}{\begin{array}{c}\text{Direct costs + Indirect costs} \\ \text{(cost of sales)}\end{array}}$$

$$= \frac{\$13{,}800{,}000}{\$225{,}500{,}000 + \$13{,}800{,}000}$$

$$= \frac{\$13{,}800{,}000}{\$239{,}300{,}000} = 0.577, \text{ or } 5.8\%$$

The six-month average ratio of indirect to total costs is 5.8%.
    For the July ratio:

$$\text{Indirect-to-direct-cost ratio} = \frac{\text{Indirect costs}}{\text{Direct costs} + \text{Indirect costs} \text{ (cost of sales)}}$$

$$= \frac{\$2,200,000}{\$33,000,000 + \$2,200,000}$$

$$= \frac{\$2,200,000}{\$35,200,000} = 0.0625, \text{ or } 6.3\%$$

July indirect costs, at 6.3% of total costs, are running slightly higher than the prior six-month average, 5.8%.

What is the ratio of overhead to cost of sales?

This ratio weighs overhead dollars against those spent in generating sales—"cost of sales."

$$\text{Total-overhead-to-cost-of-sales ratio} = \frac{\text{Total overhead (\$)}}{\text{Cost of sales (\$)}}$$

Note: This ratio can be used for any period—month, quarter, year, etc.

Example: For 19X1, XYZ Corp.'s total overhead came to $269,800,000, and its cost of sales to $945,000,000.

$$\text{Total-overhead-to-cost-of-sales ratio} = \frac{\text{Total overhead (\$)}}{\text{Cost of sales (\$)}}$$

$$= \frac{\$269,800,000}{\$945,000,000}$$

$$= 0.286, \text{ or } 28.6\%$$

Overhead costs came to 28.6% of the cost of sales.

What good does it do to compare overhead to cost of sales?

Along with direct labor, direct material, and other direct costs, overhead is an important element in the composition of cost of sales. Variances from one period to the next can be the occasion for follow-up action.

Example: The following data is available for XYZ Corp.

(in $000,000s)

Expense	19X1 $	19X0 $	Variance $	%
Total overhead	269.8	253.8	16.0	6.3
Cost of sales	945.0	865.0	80.0	9.2
Overhead-to-cost-of-sales ratio (%)	28.6	29.3	0.2	0.70

The ratio of overhead to cost of sales decreased slightly from 29.3% to 28.6% (a variance of 0.7%). This was due to the higher cost of sales, which was only partially offset by a smaller increase in overhead. From the one year to the other, the cost of sales rose at only a little greater rate than overhead.

HOW SALES AFFECT A COMPANY'S FINANCIAL STATUS

Are sales reflected on the balance sheet?

Not as a distinct entry. However, many entries on the balance can be related to sales, which represent the key entry on the income statement.

Example: For all calculations in this section, the following balance sheet will be used.

ABC Co.
Balance Sheet
19X0 (in $000,000s)

	Amount
Current Assets	
Cash	$ 3.50
Marketable securities	3.30
Accounts receivable	28.70
Inventories	
Raw materials	26.80
Work in process	10.70
Finished goods	7.30
Subtotal	44.80
Prepaid expenses	0.25
Total current assets	$ 80.55
Property, Plant, and Equipment	
Land	$ 2.30
Buildings/improvement	20.00
Machinery/equipment	31.40
Subtotal	$ 53.70

	Amount
Less: Accumulated depr'n.	17.90
Net fixed assets	$ 35.80
Deferred Charges	0.90
Total assets	**$ 117.25**
Current Liabilities	
Notes payable	$ 1.40
Current portion—LT debt	2.50
Accrued payroll	3.60
Accounts payable	20.85
Income tax payable	2.60
Total current liabilities	$ 30.95
Deferred Income Taxes	1.90
Long-Term Debt	26.70
Total liabilities	**$ 59.55**
Stockholders' Equity	
Common stock	$ 3.70
Paid-in capital	26.01
Retained earnings	27.99
Total equity capital	**$ 57.70**
Total liabilities/capital	**$117.25**

Sales and Assets

What is the cash turnover ratio?

The cash turnover ratio relates sales (the "top line" on the income statement) to a company's cash balance (an entry in the current assets section of the balance sheet).

$$\text{Cash turnover} = \frac{\text{Sales}}{\text{Cash}}$$

Example: With sales of $240,000,000, ABC Co.'s current assets section is as follows:

	Amount
Current Assets	
Cash	$ 3,500,000
Marketable securities	3,300,000
Accounts receivable	28,700,000

	Amount
Inventories	
Raw materials	26,800,000
Work in process	10,700,000
Finished goods	7,300,000
Subtotal	44,800,000
Prepaid expenses	250,000
Total current assets	$ 80,550,000

$$\text{Cash turnover} = \frac{\text{Sales}}{\text{Cash}} = \frac{\$240,000,000}{\$3,500,000} = 68.6$$

ABC Co. sales are over 68 times its cash balance.

What does the cash turnover indicate?

With this ratio, you can analyze and assess the effectiveness of an organization's use of its cash position to generate revenue. Generally, the higher the ratio, the more effective use the sales manager is making of cash.

Also, the turnover rate is helpful in determining preliminary cash balance forcasts based on sales projections.

Note: For best results an average cash position should be used.

Example: ABC Co. has ascertained that its cash position is historically 1/65 of its sales volume. Management projects a sales volume of $252,000,000 for the upcoming year.

$$\frac{1}{65} = \frac{\text{Sales}}{\text{Cash}} = \frac{\$252,000,000}{\text{Cash}}$$

Or:

$$\text{Cash} = \frac{\$252,000,000}{65} = \$3,876,923$$

ABC Co. can look for a cash position in the neighborhood of $3,800,000 or $3,900,000.

What is the fixed asset turnover?

The fixed asset turnover is a comparison of annualized sales (the "top line" of the income statement) to the average value of fixed assets (a balance sheet item).

$$\text{Fixed asset} \atop \text{turnover} = \frac{\text{Sales}}{\text{Fixed assets}}$$

Example: With annual sales of $240,000,000, ABC Co. has fixed assets of $35,800,000.

Property, Plant, and Equipment	
Land	$ 2,300,000
Buildings/improvement	20,000,000
Machinery/equipment	31,400,000
Subtotal	$ 53,700,000
Less: Accumulated depr'n.	17,900,000
Net fixed assets	**$35,800,000**

$$\text{Fixed asset} \atop \text{turnover} = \frac{\text{Sales}}{\text{Fixed assets}}$$

$$= \frac{\$240,000,000}{\$35,800,000} = 6.70$$

ABC enjoys a sales volume that is 6.70 times the value of its fixed assets.

What does the fixed asset turnover reflect?

This ratio may be used to assess performance, but with caution. For example, comparing the turnover ratios of two or more organizations may be misleading if some rent buildings while others own them. Heavy depreciation will increase fixed assets and lower the turnover ratio, while lease payments will lead to a higher ratio.

The ratio is also useful as a planning guideline. It can uncover too much or too little capacity, that is, either too much or too little plant and equipment to support a given sales volume.

How may sales be related to fixed assets?

Sales (from the income statement) may be expressed as a multiple of the average value of fixed assets (a balance sheet entry).

$$\text{Fixed-assets-to-} \atop \text{sales ratio} = \frac{\text{Sales}}{\text{Fixed assets}}$$

Example: With annual sales of $240,000,000, ABC Co. has fixed assets of $35,800,000.

Property, Plant, and Equipment	
Land	$ 2,300,000
Buildings/improvement	20,000,000
Machinery/equipment	31,400,000
Subtotal	$53,700,000
Less: Accumulated depr'n.	17,900,000
Net fixed assets	**$35,800,000**

$$\text{Fixed-assets-to-sales ratio} = \frac{\text{Sales}}{\text{Fixed assets}}$$

$$= \frac{\$240,000,000}{\$35,800,000} = 6.70$$

ABC's sales are 6.70 times that of its average fixed assets.

What is the meaning of the sales-to-fixed-assets ratio?

While fixed assets in themselves do not produce sales, without them only limited sales can be made in a product-oriented company. This ratio can provide insight as to whether an organization has too much capacity or too little for a given sales volume.

Note: When comparing ratios of many organizations in the same industry, consider the age of the assets, price levels at the time of purchase, and the depreciation policies with their related effect on fixed asset valuation. For example, a low ratio could indicate an excessive valuation of the fixed assets without a comparable increase in sales.

How is the total asset turnover computed?

The total asset turnover compares a company's sales (the income statement's "top line") to its total assets (from the balance sheet). It is usually expressed as a multiple.

$$\text{Total assets turnover ratio} = \frac{\text{Sales}}{\text{Total assets}}$$

Example: With annual sales of $240,000,000, part of ABC Co.'s balance is as follows:

	Amount
Current Assets	
Cash	$ 3,500,000
Marketable securities	3,300,000
Accounts receivable	28,700,000

	Amount
Inventories	
Raw materials	26,800,000
Work in process	10,700,000
Finished goods	7,300,000
Subtotal	44,800,000
Prepaid expenses	250,000
Total current assets	$ 80,550,000
Property, Plant, and Equipment	
Land	$ 2,300,000
Buildings/improvement	20,000,000
Machinery/equipment	31,400,000
Subtotal	$ 53,700,000
Less: Accumulated depr'n.	17,900,000
Net fixed assets	$ 35,800,000
Deferred Charges	900,000
Total assets	**$ 117,250,000**

$$\text{Total asset turnover ratio} = \frac{\text{Sales}}{\text{Total assets}}$$

$$= \frac{\$240,000,000}{\$117,250,000} = 2.05$$

ABC's total assets generate a little over twice their value in sales volume.

Of what use is the asset turnover ratio?

This ratio gauges how well an organization is making use of its total assets. The higher the multiple, the more efficient the company.

Also, given a sales forecast, the organization can project its total assets position.

Example: ABC Co. knows from past experience that its sales run about twice the value of its total assets. For the upcoming year, the sales forecast is $252,000,000.

$$\text{Total assets turnover ratio} = \frac{\text{Sales}}{\text{Total assets}}$$

Or:

$$\text{Total assets} = \frac{\text{Sales}}{\text{Total assets turnover ratio}}$$

$$= \frac{\$252{,}000{,}000}{2} = \$126{,}000{,}000$$

ABC Co. is looking for about $126,000,000 in total assets in the coming year.

Sales and Capital

What is capital?

Capital is the difference between the value of a company's assets and the total of its liabilities (both balance sheet entries). Capital represents the ownership interest of investors.

$$\text{Capital} = \text{Assets} - \text{Liabilities}$$

Example: ABC's balance shows the following total asset and total liability amounts:

	Amount
Current Assets	
Cash	$ 3.50
Marketable securities	3.30
Accounts receivable	28.70
Inventories	
Raw materials	26.80
Work in process	10.70
Finished goods	7.30
Subtotal	80.30
Prepaid expenses	0.25
Total current assets	$ 80.55
Property, Plant, and Equipment	
Land	$ 2.30
Buildings/improvement	20.00
Machinery/equipment	31.40
Subtotal	$ 53.70
Less: Accumulated depr'n.	17.90
Net fixed assets	$ 35.80
Deferred Charges	0.90
Total assets	**$117.25**

	Amount
Current Liabilities	
Notes payable	$ 1.40
Current portion—LT debt	2.50
Accrued payroll	3.60
Accounts payable	20.85
Income tax payable	2.60
Total current liabilities	$ 30.95
Deferred Income Taxes	1.90
Long-Term Debt	26.70
Total liabilities	**$ 59.55**
Stockholders' Equity	
Common stock	$ 3.70
Paid-in capital	26.01
Retained earnings	27.99
Total equity capital	**$ 57.70**
Total liabilities/capital	**$117.25**

Capital = Assets − Liabilities

$$= \$117,250,000 - \$59,550,000 = \$57,700,000$$

ABC has capital of $57,700,000.

What is the investors'-capital-to-sales ratio?

This ratio is the result of dividing stockholders' equity by sales.

$$\text{Investors'-capital-to-sales ratio} = \frac{\text{Stockholder's equity}}{\text{Sales}}$$

Example: With 19X0 sales of $240,000,000 (the "top line" of the income statement), ABC Co.'s equity was $57,700,000.

Stockholders' Equity	
Common stock	$ 3,700,000
Paid-in capital	26,010,000
Retained earnings	27,990,000
Total equity capital	**$57,700,000**

$$\text{Investors'-capital-to-sales ratio} = \frac{\text{Stockholders' equity}}{\text{Sales}}$$

$$= \frac{\$57,700,00}{\$240,000,000} = 0.2404, \text{ or } 24.0\%$$

Stockholders' equity (investors' capital) represents 24% of ABC's sales in 19X0.

What does the ratio of investors' capital to sales indicate?

This ratio reflects the percentage of sales financed by stockholders' equity. It answers the question as to whether investors are investing too much or too little for the sales volume being achieved. A high ratio indicates that sales are being fueled by capital. The lower the percentage, therefore, the more favorable the company's position.

What is the ratio of capital employed?

To compute this ratio:

- Adjust capital (stockholders' equity) by deducting the value of assets that do not contribute to operating income, such as marketable securities or other forms of investment. (These are all balance sheet entries.)

- Divide the adjusted capital value into sales (the "top line" on the income statment).

$$\frac{\text{Capital-}}{\text{employed ratio}} = \frac{\text{Sales}}{\text{Capital} - \text{Nonoperational assets}}$$

Note: To compare periods, use end-of-period figures.

Example: ABC Co.'s sales are $240,000,000. Portions of ABC Co.'s balance sheet are as follows:

	Amount
Current Assets	
Cash	$ 3,500,000
Marketable securities	**3,300,000**
Accounts receivable	28,700,000
Inventories	
Raw materials	26,800,000
Work in process	10,700,000
Finished goods	7,300,000
Subtotal	44,800,000
Prepaid expenses	250,000
Total current assets	$ 80,550,000
Property, Plant, and Equipment	
Land	$ 2,300,000
Buildings/improvement	20,000,000
Machinery/equipment	31,400,000
Subtotal	$ 53,700,000

	Amount
Less: Accumulated depr'n.	17,900,000
Net fixed assets	$ 35,800,000
Deferred Charges	900,000
Total assets	**$117,250,000**

• • •

Stockholders' Equity	
Common stock	$ 3,700,000
Paid-in capital	26,010,000
Retained earnings	27,990,000
Total equity capital	**$ 57,700,000**

*Adjust total capital by deducting the value of marketable securities:

Total equity capital	$57,700,000
Less: Marketable securities	3,300,000
Adjusted capital	$54,400,000

$$\text{Capital-employed ratio} = \frac{\text{Sales}}{\text{Capital} - \text{Nonoperational assets}}$$

$$= \frac{\$240,000,000}{\$54,400,00} = 4.41$$

Sales amounted to 4.4 times the value of assets (or capital) employed.

What does the capital-employed ratio say about an organization?

This ratio reflects how well capital (adjusted to exclude nonoperational assets) is being used to produce revenue (sales). The higher the rate, the more effectively capital is being utilized.

How is the profit return on sales computed?

The profit rate of return on sales may be computed by dividing either net income or income from operations (operating income) by sales.

$$\text{Profit return on sales} = \frac{\text{Net income or Operating income}}{\text{Sales}}$$

Example: ABC Co.'s sales are $240,000,000, with net income of $18,980,000.

$$\text{Profit return} \atop \text{on sales} = \frac{\text{Net income}}{\text{Sales}}$$

$$= \frac{\$18,980,000}{\$240,000,000} = 0.0791, \text{ or } 7.9\%$$

ABC earned a net-income profit return of 7.9% on sales. The same formula applies to operating income.

Sales and Working Capital

What is working capital?

Working capital, sometimes known as net working capital or net current assets, is equal to the difference between current assets and current liabilities, both balance sheet entries.

Working capital = Current assets − Current liabilities

Example: Portions of ABC Co.'s balance sheet are as follows:

	Amount
Current Assets	
Cash	$ 3,500,000
Marketable securities	3,300,000
Accounts receivable	28,700,000
Inventories	
Raw materials	26,800,000
Work in process	10,700,000
Finished goods	7,300,000
Subtotal	44,800,000
Prepaid expenses	250,000
Total current assets	**$80,550,000**
• • •	
Current Liabilities	
Notes payable	$ 1,400,000
Current portion—LT debt	2,500,000
Accrued payroll	3,600,000
Accounts payable	20,850,000
Income tax payable	2,600,000
Total current liabilities	**$30,950,000**

Working
  capital = Current assets − Current liabilities
       = $80,550,000 − $30,950,000 = $49,600,000

ABC Co. has working capital of $49,600,000.

What does working capital reflect?

The more working capital a company has, the greater is its liquidity.

How is average working capital computed?

Average working capital is computed by adding the working capital values at the beginning and end of an accounting period and dividing by 2.

$$\text{Average working capital} = \frac{\text{Beginning working capital} + \text{End working capital}}{2}$$

Example: ABC Co.'s working capital at the beginning of 19X0 was $48,100,000. It was $49,600,000 at the end of the year.

$$\text{Average working capital} = \frac{\text{Beginning working capital} + \text{End working capital}}{2}$$

$$= \frac{\$48,100,000 + \$49,600,00}{2}$$

$$= \frac{\$97,700,000}{2} = \$48,850,000$$

ABC's average working capital for 19X0 is $48,850,000.

What is the working capital turnover?

Working capital turnover is a ratio of sales to average working capital.

$$\text{Working-capital ratio} = \frac{\text{Sales}}{\text{Working capital}}$$

Example: ABC Co. has sales of $240,000,000 and average working capital of $48,850,000 (see preceding example).

$$\text{Working-capital ratio} = \frac{\text{Sales}}{\text{Working capital}}$$

$$= \frac{\$240,000,000}{\$48,850,000} = 4.91$$

ABC's working capital turnover is 4.91; that is, it generates almost sales equal to about 5 times the amount of its working capital.

What does the working capital turnover represent?

This turnover indicates how well the sales manager is using working capital to generate revenues—how many "times" it is turning working capital over into sales revenues. The higher the ratio, the better the sales manager looks. There is, however, no normal ratio for each industry. The "right" ratio depends on the nature of the business, along with its requirements, asset turnover, and sales demands.

Can working capital be compared to sales?

Yes. The average working capital figure can be divided by sales (usually annualized).

$$\text{Working-capital-to-sales ratio} = \frac{\text{Working capital}}{\text{Sales}}$$

Example: ABC Co. has sales of $240,000,000 and average working capital of $48,850,000 (see page 000).

$$\text{Working-capital-to-sales ratio} = \frac{\text{Working capital}}{\text{Sales}}$$
$$= \frac{\$48,850,000}{\$240,000,000} = 0.204, \text{ or } 20.4\%$$

ABC's working capital represents 20.4% of sales.

Of what use is the working-capital-to-sales ratio?

The primary use of this ratio is using it to arrive at working capital needs, given a sales projection.

Example: ABC Co.'s working capital historically runs at a level that is about 20% of sales. For the upcoming year, the sales manager forecasts sales of $252,000,000.

$$\text{Working-capital-to-sales ratio} = \frac{\text{Working capital}}{\text{Sales}}$$
$$0.20 = \frac{\text{Working capital}}{\$252,000,000}$$

Or:

Working capital = 0.20 × $252,000,000 = $50,400,000

For 19X1, ABC needs a little over $50,000,000 in working capital to meet its sales projection.

HOW SALES PROVIDE THE FIRM WITH LEVERAGE

What is leverage?

Leverage is best explained by an example. An organization borrows funds at $x\%$ interest and invests the funds in assets that yield $y\%$. If the $y\%$ yield is greater than the $x\%$ cost, then the difference represents pure gain to the equity stockholder. This is leverage—the use of certain fixed costs to enhance returns on investments or sales revenues. The purpose of leverage is that small changes in costs are associated with greater changes in return.

Example: A corporation may issue bonds to raise funds for new plant construction. The interest on the bonds and the depreciation on the plant become fixed assets, and the plant enables the company to fill a great many more orders and thereby increase sales.

What are leverage ratios?

Leverage ratios measure the degree to which a company makes use of leverage.

What is the operating leverage ratio?

The operating leverage ratio assesses the effect of fluctuating sales on operating profits.

$$\text{Operating leverage ratio} = \frac{\text{Sales} - \text{Variable expenses}}{\text{Sales} - \text{Total expenses}}$$

Since operating income equals sales less the sum of variable and fixed expenses, then:

$$\text{Operating leverage ratio} = \frac{\text{Sales} - \text{Variable expenses}}{\text{Operating income}}$$

Example: With first-quarter sales at $300,000, MNO Corp. incurs variable costs of $234,000 and fixed expenses of $36,000.

$$
\begin{aligned}
\text{Operating leverage ratio} &= \frac{\text{Sales} - \text{Variable expenses}}{\text{Sales} - \text{Fixed expenses}} \\
&= \frac{\$300{,}000 - \$234{,}000}{\$300{,}000 - (\$234{,}000 + \$36{,}000)} \\
&= \frac{\$300{,}000 - \$234{,}000}{\$300{,}000 - \$270{,}000} \\
&= \frac{\$66{,}000}{\$30{,}000} = 2.2
\end{aligned}
$$

The first-quarter operating leverage factor is 2.2.

Why is the operating leverage factor important?

Operating leverage is the leverage a company gains from sales volume. High sales volumes give an organization income with which to operate. Decreased sales volumes creates situations in which operating income is spread thin, posing a threat to a company's operating ability. The operating leverage ratio enables the sales manager to evaluate this so-called "income risk." The operating leverage factor says that income from operations changes "so many times" the percentage change sales volume. Note in the following formula that the factor is inversely proportional to operating income (income from operations):

$$\text{Operating leverage ratio} = \frac{\text{Sales} - \text{Variable expenses}}{\text{Operating income}}$$

Note: Income risk is distinguished from financial risk, which is posed by the heavy use of debt support by creditors.

Example: See the preceding example. An operating leverage factor of 2.2 means that operating income ($30,000 in the example) will change 2.2 times the percentage change in sales. If sales increase by 15%, then income from operations will increase by approximately 33%, or $9,900 (15% times 2.2): $30,000 times 0.33). For a decrease of 15% in sales, operating income would drop by $9,900.

Does the operating leverage factor change?

The operating leverage factor changes with fluctuations in sales volume and in expenses.

Example: In the second quarter of operation, MNO Corp. increases 15% to $345,000; in the third quarter, it drops by 15% to $255,000. Assume the rare occurrence that variable expenses remain at $234,000 and fixed expenses at $36,000.

For the increase in sales volume:

$$
\begin{aligned}
\text{Operating leverage ratio} &= \frac{\text{Sales} - \text{Variable expenses}}{\text{Sales} - \text{Fixed expenses}} \\[4pt]
&= \frac{\$345,000 - \$234,000}{\$345,000 - (\$234,000 + \$36,000)} \\[4pt]
&= \frac{\$345,000 - \$234,000}{\$345,000 - \$270,000} \\[4pt]
&= \frac{\$111,000}{\$75,000} = +1.48
\end{aligned}
$$

For the decrease in sales volume:

$$\begin{aligned}
\text{Operating leverage ratio} &= \frac{\text{Sales} - \text{Variable expenses}}{\text{Sales} - \text{Fixed expenses}} \\[2mm]
&= \frac{\$255{,}000 - \$234{,}000}{\$255{,}000 - (\$234{,}000 + \$36{,}000)} \\[2mm]
&= \frac{\$255{,}000 - \$234{,}000}{\$255{,}000 - \$270{,}000} \\[2mm]
&= \frac{\$21{,}000}{-\$15{,}000} = +1.40
\end{aligned}$$

When the sales volume changes (up or down), so did the operating leverage factor. At each of the revised sales levels, the operating factors change.

IS THE COMPANY MAKING MONEY ON SALES? BREAK-EVEN ANALYSIS

What is the break-even point?

In business, the break-even point is the sales volume level at which the business neither profits nor loses money; sales and total costs are exactly equal. It is a function of sales volume, and fixed and variable expenses.

$$\text{Break-even point} = \frac{\text{Fixed expenses}}{1 - \dfrac{\text{Variable expenses}}{\text{Sales}}}$$

Example: MNO Corp. has first-quarter sales for Product A of \$300,000. Its quarterly fixed expenses are \$36,000, its variable expenses \$234,000.

$$\begin{aligned}
\text{Break-even point} &= \frac{\text{Fixed expenses}}{1 - \dfrac{\text{Variable expenses}}{\text{Sales}}} \\[2mm]
&= \frac{\$36{,}000}{1 - \dfrac{\$234{,}000}{\$300{,}000}} \\[2mm]
&= \frac{\$36{,}000}{1 - 0.78} \\[2mm]
&= \frac{\$36{,}000}{0.22} = \$163{,}636
\end{aligned}$$

MNO's break-even point is \$163,636. That is, before the dollar volume of sales reaches this point, MNO loses money;

after it, MNO makes a profit. Precisely at that level, no profit or loss results.

When is the break-even point calculation made?

This computation is made to enable the sales manager to know the point at which a product, a product line, or the business itself becomes profitable.

Example: See the preceding example. MNO sales management knows that the break-even point for Product A is $163,636. If the unit price for Product A is $20, then a little over 8,180 units must be sold for the product to break even: $163,636 divided by $20 equals 8,181.8 units. Management can then compare that requirement with sales estimates. Can enough units be sold to make Product A a profitable venture for the organization?

Does the break-even point change?

Yes. The break-even point changes with:

- Fixed expenses
- Variable expenses
- Sales volume

How do fixed expenses affect the break-even point?

Expenses drive the break-even point up. Since some fixed expenses remain the same regardless of sales volume, these expenses particularly affect break-even: The greater the total fixed expenses, the higher the break-even point will be.

Example: See the preceding example. Assume that MNO Corp. has first-quarter sales for Product A of $300,000 and variable expenses of $234,000, but fixed expenses rise $14,000 (from $36,000 to $50,000).

$$\text{Break-even point} = \frac{\text{Fixed expenses}}{1 - \dfrac{\text{Variable expenses}}{\text{Sales}}}$$

$$= \frac{\$50,000}{1 - \dfrac{\$234,000}{\$300,000}}$$

$$= \frac{\$50,000}{1 - 0.78}$$

$$= \frac{\$50,000}{0.22} = \$227,272$$

MNO's break-even point increases from \$163,636 to
\$227,272. For Product A to break even, sales have to in-
crease by \$63,636 (\$227,272 less \$163,636).

How do sales affect the break-even point?

The break-even point generally declines with increased sales
volume, assuming fixed expenses do not rise (or rise disproportionately) and that variable expenses increase only as
necessary to keep pace with orders.

Example: See the preceding example. Assume that in the
second-quarter:

- Sales for Product A rise by 20%:
  (\$300,000 times 0.20 equals \$60,000)   \$360,000
- Variable expenses increase by 15.38%:
  (\$234,000 times 0.1538 equals \$36,000)   \$270,000
- Fixed expenses remain the same.   \$36,000

$$\text{Break-even point} = \frac{\text{Fixed expenses}}{1 - \dfrac{\text{Variable expenses}}{\text{Sales}}}$$

$$= \frac{\$36,000}{1 - \dfrac{\$270,000}{\$360,000}}$$

$$= \frac{\$36,000}{1 - 0.75}$$

$$= \frac{\$36,000}{0.25} = \$144,000$$

MNO's break-even point decreases from \$163,636 to
\$144,000.

Can the break-even calculation be used to determine the sales volume necessary to achieve a given level of operating income?

Yes. Given a break-even point, the sales manager can calculate the sales volume required to maintain a predetermined
level of operating income if a variable changes. Use the
complement of the factor derived for the denominator of the
break-even formula in the following equation, and solve for
Sales:

$$\text{Sales} = \frac{\text{Fixed expenses} + \text{Operating income}}{\text{Complement}}$$

Example: ABC Co. has first-quarter sales for Product × of $400,000. Its quarterly fixed expenses are $72,000, its variable expenses $238,000. Management is looking for operating income of $120,000 on this product.

$$\text{Break-even point} = \frac{\text{Fixed expenses}}{1 - \dfrac{\text{Variable expenses}}{\text{Sales}}}$$

$$= \frac{\$72,000}{1 - \dfrac{\$238,000}{\$400,000}}$$

$$= \frac{\$70,000}{1 - 0.595}$$

$$= \frac{\$72,000}{0.405} = \$177,778$$

Product × breaks even at $177,778 worth of sales. The factor in the denominator of the break-even formula is 0.405.

In the second quarter, plant expansion causes fixed expenses to rise by $30,000 to $102,000. Management must now know the sales level at which operating income of $120,000 can be maintained.

$$\text{Sales} = \frac{\text{Fixed expenses} + \text{Operating income}}{\text{Complement}}$$

$$= \frac{\$102,000 + \$120,000}{0.405}$$

$$= \frac{\$222,000}{0.405} = \$548,148$$

With increase plant (fixed) costs, sales must increase to $548,148 for Product × to yield $120,000 in operating income.

WHAT IS THE QUALITY OF SALES? ACCOUNTS RECEIVABLE

Accounts Receivable Turnover

What is the accounts receivables turnover?

The receivables turnover is the ratio of Total credit sales to receivables. (It is also known as the sales-to-receivables ratio.)

$$\text{Receivables turnover} = \frac{\text{Total (credit) sales}}{\text{Receivables balance}}$$

Example: XYZ Corp.'s sales for the first quarter of 19X1 were \$252,800,000, and its receivables balance \$110,400,400. XYZ's receivables turnover is:

$$\text{Receivables turnover} = \frac{\text{Total credit sales}}{\text{Receivables balance}}$$

$$= \frac{\$252,800,000}{\$110,400,000} = 2.29, \text{ or } 229\%$$

Note: The receivables turnover is normally expressed as an annual figure, not quarterly.

How is the receivables turnover converted to an annual figure?

There are two methods. First, the more precise procedure is to start with annualized sales and an average receivables balance.

Example: XYZ Corp.'s annual sales are \$1,077,000,000, and its average receivables for the year are \$107,300,000. Its annual receivables turnover is:

$$\text{Receivables turnover} = \frac{\text{Total credit sales}}{\text{Receivables balance}}$$

$$= \frac{\$1,077,000,000}{\$107,300,000}$$

$$= 10.04, \text{ or } 1,004\%$$

Second, quarterly figures may be used and projected for the year by multiplying the resultant ratio by 4.

$$\begin{array}{c}\text{Annual receivables}\\ \text{turnover}\end{array} = \begin{array}{c}\text{Quarterly}\\ \text{receivables turnover} \times 4\end{array}$$

Example: XYZ Corp.'s sales for the first quarter of 19X1 were \$252,800,000, and its receivables balance \$110,400,400. XYZ's receivables turnover (or turnover) is:

$$\text{Receivables turnover} = \frac{\text{Total credit sales}}{\text{Receivables balance}}$$

$$= \frac{\$252,800,000}{\$110,400,000} = 2.29, \text{ or } 229\%$$

$$\begin{array}{c}\text{Annual receivables}\\ \text{turnover}\end{array} = \begin{array}{c}\text{Quarterly}\\ \text{receivables turnover} \times 4\end{array}$$

$$= 2.29, \text{ or } 229\%, \times 4 = 9.16,$$
$$\text{or } 916\%$$

How is the receivables turnover best analyzed?

Receivables turnover is compared to the trends in sales and receivables over a number of time periods. Although annual periods are preferable, quarters can be compared too. One period is established as the baseline, and the sales and receivables amounts are assigned a "baseline" value of 100%.

Example: The following quarterly data is for XYZ Corp. The first quarter is the baseline period. Both the sales and the receivables turnover trends for that quarter are assigned the value of 100%.

(in $000,000s)

Qtr	Sales	% Trend	Receivables	% of Trend	Receivables-to-Sales Ratio
1	$252.8	100%	$110.4	100%	229%
2	$274.9	109%	$111.5	101%	247%
3	$276.2	109%	$102.3	93%	270%
4	$273.1	108%	$105.1	95%	260%

The sales trend clearly indicates increases in the last three quarters of 19X1. Receivables decreased in the last two quarters but slightly increased in the second quarter (101%). The receivables turnover trend is favorable because increases in sales did not result in higher receivables, which would have necessitated a greater capital investment in outstanding customer accounts.

Note: In ascertaining why sales and receivables values vary, the two main factors are price and sales volume.

Comparing Receivables to Sales

What is the receivables-to-sales ratio?

The receivables-to-sales ratio is calculated by dividing the average receivables by Total credit sales for a given period. It reflects the average age or level of customer accounts outstanding for the period. This ratio may be calculated for a quarter or month, but it is generally better expressed as an annual figure.

$$\text{Receivables-to-sales ratio} = \frac{\text{Average receivables}}{\text{Net credit sales}}$$

Example: XYZ Corp.'s first quarter sales are $252,800,000.

Its average receivables for the quarter are \$110,400,000. The quarterly receivables-to-sales ratio is:

$$\text{Receivables-to-sales ratio} = \frac{\text{Average receivables}}{\text{Net credit sales}}$$

$$= \frac{\$110,400,000}{\$252,800,000}$$

$$= 0.437, \text{ or } 43.7\%$$

Using the same data, quarterly receivables can also be compared to annualized sales amounts. (To annualize quarterly sales figures, simply multiply them by 4.)

Example: In the preceding example, XYZ's annualized Total credit sales are \$1,011,200,000 (\$252,800,000 times 4). This figure may be used instead of the quarterly sales in the receivables-to-sales calculation:

$$\text{Receivables-to-sales ratio} = \frac{\text{Average receivables}}{\text{Net credit sales (annualized)}}$$

$$= \frac{\$110,400,000}{\$1,011,200,000}$$

$$= 0.109, \text{ or } 10.9\%$$

Why are quarterly receivables compared to annualized sales amounts?

While sales accumulate from quarter to quarter, receivables tend to fluctuate, remaining within a given range. Comparing quarterly sales with quarterly receivables therefore represents a disproportionate amount of receivables. Annualizing sales enables you to work with a more realistic figure.

Example: The following are actual figures for XYZ sales and receivables in 19X1.

(in \$000,000s)

	First	Second	Third	Fourth	Annual
Sales	\$ 252.8	\$ 274.9	\$ 276.2	\$ 273.1	\$1,077.0
Annualized sales	\$1,011.2	\$1,099.6	\$1,104.8	\$1,092.4	—
Receivables	\$ 110.4	\$ 111.5	\$ 102.3	\$ 105.1	\$ 107.3
Receivables-to-sales ratio	43.%	40.6%	37.0%	38.5%	10.0%

The actual annual receivables-to-sales ratio in this table (10.0%) is much closer to the results of the calculation in the preceding example using the first quarter's annualized sales figure (10.9%) than to the ratio using any quarter's receivables.

How is the average receivables amount arrived at?

The average receivables is the sum of the beginning and ending balances for a period divided by 2. The period may be a month, quarter, year, or any period.

$$\text{Average receivables} = \frac{\text{Beginning receivables} + \text{End-of-period receivables}}{2}$$

Example: XYZ started 19X1 with receivables of $104,300,000 and ended it with $110,300,000. Its annual receivables are:

$$\text{Average receivables} = \frac{\text{Beginning receivables} + \text{End-of-period receivables}}{2}$$

$$= \frac{\$104,300,000 + \$110,300,000}{2}$$

$$= \frac{\$214,600,000}{2} = \$107,300,000$$

Average Collection Period

How is the average collection period calculated?

The average collection period is the average number of days between the day the invoice is sent out and the day the customer pays the bill. There are two ways to make the calculation:

Method 1:

$$\text{Average collection period} = \frac{\text{Receivables}}{\text{to sales ratio}} \times \text{Days in period}$$

Example: Using XYZ's annual receivables-to-sales ratio of 10.0% (see the preceding example), its annual average collection period is:

$$\text{Average collection period} = \frac{\text{Receivables}}{\text{to sales ratio}} \times \text{Days in period}$$

$$= 10.0\% \text{ (or .100)} \times 365 \text{ days}$$

$$= 36.5 \text{ days}$$

It takes XYZ an average of 36.5 days to collect its receivables.

Method 2: Divide average annualized receivables by average daily credit sales (which is computed by dividing the number of days in the year, 365, into annual credit sales).

$$\begin{array}{c}\text{Average}\\ \text{collection period}\end{array} = \frac{\text{Average (annualized) receivables}}{\begin{array}{c}\text{Average daily credit sales}\\ \text{(Sales/365)}\end{array}}$$

Example: If XYZ'z annualized receivables is $107,300 and its annual sales $1,077,000,000, its average collection period is:

$$\begin{array}{c}\text{Average}\\ \text{collection period}\end{array} = \frac{\text{Average (annualized) receivables}}{\begin{array}{c}\text{Average daily credit sales}\\ \text{(Sales/365)}\end{array}}$$

$$= \frac{\$107,300}{\$1,077,000,000 \,/\, 365}$$

$$= \frac{\$107,300}{2950} = 36.4 \text{ days}$$

XYZ takes 36.4 days, on average, to collect a bill. Compare this result with that of the first method.

What does the average collection period mean?

Under any circumstances, the shorter the collection period, the better for the company. This computation indicates the company's efficiency in enforcing its credit policy. The company's average can be compared from one period to another, or against industry standards.

What is the aging receivables procedure for estimating collections and cash flow?

In the aging receivables (or just aging) procedure, accounts receivable are grouped according to their ages, usually under 30 days, 31-60 days, 61-90 days, and over 90 days. For each group, the beginning-of-period and end-of-period amounts are compared, to see whether it is taking the organization more or less time to receive payment.

Example: The following data is available for XYZ Corp.:

Aging Procedure (in $000,000s)

Age of Billing	Billed 12/31/X0	% of Total	Billed 12/31/X1	% of Total	% of Variance
Under 30 days	$77.7	80	$ 89.3	85	+5
31-60 days	14.6	15	12.6	12	−3
61-90 days	4.9	5	3.2	3	−2
Totals	$97.2	100	$105.1	100	—

For each group of receivables, the percentage of variance is calculated by subtracting the percentage of total for the ending balance (12/31/X1) from that for the beginning balance (12/31/X0). For the under-30-days group, for example: 85% less 80% is 5%.

This comparison indicates a favorable trend in collections. As of 12/31/X1, outstanding receivables in the under-30-days category show a 5% increase, while the percentage of variance in each of the other two categories have declined.

In planning collections and cash flow, unfavorable trends in billing groups can trigger specific reports and/or investigations into past due accounts, with appropriate action taken.

What is the days-of-sales-in-receivables ratio (or factor)?

This ratio between sales and receivables reflects the normal number of days of uncollected sales in receivables. The calculation can be made annually for comparative purposes or monthly for greater precision. The computation itself is for the quarter:

$$\text{Days of sales in receivables ratio} = \frac{\text{Receivables balance}}{\text{Quarterly sales} / 90 \text{ (days in quarter)}}$$

Note: Use 90 days for a quarter, 360 for a year.

Example: XYZ Corp.'s first quarter sales are $252,800,000, its receivables $110,400. The days of sales in receivables is:

$$\text{Days of sales in receivables ratio} = \frac{\text{Receivables balance}}{\text{Quarterly sales} / 90 \text{ (days in quarter)}}$$

$$= \frac{\$11,040,000}{\$252,800,000 / 90 \text{ days}}$$

$$= \frac{\$110,400,000}{\$280,888.89} = 39.3 \text{ days}$$

The ratio 39.3 reflects the average numbers of days it takes XYZ to receive payment on accounts receivable for the quarter.

How is the days-of-sales-in-receivables ratio put to use?

This ratio, if proven consistent over time, can provide at least a preliminary basis for estimating ending receivable balances, given sales projections. The process is:

$$\text{Ending receivable balance} = \text{Days-of-sales ratio} \times \frac{\text{Sales projection}}{\text{Days in period}}$$

Note: Use 90 days for a quarter, 360 for a year.

Example: XYZ projects second-quarter of $274,900,000, and a days-of-sales ratio of 36.5 has proven to be reliable over the past few years. The second quarter's ending receivable balance is estimated as follows:

$$\text{Ending receivable balance} = \text{Days-of-sales ratio} \times \frac{\text{Sales projection}}{\text{Days in period}}$$

$$= 36.5 \text{ (days)} \times \frac{\$274,900,000}{90 \text{ days}}$$

$$= 36.5 \times \$305,444.44 = \$11,148,722$$

For the second quarter, XYZ Corp. has $11,148,722—a little over $11 million—in receivables.

Liquidation Limit

What is the liquidation limit?

The liquidation limit is the percentage of billed sales that will be collected in the same period as they are billed. Expressed as a percentage, this limit must be determined by each organization in light of its collections history.

Example: MNO Corp. has established over a number of years that, on average, it collects 60% of its billings in the same period. The MNO liquidation limit is therefore 60%.

Note: The liquidation limit is the complement of the liquidation lag value.

What is the liquidation lag value of billed sales?

The liquidation lag value is the portion of billed sales that will be collected sometime after the billing period. Expressed as a percentage, this ratio must be determined by an organization in light of its collection record.

Example: MNO Corp. has established over a number of years that, on average, it collects 40% of its billings in the period following the billing period. The MNO liquidation lag value is therefore 40%.

Note: The liquidation lag value is the complement of the liquidation limit.

How are the liquidation limit and liquidation lag value used?

Either of these ratios can be used as a planning guideline in making cash flow projections.

Example: MNO Corp. estimates that in the upcoming year billings will average $120,000 per month. With a liquidation limit of 60%, it may reasonably expect to recoup $72,000 each month, having that amount available for cash flow purposes: $120,000 in billings times 0.60 liquidation limit equals $72,000.

Conversely, the liquidation lag value of billed sales is $48,000: $120,000 billed sales times 0.40 liquidation lag value equals $48,000.

Sales Backlog

How is backlog effectiveness measured?

To evaluate an organization's ability to handle its backlog, you must analyze historically the days-of-sales-in-backlog factor.

$$\text{Days of sales in backlog} = \frac{\text{Backlog balance}}{\text{Sales volume / Days in period}}$$

Note: Use 90 days for a quarter, 360 for a year.

Example: For the past two years, ABC Co. showed the following figures:

	(in $000s)		
	Backlog Balance	*Total Sales*	*Days in Period*
19X0	$130.0	$1,070.0	360
19X1	$160.0	$1,250.0	360

For 19X0, its days-sales-in-backlog factor is:

$$\begin{aligned} \text{Days of sales in backlog} &= \frac{\text{Backlog balance}}{\text{Sales volume / Days in period}} \\ &= \frac{\$130,000}{\$1,070,000 \ / \ 360 \text{ days}} \\ &= \frac{\$130,000}{\$2,972.22 \text{ per day}} = 43.7 \text{ days} \end{aligned}$$

ABC Co. has 43.7 days' worth of sales in backlog. For 19X1, it is 46.1 (computed in the same way as for 19X0).

Note: A high backorder ratio may be misleading if some sales are for long-range delivery.

CAN ORDERS BE FILLED?
SALES AND INVENTORY

What is the sales-to-inventory ratio?

By comparing inventory to sales volume, this ratio indicates whether there is too little or too much inventory to support the given level of sales. It is a measure of sales efficiency. The objective is to have the smallest level of inventory while still meeting sales requirements efficiently.

The ratio of sales to inventory is considered a rough measure of performance. Comparing sales and inventory is difficult because the two amounts have different bases. Inventory is valued at cost or market, whichever is lower; sales at selling price (that is, cost plus gross margin). Further, to compare periods, you must take into account prevailing business conditions. For example, a change in the price level at which new stock is acquired changes the relationship between sales and inventory. The dollar relationship could vary markedly without any actual change in the physical volume of sales or inventory. Finally, seasonal fluctuations in inventory values can also throw calculations off.

Note: Cost of sales is generally used for this estimate, but sale may substitute for it.

$$\text{Sales-to-inventory ratio} = \frac{\text{Sales}}{\text{Average inventory balance}}$$

Example: ABC Corp. shows the following data:

(in $000,000s)

	First	Second	Third	Fourth	Annual Period
			Quarter		
Sales volume	$ 252.8	$ 274.9	$ 276.2	$ 273.1	$1,077.0
Annualized sales	$1,011.2	$1,099.6	$1,104.8	$1,092.4	$1,077.0
Inventory balances	$ 260.0	$ 268.5	$ 256.9	$ 243.4	$ 257.2
Sales-to-inventory ratio	.97	1.0	1.1	1.1	4.2
Annualized ratio	3.9	4.1	4.3	4.5	4.2

The sales-to-inventory ratio for the first quarter is computed as follows:

$$\text{Sales-to-inventory ratio} = \frac{\text{Sales}}{\text{Average inventory balance}}$$

$$= \frac{\$252,800,000}{\$260,000,000} = 0.97$$

Ratios for the other quarters and the year are computed in the same way.

Does the sales-to-inventory ratio have to be annualized?

Yes, because sales accumulate over the year and inventory balances remain more or less constant from quarter to quarter. There are two ways to annualize the quarterly ratio. (1) Multiply it by 4:

$$\text{Annual ratio} = \text{Quarterly ratio} \times 4$$

(2) Multiply the quarterly sales volume by 4 and use the ratio formula.

$$\text{Annual sales-to-inventory ratio} = \frac{\text{Quarterly sales} \times 4}{\text{Average inventory balance}}$$

Example: ABC Corp.'s quarterly ratios are:

(in $000,000s)

	First	Second	Third	Fourth	Annual Period
		Quarter			
Sales volume	$ 252.8	$ 274.9	$ 276.2	$ 273.1	$1,077.0
Annualized sales	$1,011.2	$1,099.6	$1,104.8	$1,092.4	$1,077.0
Inventory balances	$ 260.0	$ 268.5	$ 256.9	$ 243.4	$ 257.2
Sales-to-inventory ratio	.97	1.0	1.1	1.1	4.2
Annualized ratio	3.9	4.1	4.3	4.5	4.2

Method 1: Multiply the ratio by 4: Use the first quarter's figures as an example.

$$\text{Annual ratio} = \text{Quarterly ratio} \times 4$$
$$= .97 \times 4 = 3.9$$

Method 2: Multiply the quarterly sales volume by 4 and use the ratio formula. Again, use the first quarter.

$$\text{Annual sales-to-inventory ratio} = \frac{\text{Quarterly sales} \times 4}{\text{Average inventory balance}}$$
$$= \frac{\$252,800,000 \times 4}{\$257,200,000}$$
$$= \frac{\$1,011,200,000}{\$257,200,000} = 3.9$$

CHAPTER 4

CONTAINING EXPENSES: COST ANALYSIS

WORDS TO KNOW

Break-even point. The sales volume at which neither a profit nor a loss is made.

COGS. *See* cost of sales.

Cost of goods sold (COGS). *See* Direct cost.

Cost of sales (COS). *See* Direct cost.

Direct cost (cost of sales [COS], cost of goods sold [COGS]). Cost that relates directly to the making of the company's product.

Direct labor. *See* Direct personnel.

Direct material. An element of cost of sales, the cost of materials used in making a product or in rendering a service.

Direct personnel (labor). The part of cost of sales paid to employees who are directly involved in the production of goods.

Fixed expense. An expense of doing business that is not directly related to the prevailing level of production and that does not fluctuate with production.

G&A. *See* General and administrative expense.

General and administrative expense. An indirect cost associated with running a business, other than production or sales.

Gross profit. Sales less cost of sales.

Indirect cost (operating expense). A cost that cannot be directly attributed to production, such as selling expenses or general and administrative (G&A) costs.

Indirect personnel (labor). The portion of payroll cost paid to workers who are not directly involved in making the company's product.

Net income. Revenues and unearned income, less all expenses, including taxes.

Net income before taxes (pretax income, pretax earnings). Revenues and unearned income, less all expenses, but before taxes are deducted.

Other indirect costs (OIC, or overhead). Indirect costs other than selling or G&A.

Total overhead. *See* Other indirect costs.

Operating expense. *See* Indirect cost.

Operating income (income from operations). Sales revenues less direct and indirect expenses.

Overhead. *See* Other direct costs.

Pretax earnings (income). *See* Net income before taxes.

Sales. *See* Total credit sales.

Selling expenses. An indirect cost associated with sales, selling expenses include the costs of marketing and contract administration.

Total credit sales (sales, total sales, total net sales, volume). All sales revenues less allowances for returns and bad debt.

Variable expense. An expense that fluctuates in proportion to the prevailing level of production.

Volume. *See* Total credit sales.

EVALUATING THE IMPACT OF PERSONNEL (LABOR)

What is direct labor?

Direct personnel (or labor) is the cost of labor directly related to the production of goods or to the rendering of services, such as assembly line workers or technicians. Direct labor includes employees directly involved in the making of a product or in the rendering of a service. Direct labor payroll falls into the category of direct costs (cost of sales, cost of goods sold).

Examples: In a manufacturing firm, direct labor would consist of, among others, the assembly line workers; in a fast-food service chain, the cooks and counter attendants.

What is indirect labor?

Indirect personnel (or labor) is the cost of labor that does contribute to production, such as foreman, accountants, salespeople, and the like. Indirect labor is made up of employees who are necessary for running a business but who are not directly involved in production or service. Indirect labor wages and salaries are indirect costs. Indirect personnel costs are part of factory overhead (or just overhead), and they should be monitored so as not to become excessive.

Examples: Receptionists, accounting department clerks, or maintenance workers.

How are direct labor and indirect labor compared?

These types of costs can be compared in terms of their headcounts.

$$\text{Indirect-to-direct-labor ratio} = \frac{\text{Indirect labor headcount}}{\text{Direct labor headcount}}$$

Generally, a low ratio is assumed to be an indicator of productive and effective use of indirect personnel. Further, if indirect manpower is reasonably reduced and controlled, the effect on total overhead expenses and rate (relative to product cost and competitive sales price) can be significant.

Example: In January XYZ Corp. has 32,909 employees. Of that total, 22,312 were classified as direct labor, 10,597 as indirect labor.

$$\text{Indirect-to-direct-labor ratio} = \frac{\text{Indirect labor headcount}}{\text{Direct labor headcount}}$$

$$= \frac{10,597}{22,312} = 0.475, \text{ or } 47.5\%$$

Of XYZ's total workforce, indirect labor represents 47.5% of direct labor.

Can indirect labor costs be compared to direct labor costs?

Yes. The indirect-to-direct-personnel ratio (which may be expressed as a decimal or a percentage) measures the proportion of indirect labor needed to maintain the current sales volume.

$$\text{Indirect-to-direct personnel ratio} = \frac{\text{Indirect personnel cost}}{\text{Direct personnel cost}}$$

Example: This quarter, ABC Corp. incurred an indirect personnel cost of $16,522,000 and a direct personnel cost of $34,737,000.

$$\text{Indirect-to-direct personnel ratio} = \frac{\text{Indirect personnel cost}}{\text{Direct personnel cost}}$$

$$= \frac{\$16,522,000}{\$34,737,000} = .4756, \text{ or } 47.6\%$$

How is the indirect-to-direct-personnel ratio used?

This ratio is used to project indirect personnel requirements by multiplying direct personnel costs by an average ratio.

$$\begin{matrix} \text{Indirect personnel} \\ \text{requirements} \end{matrix} = \begin{matrix} \text{Direct} \\ \text{personnel costs} \end{matrix} \times \begin{matrix} \text{Average indirect-} \\ \text{to-direct-personnel} \\ \text{ratio} \end{matrix}$$

Example: If ABC Corp. accepts 47.6% as a valid ratio, it can be applied to the next quarter's projected direct personnel costs (of $37,500,000) to estimate indirect labor expenses.

$$\begin{matrix} \text{Indirect personnel} \\ \text{requirements} \end{matrix} = \begin{matrix} \text{Direct} \\ \text{personnel costs} \end{matrix} \times \begin{matrix} \text{Average indirect-} \\ \text{to-direct-personnel} \\ \text{ratio} \end{matrix}$$

$$= \$37,500,000 \times .476 = \$17,850,000$$

ABC may expect indirect labor costs to be in the neighborhood of $17,850,000 in the upcoming quarter.

Can direct and indirect labor be compared to total labor?

Yes. Either type of labor cost can be expressed as a ratio or percentage of total labor cost, measured in terms of head count.

$$\begin{matrix} \text{Direct-labor-to-} \\ \text{total-labor ratio} \end{matrix} = \frac{\text{Direct labor headcount}}{\text{Total labor headcount}}$$

Or:

$$\begin{matrix} \text{Indirect-labor-to-} \\ \text{total-labor ratio} \end{matrix} = \frac{\text{Indirect labor headcount}}{\text{Total labor headcount}}$$

Example: In January XYZ Corp. has 32,909 employees. Of that total, 22,312 were classified as direct labor, 10,597 as indirect labor.

$$\begin{matrix} \text{Direct-labor-to-} \\ \text{total-labor ratio} \end{matrix} = \frac{\text{Direct labor headcount}}{\text{Total labor headcount}}$$

$$= \frac{22,312}{32,909} = 0.678, \text{ or } 67.8\%$$

$$\begin{matrix} \text{Indirect-labor-to-} \\ \text{total-labor ratio} \end{matrix} = \frac{\text{Indirect labor headcount}}{\text{Total labor headcount}}$$

$$= \frac{10,957}{32,909} = 0.322, \text{ or } 32.2\%$$

In January, XYZ's direct labor is about two-thirds (67.8%) of its total payroll, its indirect labor about one-third (33.3%).

Also, trends in this ratio indicate to the cost manager whether indirect personnel expenses are growing in or out of proportion to the production workforce. Inasmuch as indirect labor costs generally represent the largest percentage of all individual overhead costs, this is an area that bears close monitoring. Small percentage reductions can mean large dollar contributions to the profit margin.

Example: The following data is available for XYZ Corp.:

(in $000,000s)

	19X1	19X0	Variance	
Expense	$	$	$	%
Total overhead	269.8	253.8	16.0	6.3
Direct labor $	198.0	181.6	16.4	9.0
Indirect labor $	125.0	120.0	5.0	4.2
Indirect-to-direct-labor ratio	63.1	66.1	3.0	4.5

The decrease in the ratio from 66.1% to 63.1% (a 3-point, or 4.5% decrease) is favorable, reflecting control over overhead costs. Indirect labor expenses are growing at a slightly slower pace than those of direct labor.

HOW COSTS-OF-SALES (DIRECT EXPENSES) AFFECT PROFITABILITY

What is cost of sales?

Sometimes known as cost of goods sold, cost of sales consists of the expenses that can be directly attributed to the making of the company's product or the rendering of its service. Examples of such "direct" costs are assembly line workers, raw materials that go into the product, equipment used to produce goods, and so on.

How is cost of sales compared to sales?

The total cost of sales is divided by the "top line," sales or revenues.

$$\text{Cost-of-sale-to-sale ratio} = \frac{\text{Cost of sales}}{\text{Sales}}$$

Example: The following monthly data is available for XYZ Corp.

(in $000,000s)

	Jan.
Sales	$44.0
Direct labor	9.6
Overhead	13.0
Material & ODC	15.8
Cost of sales	$38.4
Gross profit	5.6
G&A/selling expenses	2.7
Income from operations	$ 2.9

$$\text{Cost-of-sales-to-sale ratio} = \frac{\text{Cost of sales}}{\text{Sales}}$$
$$= \frac{\$38,400,000}{\$44,000,000} = 0.8727, \text{ or } 87.3\%$$

How is the cost-of-sales-to-sales ratio used?

The ratio is useful in two ways: First, if the organization has established an average ratio of cost of sales (or cost of goods sold, COGS) to sales, it confirms whether an actual cost of sales figure is above or below the historical average. Second, a validated average ratio provides a fairly reliable planning statistic to "ballpark" a total cost of sales value based on a projected sales volume.

How is the cost-of-sales-to-sales ratio used to evaluate actual data?

With actual data on hand and a valid historical ratio, an organization can compare them to determine whether the actual figure is above or below average.

Example: XYZ Corp. uses an historically validated cost-of-sales-to-sales ratio of 88.1%. That is, on average, its cost of sales runs 88.1% of total sales volume. For the month of January, XYZ's cost-of-sales-to-sales ratio is 87.3% (see preceding example). This is 0.8% less than the average (88.1% less 87.3%).

How would the cost-of-sales-to-sales ratio assist planners in making projections?

Planners can apply the organization's historically average ratio to the projected sales volume for a given upcoming period, to arrive at an estimated cost of sales.

Example: XYZ Corp.'s sales manager projects $36,500,000 in sales for the month of February. The company's average cost-of-sales-to-sales ratio is 88.1%.

$$\text{Cost-of-sale-to-sale ratio} = \frac{\text{Cost of sales}}{\text{Sales}}$$

$$0.881 = \frac{\text{Cost of sales}}{\$36,500,000}$$

Or:

Cost of sales = 0.881 × $36,500,000 = $32,156,500

For the month of February, XYZ can expect cost of sales in the neighborhood of $32,156,500.

Can types of costs of sales be evaluated in terms of sales?

Yes. In fact, in many cases it is generally more useful to compare individual types of costs to sales, rather than the overall cost of sales. For each category, however, the formula is the same.

Cost of sales consists of several categories:

- Direct labor (personnel)
- Overhead (factory overhead)
- Material and other direct costs (ODC)

$$\text{Cost-of-sales-to-sale ratio} = \frac{\text{Cost of sales}}{\text{Sales}}$$

Example: The following monthly data is available for XYZ Corp.:

(in $000,000s)

	Jan.
Sales	$44.0
Direct labor	9.6
Overhead	13.0
Material & ODC	15.8
Cost of sales	$38.4
Gross profit	5.6
G&A/selling expenses	2.7
Income from operations	$ 2.9

$$\text{Cost-of-sales-to-sale ratio} = \frac{\text{Cost of labor}}{\text{Sales}}$$

$$= \frac{\$9,600,000}{\$44,000,000} = 0.2181, \text{ or } 21.8\%$$

$$\text{Cost-of-sales-to-sale ratio} = \frac{\text{Cost of overhead}}{\text{Sales}}$$

$$= \frac{\$13,000,000}{\$44,000,000} = 0.2954, \text{ or } 29.5\%$$

$$\text{Cost-of-sales-to-sale ratio} = \frac{\text{Cost of material \& ODC}}{\text{Sales}}$$

$$= \frac{\$15,800,000}{\$44,000,000} = 0.3590, \text{ or } 35.9\%$$

Any of the individual cost elements may be used to check the reasonableness of sales projections and/or to estimate costs for upcoming periods.

Can an individual type of cost be expressed as a ratio of total cost of sales?

Yes. To monitor cost elements, each type of expense may be expressed as a percentage of overall cost of sales.

$$\text{Direct-cost-to-cost-of-sales ratio} = \frac{\text{Individual direct cost}}{\text{Cost of sales}}$$

Example: XYZ Corp. shows the following monthly data:

(in $000,000s)

	Jan.
Sales	$44.0
Direct labor	9.6
Overhead	13.0
Material & ODC	15.8
Cost of sales	$38.4

$$\text{Direct-cost-to-cost-of-sales ratio} = \frac{\text{Direct labor}}{\text{Cost of sales}}$$

$$= \frac{\$9,600,000}{\$38,400,000} = .250, \text{ or } 25\%$$

$$\text{Direct-cost-to-cost-of-sales ratio} = \frac{\text{Overhead expenses}}{\text{Cost of sales}}$$

$$= \frac{\$13,000,000}{\$38,400,000} = .339, \text{ or } 33.9\%$$

$$\text{Direct-cost-to-cost-of-sales ratio} = \frac{\text{Material \& ODC}}{\text{Cost of sales}}$$

$$= \frac{\$15,800,000}{\$38,400,000} = .411, \text{ or } 41.1\%$$

Note: Individual cost rates add up to 100% (25.0 plus 33.9 plus 44.1).

What use is it to monitor individual cost-of-sale elements?

While the overall ratio of cost of sales to sales may remain in line with the historical average, an individual cost element may be increasing disproportionately.

Example: XYZ Corp. shows the following monthly and six-month data:

(in $000,000s)			
	Jan.	Jan. Ratios*	Six-Month Average
Sales	44.0	—	225.3
Direct labor	9.6	0.25	59.0
Overhead	13.0	0.34	51.0
Material & ODC	15.8	0.41	86.9
Cost of sales	$38.4		$196.9
Cost-of-sales-to-sales ratio	0.87		
See preceding example for calculations.			

The six-month ratios for cost-of-sale elements are calculated and compared to January's:

$$\text{Direct-cost-to-cost-of-sales ratio} = \frac{\text{Direct labor}}{\text{Cost of sales}}$$

$$= \frac{\$59,000,000}{\$196,900,000} = 0.299, \text{ or } 30\%$$

$$\text{Direct-cost-to-cost-of-sales ratio} = \frac{\text{Overhead expenses}}{\text{Cost of sales}}$$

$$= \frac{\$51,000,000}{\$196,900,000} = 0.259, \text{ or } 26\%$$

$$\text{Direct-cost-to-cost-of-sales ratio} = \frac{\text{Material \& ODC}}{\text{Cost of sales}}$$

$$= \frac{\$86,900,000}{\$196,900,000} = 0.441, \text{ or } 44\%$$

Note: Individual cost rates add up to 100% (30 plus 26 plus 44).

(in $000,000s)

	Jan.	Jan. Ratios*	Six-Month Average	Six-Month Ratios
Sales	44.0		225.3	
Direct labor	9.6	0.25	59.0	0.30
Overhead	13.0	0.34	51.0	0.26
Material & ODC	15.8	0.41	86.9	0.44
Cost of sales	$38.4		$196.9	
Cost-of-sales-to-				
sales ratio	0.87			

*See preceding example for calculations.

While direct labor and materials for January (0.25 and 0.41) were lower than the six-month ratios (0.30 and 0.44), overhead showed an 8-point jump (0.34 in January compared to 0.26 for the half-year).

This increase in overhead would not be detected if only the cost-of-sales-to-sales ratio were computed:

$$\text{Cost-of-sale-to-sale ratio} = \frac{\text{Cost of sales}}{\text{Sales}}$$

$$= \frac{\$196,900,000}{\$225,300,000} = 0.874, \text{ or } 87\%$$

The January ratio (0.87) matches the six-month ratio exactly, leading one to believe that cost of sales is well in hand.

Can the total cost of sales be compared to product units?

Yes. An organization can compute how much in total cost of sales (or cost of goods sold) is represented by each unit produced.

$$\text{Cost of sales per unit} = \frac{\text{Cost of sales}}{\text{Units produced}}$$

Example: In February, Hudson Co. produced 7,400 widgets, and its cost of sales were:

(in $000s)

Direct labor dollars	$ 8,000
Overhead expense	10,900
Material and ODC	13,100
Cost of sales	$32,000

$$\text{Cost of sales per unit} = \frac{\text{Cost of sales}}{\text{Units produced}}$$

$$= \frac{\$32,000}{7,400 \text{ units}} = \$4.32 \text{ per unit}$$

Hudson pays $4.32 in cost of sales per unit.

Can individual elements of cost of sales be compared to units produced?

Yes. The formula is similar to the one for total cost of sales.

$$\text{Cost of sales per unit} = \frac{\text{Individual cost of sales}}{\text{Units produced}}$$

Example: In February, Hudson Co. produced 7,400 widgets, and its cost of sales were:

(in $000s)	
Direct labor dollars	$ 8,000
Overhead expense	10,900
Material and ODC	13,100
Cost of sales	$32,000

For direct labor dollars:

$$\text{Cost of sales per unit} = \frac{\text{Individual cost of sales}}{\text{Units produced}}$$

$$= \frac{\$8,000}{7,400 \text{ units}} = \$1.08 \text{ per unit}$$

Hudson pays $1.08 in direct labor dollars per unit produced. Other cost of sale elements are computed in the same way:

(in $000s)	$	$ Per Unit
Direct labor dollars	$ 8,000	$1.08
Overhead expense	10,900	1.47
Material and ODC	13,100	1.77
Cost of sales	$32,000	$4.32

Can total cost of sales be expressed in terms of labor hours?

Yes. The total cost of sales is divided by direct labor hours.

$$\text{Cost-of-sales-per-direct-labor-hour ratio} = \frac{\text{Total cost of sales}}{\text{Direct labor hours}}$$

Example: For the month of February, XYZ Corp. incurred total cost of sales of $32,000, and paid for 3,000 direct labor hours.

$$\begin{aligned}
\text{Cost-of-sales-per-direct-labor-hour ratio} &= \frac{\text{Total cost of sales}}{\text{Direct labor hours}} \\
&= \frac{\$32,000}{3,000 \text{ direct labor hours}} \\
&= \$10.67 \text{ per direct labor hour}
\end{aligned}$$

In February, for every direct labor hour worked, XYZ spent $10.67 in total cost of sales.

HOW INDIRECT COSTS AFFECT PROFITABILITY

What are indirect expenses?

Indirect costs are expenses that are incurred to operate a business but that do not relate directly to the making of the company's product. Examples are administrative, sales, and accounting staff, or office equipment, company cars, and benefit plans. Usually, indirect expenses consist of:

- General and administrative (G&A) costs, such as the cost of payroll computer systems, the wages of bookkeepers, or retainers for corporate attorneys.

- Selling expenses, such as general advertising, a salesperson's company car, or commissions.

- Other indirect costs (OIC), which cannot be attributed to the making of a specific product. Examples are depreciation on a plant in which many products are made, utility and heating expenses, or delivery fleet lease payments and maintenance costs.

Indirect expenses = G&A + selling expenses + OIC

Example: Hudson Co.'s annual selling expenses are $5,400,000, and its G&A costs $4,900,000. It also incurs depreciation and other types of expenses that cannot be attributed to specific products to the tune of $2,300,000.

$$\begin{aligned}
\text{Indirect expenses} &= \text{G\&A} + \text{selling expenses} + \text{OIC} \\
&= \$4,900,000 + \$5,400,000 + \$2,300,000 \\
&= \$12,600,000
\end{aligned}$$

Indirect Costs per Product Unit

How are indirect expenses compared to product units?

Indirect expenses may be compared to product units by means of the so-called "labor hour approach." This is a quick way to estimate total cost based on the labor rate (assuming the dollar-per-hour rate is reliable).

$$\text{Cost of sales per unit} = \frac{\text{Indirect expenses}}{\text{Units produced}}$$

Example: Hudson Co.'s annual selling expenses are $5,400,000, its G&A costs $4,900,000, and other indirect costs $2,300,000. The company produced 20,100,00 widgets during the year.

$$\begin{aligned}
\text{Cost of sales per unit} &= \frac{\text{Indirect expenses}}{\text{Units produced}} \\
&= \frac{\$12,600,000}{20,100,000 \text{ units}} \\
&= \$0.626 \text{ per unit}
\end{aligned}$$

For every unit produced in 19X1, Hudson paid $0.626 in indirect costs.

How are indirect costs per product unit used in connection with direct costs per product unit?

Along with direct costs per product unit (see pages 000-000), indirect costs per product provide projections of total cost and operating income. They can also be used in pricing and customer quotations.

$$\text{Total cost per unit} = \frac{\text{Indirect cost}}{\text{per unit}} + \frac{\text{Direct cost}}{\text{per unit}}$$

Example: Hudson's indirect costs per product are $.637. (See preceding example.) The company's direct costs (cost of sales) per product are $4.32. (See page 166 for the computation.)

$$\text{Total cost per unit} = \frac{\text{Indirect cost}}{\text{per unit}} + \frac{\text{Direct cost}}{\text{per unit}}$$

$$= \$.637 + \$4.32 = \frac{\$4.957}{\text{per unit}}$$

For every unit produced, Hudson pays total cost of $4.96.

Can individual indirect costs be related to units produced?

Yes. Any one cost can be monitored by dividing it by the number of product units.

$$\text{Indirect expense per unit} = \frac{\text{Indirect cost element}}{\text{Units produced}}$$

Example: Hudson Co.'s annual selling expenses are $5,400,000, and its G&A costs $4,900,000. It also incurs depreciation and other indirect costs (OIC) that cannot be attributed to specific products to the tune of $2,300.000.

For selling expenses:

$$\text{Indirect expense per unit} = \frac{\text{Indirect cost element}}{\text{Units produced}}$$

$$= \frac{\$5,400,000}{20,100,000 \text{ units}} = \frac{\$.269}{\text{per unit}}$$

Other indirect cost elements are computed in the same way:

	(in $000s)	
	$	*$ Per Unit*
Selling expenses	$ 5.4	$.269
G&A	$ 4.9	$.244
OIC	$ 2.3	$.114
Total cost	$12.6	$.627

Selling, General and Administrative (G&A) Expenses

What are selling, general, and administrative expenses?

General and administrative costs are those associated with operating the business, controller's staffs or procurement. Selling expenses are those related to marketing and administering contracts. Selling, general, and administrative expenses are listed as operating expenses (along with cost of goods sold and depreciation) on the income statement. In many companies, they are itemized as part and parcel of the overall expense reporting format.

Example: XYZ Corp.'s overall cost reporting format for 19X1 is as follows:

(in $000,000s)

Expense	$	% of Total Expense*
Indirect labor	$27.0	47.4
Misc. labor benefits	3.7	6.5
Retirement plan	1.3	2.3
Management incentive	**0.7**	**1.2**
Supplies	5.4	9.5
Taxes & insurance	2.7	0.6
Depreciation	0.8	1.4
Equipment rentals	2.2	3.9
Utilities	0.8	1.4
Telephone & telegraph	2.7	4.7
Travel	1.4	2.5
Professional/outside services	2.0	3.5
Entertainment	0.6	1.0
Dues and donations	0.5	0.9
Miscellaneous	0.6	1.1
Advertising/promotion	**3.0**	**5.3**
Sales commissions	**1.2**	**2.1**
Total expenses	$56.60	95.3

*Individual expenses are calculated as ratios of overall expenses; percentages do not total to 100% due to rounding.

In the preceding listing, "Management incentive" is a G&A expense, while "advertising/promotion" and "Sales commissions" are selling expenses. The company choose to isolate other G&A expenses, such as executives' compensation.

How is the rate of selling, G&A per direct labor hour computed?

The sum of selling, general, and administrative expenses is divided by the total number of direct labor hours performed within the period. The result is a rate, expressed as dollars per direct labor hour.

$$\text{Selling-G\&A-per-direct-labor-hour rate} = \frac{\text{Selling, G\&A}}{\text{Direct labor hours}}$$

Example: In 19X1, XYZ Corp. incurred G&A expenses of $1,200,000 and selling expenses of $4,200,000. During the year, it paid for 39,400,000 direct labor hours.

$$\begin{aligned}
\text{Selling-G\&A-per-} \atop \text{direct-labor-hour rate} &= \frac{\text{Selling, G\&A}}{\text{Direct labor hours}} \\[2mm]
&= \frac{\$4,200,000 + \$1,200,000}{39,400,000} \\[2mm]
&= \frac{\$5,400,000}{39,400,000} = \begin{matrix} 0.137, \text{ or} \\ \$0.14/\text{hour} \end{matrix}
\end{aligned}$$

For every direct labor hour performed, XYZ Corp. spends 14 cents on selling, general, and administrative expenses.

Of what benefit is the rate of selling/G&A per direct labor hour?

As direct labor hours and sales activity increase, they affect G&A and selling expenses. If a combined G&A and selling expense "rate" can be historically validated, it can expresses what these expenses "should" be as a dollar rate per direct labor hour. Companies can use this rate per hour or the ratio of selling/G&A to direct labor *dollars* (see next section). But the comparison to direct labor *hours* is more commonly used because an increase in hourly labor rate does not act as a "hidden" source of higher labor costs.

Can selling, general, and administrative expenses be compared to direct labor dollars?

Yes. The sum of selling and G&A costs can be divided by the total direct labor dollars spent in a period. The result is a ratio, expressed as a decimal or percentage.

$$\text{Selling-G\&A-to-direct-} \atop \text{labor-dollars ratio} = \frac{\text{Selling, G\&A (\$)}}{\text{Direct labor dollars}}$$

Example: In 19X1, XYZ Corp. incurred G&A expenses of $1,200,000 and selling expenses of $4,200,000. During the year, it paid $198,000,000 in direct labor costs.

$$\begin{aligned}
\text{Selling-G\&A-per-} \atop \text{direct-labor-dollar rate} &= \frac{\text{Selling, G\&A (\$)}}{\text{Direct labor dollars}} \\[2mm]
&= \frac{\$4,200,000 + \$1,200,000}{\$198,000,000} \\[2mm]
&= \frac{\$5,400,000}{\$198,000,000} \\[2mm]
&= \quad 0.027, \text{ or } 2.7\%
\end{aligned}$$

The ratio of selling, general, and administrative expenses to direct labor dollars is 2.7%. Expressed another way: For every direct labor dollar spent, XYZ Corp. spends 2.7% (or 2.7 cents) on selling, general, and administrative expenses.

What purpose is served by the ratio of selling/G&A to direct labor dollars?

If the ratio can be accepted as a guideline, it enables the cost manager to insert an estimated dollar figure in expense projections.

Example: XYZ Corp. estimates that it will spend $205,000,000 on direct labor dollars in the coming year. Also, the ratio of selling, general, and administrative costs to direct labor dollars has been, on average, 2.7%.

$$\text{Selling-G\&A-to-direct-labor-dollars ratio} = \frac{\text{Selling, G\&A (\$)}}{\text{Direct labor dollars}}$$

$$0.027 = \frac{\text{Selling, G\&A (\$)}}{\$205,000,000}$$

Or:

$$\text{Selling, G\&A (\$)} = 0.027 \times \$205,000,000 = \$5,535,000$$

XYZ can reasonably expect to pay $5,535,000 in selling, general, and administrative expenses in the year to come.

Can selling, general, and administrative expenses be compared to gross profit?

Yes. The sum of selling, general, and administrative costs is divided by the company's gross profit for the period. The result is a ratio, which may be expressed as a decimal or percentage.

$$\text{Selling-G\&A-to-gross-profit ratio} = \frac{\text{Selling, G\&A (\$)}}{\text{Gross profit}}$$

Example: In 19X1, XYZ Corp. incurred G&A expenses of $1,200,000 and selling expenses of $4,200,000. Its gross profit for the year was $155,000,000.

$$\begin{aligned}\text{Selling-G\&A-to-gross-profit ratio} &= \frac{\text{Selling, G\&A (\$)}}{\text{Gross profit}} \\ &= \frac{\$4,200,000 + \$1,200,000}{\$155,000,000} \\ &= \frac{\$5,400,000}{\$155,000,000} = 0.0348, \text{ or } 3.5\%\end{aligned}$$

Does this ratio benefit the cost manager?

Yes. If the ratio of selling, general, and administrative costs to gross profit proves to be valid over time, you may apply it to the profit for pr:liminary values until actual or better data is on hand.

Example: XYZ Corp. projects a gross profit of $169,000,000. Over the years, selling, general, and administrative expenses have come to an average of 3.5% of gross profit.

$$\text{Selling-G\&A-to-gross-profit ratio} = \frac{\text{Selling, G\&A (\$)}}{\text{Gross profit}}$$

$$0.035 = \frac{\text{Selling, G\&A (\$)}}{\$169,000,000}$$

Or:

$$\text{Selling, G\&A (\$)} = 0.035 \times \$169,000,000 = \$5,915,000$$

XYZ Corp. may reasonably expect to incur about $5,900,000 in selling, general, and administrative expenses in the coming year.

Can selling, general, and administrative expenses be related to total sales?

Yes. The sum of these expenses is divided by total sales, to produce a ratio that can be expressed as a decimal or percentage.

$$\text{Selling-G\&A-to-total-sales ratio} = \frac{\text{Selling, G\&A (\$)}}{\text{Total sales}}$$

Example: In 19X1, XYZ Corp. incurred G&A expenses of $1,200,000 and selling expenses of $4,200,000. Its total sales for the year were $1,100,000,000.

$$
\begin{aligned}
\text{Selling-G\&A-to-total-sales ratio} &= \frac{\text{Selling, G\&A (\$)}}{\text{Total sales}} \\
&= \frac{\$4,200,000 + \$1,200,000}{\$1,100,000,000} \\
&= \frac{\$5,400,000}{\$1,100,000,000} = 0.0049, \text{ or } 0.049\%
\end{aligned}
$$

Does this ratio benefit the cost manager?

Yes. If the ratio of selling, general, and administrative costs to total sales proves to be valid over time, you may apply it to the profit for preliminary values until actual or better data is on hand.

Example: XYZ Corp. projects total sales of $1,210,000,000. Over the years, selling, general, and administrative expenses have come to an average of 0.049%.

$$\text{Selling-G\&A-to-total-sales ratio} = \frac{\text{Selling, G\&A (\$)}}{\text{Total sales}}$$

$$0.0049 = \frac{\text{Selling, G\&A (\$)}}{\$1,210,000,000}$$

Or:

$$\text{Selling, G\&A (\$)} = 0.005 \times \$1,210,000,000$$
$$= \$6,050,000$$

XYZ Corp. may reasonably expect to incur about $6,000,000 in selling, general, and administrative expenses in the coming year.

Note: Compare this estimate with that of the preceding example.

Can selling, general, and administrative expenses be compared to net income?

Yes. The sum of these expenses is divided by net income, to produce a ratio that can be expressed as a decimal or percentage.

$$\text{Selling-G\&A-to-net-income ratio} = \frac{\text{Selling, G\&A (\$)}}{\text{Net income}}$$

Example: In 19X1, XYZ Corp. incurred G&A expenses of $1,200,000 and selling expenses of $4,200,000. Its net income for the year was $49,025,000.

$$\begin{aligned}
\text{Selling-G\&A-to-net-income ratio} &= \frac{\text{Selling, G\&A (\$)}}{\text{Net income}} \\
&= \frac{\$4,200,000 + \$1,200,000}{\$49,025,000} \\
&= \frac{\$5,400,000}{\$49,025,000} = 0.11, \text{ or } 11\%
\end{aligned}$$

Selling, general, and administrative expenses are running about 11% of net income.

Does this ratio benefit the cost manager?

Yes. If the ratio of selling, general, and administrative costs to net income proves to be valid over time, you may apply it to the profit for preliminary values until actual or better data is on hand.

Example: XYZ Corp. projects next year's net income $53,900,000. Over the years, selling, general, and administrative expenses have come to an average of 11%.

$$\begin{array}{l} \text{Selling-G\&A-to-} \\ \text{net-income ratio} \end{array} = \frac{\text{Selling, G\&A (\$)}}{\text{Net income}}$$

$$0.11 = \frac{\text{Selling, G\&A (\$)}}{\$53,900,000}$$

Or:

$$\text{Selling, G\&A (\$)} = 0.11 \times \$53,900,000 = \$5,929,000$$

XYZ Corp. may reasonably expect to incur about $5,900,000 in selling, general, and administrative expenses in the coming year.

Note: Compare this estimate with those of the preceding two examples.

Can selling expenses and G&A costs be compared individually to total sales, gross profit, or net income?

Either type of expense can be compared to total sales, gross profit, or net income. In any of these cases, the individual expense is divided by total sales, gross profit, or net income. (Only one formula and example are shown.)

$$\begin{array}{l} \text{Selling-expenses-} \\ \text{to-total-sales ratio} \end{array} = \frac{\text{Selling expenses}}{\text{Total sales}}$$

Example: The following data is available for XYZ Corp.:

Total sales		$1,100,000,000
Net income		49,025,000
Selling expenses:		
Advertising & promotion	$3,000,000	
Selling commissions	1,200,000	
Total selling expenses		4,200,000

$$\text{Selling-expenses-} \atop \text{to-total-sales ratio} = \frac{\text{Selling expenses}}{\text{Total sales}}$$

$$= \frac{\$4,200,000}{\$1,100,000,000} = 0.00382, \text{ or } 0.38\%$$

XYZ's selling expenses come to about 0.38% of total sales.

By applying the preceding general formula, an array of ratios can be developed and trend analysis applied.

Example: XYZ Corp. has put together the following data for the years 19X0 and 19X1:

(in $000s)

	19X1	19X0	Variance ($)	Variance (%)
Total sales	$1,100,000	$995,000	$105,000	+10.6
Net income	49,025	38,350	10,675	+27.8
Selling expenses:				
Adv. & promo.	3,000	2,800	200	+ 7.1
Commissions	1,200	1,400	(200)	−14.3
Total	4,200	4,200		
Ratios to Total Sales				
Adv. & promotion	.27%	.28%	−0.01%	− 3.6%
Commisions	.11%	.14%	−0.03%	−21.4%
Ratios to Net Income				
Adv. & promotion	6.1%	7.3%	−1.2%	−16.4%
Commissions	2.4%	3.7%	−1.3%	−35.1%

Ratio to sales:

• The decline in advertising and promotion of 3.6% may have resulted from a greater proportional increase in sales.

• The decrease in commission expense ratio is accounted for by the increase in total sales, which was greater than the increase in commission dollars.

Ratio to net income:

• The ratio of commissions to net income went down primarily because the 27.8% rise in net income more than offset the 7.1% increase in commissions.

• The 35.1% decrease in sales commissions is due to the 27.8% increase in net income versus a 14.3% decline in commissions.

Assuming these these expense ratios are consistent from one period to another, their analysis enables the cost manager to:

- Assess trends in the relationships between selling expenses and sales volume and/or net income.
- Establish expense limitations and controls.
- Use guidelines based on historical experience for expense surveillance and for planning a realistic selling expense budget.

Overhead

What are overhead expenses?

Overhead expenses represent indirect services and support for operational activities; they do not contribute directly— or they cannot be identified as directly contributing—to the manufacture of a product. Typical overhead expenses are:

- Retirement plans
- Fringe benefits
- Management incentives
- Supplies
- Taxes
- Insurance
- Repair and maintenance
- Depreciation
- Equipment rentals
- Utilities
- Telephone
- Travel
- Professional/outside services
- Entertainment
- Dues and donations
- Miscellaneous expenses

Such expenses can be elusive to monitor, plan, and control. Yet they need not present a problem if you (a) accumulate accurate source data and (b) make use of overhead expense ratios.

Some of these overhead expenses are categorized as "general and administrative (G&A) expenses," others as "selling expenses."

Can individual overhead expenses be compared to total overhead expenses?

Yes. Any of the individual expenses listed in the preceding section can be expressed as a ratio to total overhead.

$$\text{Individual-to-total-overhead-expense ratio} = \frac{\text{Individual overhead expense (\$)}}{\text{Total overhead expense}}$$

Example: XYZ Corp. shows the following overhead expense data for 19X1:

	(in $000,000s)	
Expense	*19X1 $*	*Ratio to Total (%)*
Indirect labor	$125.0	46.3
Misc. labor benefits	50.0	18.5
Retirement plan	12.5	4.6
Management incentive	2.5	0.9
Supplies	18.5	6.9
Taxes & insurance	14.2	5.3
Repair & maintenance	12.5	4.6
Depreciation	13.2	4.9
Equipment rentals	2.4	0.9
Utilities	4.2	1.6
Telephone	4.0	1.5
Travel	3.8	1.4
Professional/outside services	4.7	1.8
Entertainment	0.9	0.3
Dues and donations	0.8	0.3
Miscellaneous	0.6	0.2
Total overhead	269.8	100.0

Each of these individual overhead expense ratios was calculated in the same way. Take Indirect labor as an example:

$$\text{Individual-to-total-overhead-expense ratio} = \frac{\text{Individual overhead expense (\$)}}{\text{Total overhead expense}}$$

$$\text{Individual-to-total overhead-expense ratio} = \frac{\text{Indirect labor (\$)}}{\text{Total overhead expense}}$$

$$= \frac{\$125,000,000}{\$269,800,000} = .4633, \text{ or } 46.3\%$$

What purpose does it serve to compute ratios for individual expenses?

Individual overhead expense ratios, preferably calculated automatically by means of an electronic spreadsheet, enable the cost manager to arrive at historically validated guideline ratios and to compare actual ratios against them. In the absence of guidelines, the cost manager can monitor changes in expense levels from one period to the next.

$$\text{Variance (\%)} = \frac{\text{Present period's actual} - \text{Prior period's actual}}{\text{Prior period's actual}}$$

Note: The numerator in the preceding formula may be positive or negative. If positive, it represents an increase in the expense; if negative, a decrease.

Example: XYZ Corp. shows the following individual overhead expense data for 19X0 and 19X1:

		Ratio		*Ratio*		
	19X1	*to*	*19X0*	*to*	*Variance*	
Expense	*$*	*Total*	*$*	*Total*	*$*	*%*
Indirect labor	125.0	46.3	120.0	47.3	5.0	4.2
Misc. labor benefits	50.0	18.5	45.0	17.7	5.0	11.1
Retirement plan	12.5	4.6	11.0	4.3	1.5	13.6
Management incentive	2.5	0.9	2.2	0.9	0.3	13.6
Supplies	18.5	6.9	18.0	7.1	0.5	2.8
Taxes & insurance	14.2	5.3	13.8	5.4	0.4	2.9
Repair & maintenance	12.5	4.6	11.8	4.7	0.7	5.9
Depreciation	13.2	4.9	12.5	4.9	0.7	5.6
Equipment rentals	2.4	0.9	1.9	0.7	0.5	26.3
Utilities	4.2	1.6	3.8	1.5	0.4	10.5
Telephone	4.0	1.5	3.9	1.5	0.1	2.6
Travel	3.8	1.4	3.7	1.5	0.1	2.7
Professional/outside services	4.7	1.8	4.2	1.7	0.5	11.9
Entertainment	0.9	0.3	0.8	0.3	0.1	12.5
Dues and donations	0.8	0.3	0.7	0.3	0.1	14.3
Miscellaneous	0.6	0.2	0.5	0.2	0.1	20.0
Total overhead	269.8	100.0	253.8	100.0	16.0	6.3

(in $000,000s)

Each of these ratios, for 19X0 and 19X1, is arrived at by the same formula (see preceding example). The dollar variance (19X0 less 19X1 actuals) is used to find the percentage of variance. Let's take Indirect labor as an example:

$$\text{Variance (\%)} = \frac{\text{Present period's actual} - \text{Prior period's actual}}{\text{Prior period's actual}}$$

$$= \frac{\text{19X1 Indirect labor} - \text{19X0 Indirect labor}}{\text{19X0 Indirect labor}}$$

$$= \frac{\$125,000,000 - \$120,000,000}{\$120,000,000}$$

$$= \frac{\$5,000,000^*}{\$120,000,000} = 0.4166, \text{ or } 4.2\%$$

What does a comparison of two periods' overhead cost ratios tell the cost manager?

Comparing ratios for successive periods helps the cost manager analyze expenses and plan operational budgets. What is not apparent when expressed in terms of dollars might become clear when cast in terms of percentages and rates.

Example: XYZ Corp. shows the following individual overhead expense and related data for 19X0 and 19X1:

(in $000,000s)

Expense	19X1 $	Ratio to Total	19X0 $	Ratio to Total	Variance $	Variance %
Indirect labor	125.0	46.3	120.0	47.3	5.0	4.2
Misc. labor benefits	50.0	18.5	45.0	17.7	5.0	11.1
Retirement plan	12.5	4.6	11.0	4.3	1.5	13.6
Management incentive	2.5	0.9	2.2	0.9	0.3	13.6
Supplies	18.5	6.9	18.0	7.1	0.5	2.8
Taxes & insurance	14.2	5.3	13.8	5.4	0.4	2.9
Repair & maintenance	12.5	4.6	11.8	4.7	0.7	5.9
Depreciation	13.2	4.9	12.5	4.9	0.7	5.6
Equipment rentals	2.4	0.9	1.9	0.7	0.5	26.3
Utilities	4.2	1.6	3.8	1.5	0.4	10.5
Telephone	4.0	1.5	3.9	1.5	0.1	2.6
Travel	3.8	1.4	3.7	1.5	0.1	2.7
Professional/outside services	4.7	1.8	4.2	1.7	0.5	11.9
Entertainment	0.9	0.3	0.8	0.3	0.1	12.5
Dues and donations	0.8	0.3	0.7	0.3	0.1	14.3
Miscellaneous	0.6	0.2	0.5	0.2	0.1	20.0
Total overhead	269.8	100.0	253.8	100.0	16.0	6.3
Direct labor hours	39.4		37.3		2.1	5.6
Direct labor $	198.0		181.6		16.4	9.0
Sales volume	1,100.0		995.0		105.0	10.6

*Since the numerator is a positive number, variance represents an increase in Indirect labor costs.

From these ratios and other data, the following conclusions might be drawn:

- The variance in total expense between 19X0 and 19X1 was $16,000, which represented a 6.3% increase. In dollars, the largest variances occurred in indirect labor (4.2%), retirement place (13.6%), and other labor benefits (11.1%).

- The relatively modest dollar increases in other expense accounts can be considered the effects of a 5.6% rise in direct labor hours and a 10.6% greater sales volume, which indicates higher productivity.

- The ratios of individual expense accounts to their totals remained modestly consistent from one year to the next, indicating that the actual performance results of the company were probably in accord with the operational plan.

- If ratios like the ones in the table remain reasonably consistent over time, they may provide a sound basis for developing an expense budget, or at least a preliminary one. Budget-to-actual comparisons can then highlight variances for further analysis and possible corrective action.

How are overhead costs compared to sales?

Like G&A or selling expenses, overhead (other indirect costs) can be compared to sales.

$$\text{Indirect-cost-to-sales ratio} = \frac{\text{Overhead cost}}{\text{Sales}}$$

Example: During the first six months of 19X1, XYZ Corp. had sales of $256,000,000 and total other indirect costs of $13,800,000.

$$\text{Indirect-cost-to-sales ratio} = \frac{\text{Overhead cost}}{\text{Sales}}$$

$$= \frac{\$13,800,000}{\$256,000,000} = 0.0539, \text{ or } 5.4\%$$

XYZ'z indirect costs were 5.4% of its total sales.

Can overhead be compared to total costs?

Yes. Rising "overhead," if not detected, can erode profit margins. Comparing indirect with direct costs is one way of monitoring this outflow of funds.

HOW INDIRECT COSTS AFFECT PROFITABILITY

$$\text{Indirect-to-direct-cost ratio} = \frac{\text{Indirect costs}}{\substack{\text{Direct costs} + \text{Indirect costs} \\ \text{(cost of sales)}}}$$

Example: In July, XYZ Corp.'s total cost of sales is $33,000,000, its indirect costs $2,200,000. Over the previous half-year, its six-month cost of sales was $225,500,000, indirect costs $13,800,000.

The six-month ratio:

$$\text{Indirect-to-direct-cost ratio} = \frac{\text{Indirect costs}}{\substack{\text{Direct costs} + \text{Indirect costs} \\ \text{(cost of sales)}}}$$

$$= \frac{\$13,800,000}{\$225,500,000 + \$13,800,000}$$

$$= \frac{\$13,800,000}{\$239,300,000} = 0.577, \text{ or } 5.8\%$$

The six-month average ratio of indirect to total costs is 5.8%.

For the July ratio:

$$\text{Indirect-to-direct-cost ratio} = \frac{\text{Indirect costs}}{\substack{\text{Direct costs} + \text{Indirect costs} \\ \text{(cost of sales)}}}$$

$$= \frac{\$2,200,000}{\$33,000,000 + \$2,200,000}$$

$$= \frac{\$2,200,000}{\$35,200,000} = 0.0625, \text{ or } 6.3\%$$

July indirect costs, at 6.3% of total costs, are running slightly higher than the prior six-month average, 5.8%.

What is the ratio of overhead to cost of sales?

This ratio weighs overhead dollars against those spent in generating sales—"cost of sales."

$$\text{Total-overhead-to-cost-of-sales ratio} = \frac{\text{Total overhead (\$)}}{\text{Cost of sales (\$)}}$$

Note: This ratio can be used for any period—month, quarter, year, etc.

Example: For 19X1, XYZ Corp.'s total overhead came to $269,800,000, and its cost of sales to $945,000,000.

$$\text{Total-overhead-to-cost-of-sales ratio} = \frac{\text{Total overhead (\$)}}{\text{Cost of sales (\$)}}$$

$$= \frac{\$269,800,000}{\$945,000,000} = 0.286, \text{ or } 28.6\%$$

Overhead costs came to 28.6% of the cost of sales.

What good does it do to compare overhead to cost of sales?

Along with direct labor, direct material, and other direct costs, overhead is an important element in the composition of cost of sales. Variances from one period to the next can be the occasion for follow-up action.

Example: The following data is available for XYZ Corp.

(in $000,000s)

	19X1 $	19X0 $	Variance $	Variance %
Expense				
Total overhead	269.8	253.8	16.0	6.3
Cost of sales	945.0	865.0	80.0	9.2
Overhead-to-cost-of-sales ratio (%)	28.6	29.3	0.2	0.7

The ratio of overhead to cost of sales decreased slightly from 29.3% to 28.6% (a variance of 0.7%). This was due to the higher cost of sales, which was only partially offset by a smaller increase in overhead. From the one year to the other, the cost of sales rose at only a little greater rate than overhead.

How are overhead costs applied to a product before the expenses are known?

Overhead expenses are applied to a product before expenses are incurred by means of the application rate. The unit of measurement may be units, direct labor hours, or dollars.

$$\text{Application rate} = \frac{\text{Overhead expenses}}{\text{Production}}$$

To calculate a predetermined rate, divide the estimated overhead by the estimated production (again in units, direct labor hours, or dollars).

$$\text{Predetermined rate} = \frac{\text{Estimated overhead}}{\text{Estimated production}}$$

These formulas are, however, conceptual. In actuality, overhead may be expressed as a rate or percentage of:

- Direct labor hour
- Direct labor dollars
- Prime costs
- Machine hour
- Unit cost rate

Note: The ratios of overhead to sales and cost of sales are explained on pages 182–184.

What is the ratio of total overhead to direct labor hours?

This ratio compares the total overhead cost to direct labor hours. Direct labor dollars are the dollars paid to employees directly engaged in the making of the product or in the rendering of the service. Expressed as so many dollars per hour, it reflects how much money in overhead expense the company spends for every direct labor hour performed.

$$\text{Total overhead to direct labor hours ratio} = \frac{\text{Total overhead (\$)}}{\text{Direct labor (hours)}}$$

Example: For 19X1, XYZ Corp.'s total overhead expense came to $269,800,000, and its all-in direct labor hours were 39,400,000 (the number of hours worked by all direct personnel during the year).

$$\text{Total overhead to direct labor hours ratio} = \frac{\text{Total overhead (\$)}}{\text{Direct labor (hours)}}$$
$$= \frac{\$269,800,000}{39,400,000} = \$6.85 \text{ per hour}$$

XYZ Corp. spent $6.85 in overhead expenses for every hour worked by direct personnel.

Note: This ratio can be used for any period—month, quarter, year, etc.

What benefit is there to comparing overhead to direct labor hours?

With a historically validated ratio, the cost manager can:

- Determine whether overhead is increasing or merely keeping pace with direct labor hours. (Disproportionate increases in indirect expenses may mean a lack of control over costs.)

● Estimate product costs per direct labor hour.
● Develop a factory overhead budget.

Example: The following data applies to XYZ Corp. (see preceding example for complete table):

		(in $000,000s)				
		Ratio		Ratio		
	19X1	*to*	*19X0*	*to*	*Varianec*	
Expense	*$*	*Total*	*$*	*total*	*$*	*%*
Total overhead	269.8	100.0	253.8	100.0	16.0	6.3
Direct labor hours	39.4		37.3		2.1	5.6
Direct labor $	198.0		181.6		16.4	
9.0						
Sales volume	1,100.0		995.0		105.0	10.6

In 19X1, the ratio of total overhead to direct labor hours in XYZ Corp. was $6.85 (see preceding example). This was up slightly from $6.80 in 19X0—a 0.74% increase. Although total overhead increased 6.3%, the ratio did not rise greatly because of the offsetting increase in direct labor hours (39,400,000 in 19X1 from 37,300,000 in 19X0).

What is the ratio of total overhead to direct labor dollars?

This ratio compares the dollars spent on total overhead to those spent on direct labor.

$$\text{Total overhead to direct labor dollars ratio} = \frac{\text{Total overhead (\$)}}{\text{Direct labor (\$)}}$$

Example: For 19X1, XYZ Corp.'s total overhead expense came to $269,800,000, and its total direct labor costs were $198,000,000 (the number of dollars paid to all direct personnel during the year).

$$\text{Total overhead to direct labor dollars ratio} = \frac{\text{Total overhead (\$)}}{\text{Direct labor (\$)}}$$

$$= \frac{\$269,800,000}{\$198,000,000}$$

$$= 136.2, \text{ or } 136\%$$

XYZ spends a little over 1.36 times as much on overhead as it does on direct labor.

Note: This ratio can be used for any period—month, quarter, year, etc.

What does the cost manager learn from the ratio of total overhead to direct labor dollars?

This ratio may be useful in bidding and estimating contract costs.

Example: The following data applies to XYZ Corp. (see preceding example for complete table):

(in $000,000s)

Expense	*19X1* $	*19X0* $	*Variance* *Diff.*	*%*
Total overhead	269.8	253.8	16.0	6.3
Direct labor dollars	198.0	181.6	16.4	9.0
Ratio of total overhead to direct labor dollars	136.2	139.7	(3.5)	2.5

In 19X1, the ratio of total overhead to direct labor dollars is 136.2%; in 19X0, 137.9%. The variance of 3.5% represents a 2.5% decrease. The rate reduction is attributed largely to a 9.0% increase in direct labor dollars ($181,600,000 to $198,000,000) versus an offsetting increase of only 6.3% in total overhead ($253,800,000 to $269,800,000).

Indirect costs may be applied to a product on the basis of ratios, either before or after the expenditures are ascertained.

How is overhead computed in terms of prime cost?

Prime cost is the sum of direct labor plus material and other direct costs.

$$\text{Overhead-to-prime-cost ratio} = \frac{\text{Overhead (\$)}}{\text{Prime cost (\$)}}$$

Or:

$$\text{Overhead-to-prime cost ratio} = \frac{\text{Overhead (\$)}}{\text{Direct labor dollars} + \text{Direct materials \& ODC}}$$

Example: In January of 19X1, XYZ Corp. incurred $38,400,000 in overhead expenses, paid $9,600,000 in direct labor, and incurred $15,800,000 in materials and other direct costs.

$$\text{Overhead-to-prime} = \frac{\text{Overhead (\$)}}{\begin{array}{c}\text{Direct labor} \\ \text{dollars}\end{array} + \begin{array}{c}\text{Direct} \\ \text{materials \& ODC}\end{array}}$$

$$= \frac{\$38,400,000}{\$9,600,000 + \$15,800,000}$$

$$= \frac{\$38,400,000}{\$25,400,000} = 1.512, \text{ or } 151\%$$

For every dollar spent on prime costs, XYZ spent $1.51 on overhead. If this rate can be validated as accurate, it can serve as a guideline in planning and as a tool in checking actual figures, once on hand.

What is the machine hour rate method?

The machine hour rate is the cost per hour of running the company's production equipment. The rate includes:

- Specific charges to each machine, such as lease payments or depreciation, maintenance costs, or power requirements.

- Heating, lighting, and building costs.

- All other general and service costs, including indirect supplies and miscellaneous labor, supervision, and engineering support.

Each of these types of costs can be generated by the affected departments.

The total of all machine-related and prorated costs are then divided by the number of hours the machinery runs over the year (or the period in question).

$$\text{Machine hour rate} = \frac{\begin{array}{c}\text{Machine-} \\ \text{related expense}\end{array} + \begin{array}{c}\text{Heating,} \\ \text{light, plant}\end{array} + \text{Overhead}}{\text{Annual machine hours}}$$

Example: Each of the four main presses of Acme Printing Co. run 3,300 hours in a year.

- Machine-related expenses are depreciation, $12,500; service contracts and costs, $5,000; power, $1,350.

- Prorated heating, light, and plant costs amount to $3,500.

- Supervisory labor, downtime for maintenance and repair, and service supplies and parts come to $6,700.

$$\begin{array}{l} \text{Machine} \\ \text{hour rate} \end{array} = \dfrac{\begin{array}{c} \text{Machine-} \\ \text{related expense} \end{array} + \begin{array}{c} \text{Heating,} \\ \text{light, plant} \end{array} + \text{Overhead}}{\text{Annual machine hours}}$$

$$= \dfrac{\$18,850 + \$3,500 + \$6,700}{3,300 \text{ hours}}$$

$$= \dfrac{\$29,050}{3,300 \text{ hours}} = \$8.80 \text{ per hour}$$

What is the product unit cost rate?

The simplest and most direct way to apply overhead is on the basis of the product quantities produced, expressed as a rate of dollars spent per units produced. The calculations may involve actual or estimated figures, and they may be for the total plant, a department, or a cost center.

$$\text{Product unit cost} = \dfrac{\text{Overhead (\$)}}{\text{Units of product}}$$

Example: XYZ Corp. made 8,800 widgets in January. Its overhead $13,000,000.

$$\begin{aligned} \text{Product unit cost} &= \dfrac{\text{Overhead (\$)}}{\text{Units of product}} \\ &= \dfrac{\$13,000,000}{8,800 \text{ units}} = \$1,477.27 \text{ per unit} \end{aligned}$$

XYZ spends $1,477 in overhead for every unit produced.

What if a firm cannot use units produced in the product unit cost method?

Units produced is only one possible factor. The rate can also be expressed in terms of pounds, gallons, feet, or other types of units.

$$\text{Product unit cost} = \dfrac{\text{Overhead (\$)}}{\text{Units}}$$

Example: A division of Apex, Inc. produces three products, each of a different weight but of basically the same type. Management knows that their overhead is running $2,146.49 per month. They must be able to compute their cost per unit. The units produced are as follows:

| | Product | | | |
	A	B	C	Total
Units produced	500	400	600	
Unit weight (lbs.)	3	5	2	
Weight produced	1,500	2,000	1,200	4,700

$$\text{Product unit cost} = \frac{\text{Overhead (\$)}}{\text{Pounds}}$$

$$= \frac{\$2,146.49}{4,700 \text{ lbs.}} = \$.4567 \text{ per pound}$$

Apex's overhead cost per pound is $.4567.

| | Product | | | |
	A	B	C	Total
Units produced	500	400	600	
Unit weight (lbs.)	3	5	2	
Weight produced	1,500	2,000	1,200	4,700
Cost per pound	$.4567	$.4567	$.4567	$.4567
Overhead cost applied to lbs.	$685.05	$913.50	$548.04	$2,146.49

For Product A:

$$\text{Product unit cost} = \frac{\text{Overhead (\$)}}{\text{Units of product}}$$

$$= \frac{\$685.05}{500 \text{ lbs.}} = \$1.37 \text{ per unit}$$

Apex spends $1.37 in overhead dollars for every unit of Product A. The cost per unit for Products B and C are computed in a similar fashion.

| | Product | | | |
	A	B	C	Total
Units produced	500	400	600	
Unit weight (lbs.)	3	5	2	
Weight produced	1,500	2,000	1,200	4,700
Cost per pound	$.4567	$.4567	$.4567	$.4567
Overhead cost applied to lbs.	$685.05	$913.50	$548.04	$2,146.49
Cost per unit	$ 1.37	$ 2.28	$ .91	

How is the rate of fringe benefits to direct labor hours calculated?

The total dollar cost of fringe benefits (retirement plan, the cost manager incentives, and other labor benefits) is divided by total direct labor hours. The rate is expressed in terms of the dollars spent on benefits for every hour of direct labor performed.

$$\text{Fringe-benefits-to-direct-labor-hours rate} = \frac{\text{Fringe benefits (\$)}}{\text{Direct labor hours}}$$

Example: In 19X1, XYZ Corp. paid for 39,400,000 direct labor hours and spent the following on fringe benefits:

Retirement plan	$12,500,000
Management incentives	$ 2,500,000
Miscellaneous labor benefits	$50,000,000
Total fringe benefits	$65,000,000

$$\text{Fringe-benefits-to-direct-labor-hours rate} = \frac{\text{Fringe benefits (\$)}}{\text{Direct labor hours}}$$
$$= \frac{\$65,000,000}{39,000,000} = \frac{\$1.65}{\text{per hour}}$$

For every hour of direct labor performed, XYZ spends $1.65 on fringe benefits.

What does the fringe-benefit-to-direct-labor-hours rate tell the cost manager?

Either comparisons of rates from period to period or comparisons of actual to estimated rates can help the cost manager assess its performance in controlling these costs and in planning future fringe benefit allocations.

Example: The following data is available for XYZ Corp.:

	19X1	19X0	Variance	
Expense	$	$	$	%
Total overhead	269.8	253.8	16.0	6.3
Direct labor hours	39.4	37.3	2.1	5.6
Fringe benefits	65.0	58.2	6.8	11.7
Fringe-benefits-to-direct-labor-hours ratio	1.65	1.56	0.06	3.8

(in $000,000s)

The rate of fringe benefits to direct labor hours increased from $1.56 in 19X0 to $1.65 in 19X1—3.8%. This compares favorably with the 5.6% rise in direct labor hours over the same timespan.

How is the ratio between fringe benefits and total labor dollars computed?

The total dollar cost of fringe benefits (retirement plan, the cost manager incentives, and other labor benefits) is divided by total labor dollars. Total labor cost is the sum of direct and indirect labor. The rate is expressed in terms of the dollars spent on benefits for every hour of direct labor performed.

$$\text{Fringe-benefits-to-direct-labor-dollars rate} = \frac{\text{Fringe benefits (\$)}}{\text{Total labor \$}}$$

Note: Total labor dollars are used because both direct and indirect personnel share in the retirement and other labor benefits (vacations, sick leave, insurance, and the like).

Example: In 19X1, XYZ Corp. paid $198,000,000 in direct labor dollars, $125,000,000 for indirect labor, and the following on fringe benefits:

Retirement plan	$12,500,000
Management incentives	$ 2,500,000
Miscellaneous labor benefits	$50,000,000
Total fringe benefits	$65,000,000

$$
\begin{aligned}
\text{Fringe-benefits-to-direct-labor-dollars rate} &= \frac{\text{Fringe benefits (\$)}}{\text{Total labor \$}} \\
&= \frac{\$65,000,000}{\$198,000,000 + \$125,000,000} \\
&= \frac{\$65,000,000}{\$323,000,000} = 0.201, \text{ or } 20.1\%
\end{aligned}
$$

For every dollar XYZ pays for total labor, it incurs an additional $.201 cost in fringe benefits.

What does the fringe-benefit-to-total-labor-dollars rate tell the cost manager?

By highlighting the proportion of fringe benefits to total labor dollars, this ratio is more useful for monitoring than for planning or control. Fringe benefits are largely beyond the control of the cost manager since the pertinent guidelines are governed by the organization's policies and procedures, by law and tax codes, and by negotiations with labor.

Example: The following data is available for XYZ Corp.:

	19X1	*19X0*	*Variance*	
Expense	$	$	$	%
Total overhead	269.8	253.8	16.0	6.3
Direct labor hours	39.4	37.3	2.1	5.6
Direct labor $	198.0	181.6	16.4	9.0
Indirect labor $	125.0	120.0	5.0	4.2
Fringe benefits	65.0	58.2	6.8	11.7
Fringe-benefits-to-total-labor-dollars ratio (%)	20.1	19.3	0.8	4.1

(in $000,000s)

The rate of fringe benefits to total labor dollars increased from 19.3% in 19X0 to 20.1% in 19X1—4.1%. This rise is due primarily to the 9.0% increase in direct labor hours.

WEIGHING THE IMPACT OF COSTS ON OPERATING (OPERATIONAL) INCOME

What is operating (operational) income?

Operational (or operating) income is equal to sales (or revenues) less cost of sales and indirect costs.

$$\text{Operational income} = \text{Sales} - \left(\text{Cost of sales} + \text{Indirect costs} \right)$$

Example: XYZ Corp. had sales (revenues) of $45,000,000 in May, with total cost of sales of $40,000,000 and indirect costs of $2,100,000.

$$\begin{aligned} \text{Operational income} &= \text{Sales} - \left(\text{Cost of sales} + \text{Indirect costs} \right) \\ &= \$45,000,000 - (\$40,000,000 + \$2,100,000) \\ &= \$45,000,000 - \$42,100,000 = \$2,900,000 \end{aligned}$$

XYZ's operational income in May is $2,900,000.

HOW TO EVALUATE PURCHASES, PAYABLES, AND DISBURSEMENTS

What is the days-purchases-in-payables ratio?

This ratio relates the amounts payable to an organization's total purchases for a given period. When vaildated by historical data, this factor acts as a guideline in verifying the reasonableness of payables figures that are developed by other means.

$$\text{Days-purchases-in-payables ratio} = \frac{\text{Accounts payable, ending balance}}{\text{Period purchases / Days in period}}$$

Note: Accounts payable, ending balance is calculated as follows:

> Accounts payable, beginning balance
> + Purchases for the period
> − Cash disbursements for the period
>
> Accounts payable, ending balance

Example: ABC Co. started the quarter with an accounts payable of $42,000,000. During the quarter, the company made purchases of $78,300,000, and cash disbursements of $79,600,000.

Accounts payable, beginning balance	$42,000,000
+ Purchases for the period	78,300,000
− Cash disbursements for the period	79,600,000
Accounts payable, ending balance	$40,700,000

$$
\begin{aligned}
\text{Days-purchases-in-payables ratio} &= \frac{\text{Accounts payable, ending balance}}{\text{Period purchases / Days in period}} \\
&= \frac{\$40,700,000}{\$78,300,000 \ / \ 90 \text{ days}} \\
&= \frac{\$40,700,000}{\$870,000 \text{ per day}} = 46.8 \text{ days}
\end{aligned}
$$

For the quarter, ABC has 46.8 days' worth of purchases payable.

What is the ratio of daily purchases versus daily disbursements?

Called the days-purchases-in-disbursements ratio, this relates how much a company purchases to how much cash it actually disburses in a given period. It is expressed in terms of days' worth of purchase.

$$\text{Days-purchases-in-disbursements} = \frac{\text{Cash disbursements}}{\text{Period purchases / Days in period}}$$

Example: During the quarter, ABC Co. made purchases of $78,300,000 and cash disbursements of $79,600,000.

$$\text{Days-purchases-in-disbursements} = \frac{\text{Cash disbursements}}{\text{Period purchases / days in period}}$$

$$= \frac{\$79,600,000}{\$78,300,000 \text{ / 90 days in period}}$$

$$= \frac{\$79,600,000}{\$870,000} = 91.5 \text{ days}$$

91.5 days' worth of a quarter's purchases have resulted in cash disbursements. In effect, its purchases and cash disbursements are running just about one for one: 91.5 days' worth of disbursements versus 90 days' worth of purchases. If this factor is historically consistent, ABC can expect to pay for all its purchases within a quarter.

What are cash disbursements?

Cash disbursements are any items that result in the flow of cash out of the organization: accounts payable, payroll, federal income taxes, other taxes, deferred compensation fund payments, loan payments, interest payments, lease payments, insurance premium installments, and so on.

Example: MNO Corp.'s cash disbursement for the first quarter are as follows:

Accounts payable	$ 85,100
Gross payroll	51,000
Income and other taxes	3,400
Retirement fund	3,500
Interest payment	1,100
Total cash disbursements	$144,100

What is the accounts-payable-turnover ratio?

This ratio indicates the number of times the accounts payable "turned over"—that is, were paid—in a period.

$$\text{Accounts-payable-turnover ratio} = \frac{\text{Period purchases}}{\text{Accounts payable, ending balance}}$$

Example: ABC Co. ended the quarter with an accounts payable balance of $40,700,000. During the quarter, it made purchases of $78,300,000.

$$\text{Accounts-payable-turnover ratio} = \frac{\text{Period purchases}}{\text{Accounts payable, ending balance}}$$

$$= \frac{\$78,300,000}{\$40,700,000} = 1.9$$

During the quarter, ABC made purchases that were 1.9 its ending accounts payable amount.

How is the accounts-payable-turnover ratio used?

This ratio can be used not only for comparative purposes (from period to period or with industry standards), but also for estimating ending payable balances, given estimated sales.

Example: ABC Co.'s accounts-payable-turnover ratio has been validated by historical data to be 1.9. For the upcoming quarter, purchases are projected at $77,100,000. The end-of-quarter accounts payable balance is estimated as follows:

$$\text{Accounts-payable-turnover ratio} = \frac{\text{Period purchases}}{\text{Accounts payable, ending balance}}$$

$$1.9 = \frac{\$77,100,000}{\text{Accounts payable, ending balance}}$$

Or:

$$\text{Accounts payable, ending balance} = \frac{\$77,100,000}{1.9} = \$40,578,947$$

During the quarter, ABC made purchases that were 1.9 its ending accounts payable amount.

How is the ratio of disbursements to accounts payable computed?

To calculate this ratio for a given period, divide actual disbursements by the accounts payable during the period.

$$\text{Disbursements-to-accounts-payable ratio} = \frac{\text{Disbursements}}{\text{Accounts payable}}$$

Example: During the first quarter of its fiscal year, MNO Corp. made actual cash disbursements of $85,100, against an accounts payable total of $82,200.

$$\text{Disbursements-to-accounts-payable ratio} = \frac{\text{Disbursements}}{\text{Accounts payable}}$$

$$= \frac{\$85,100}{\$82,200} = 1.04, \text{ or } 104\%$$

MNO Corp. overpaid is obligations by 4% in the first quarter.

What is the purpose of the disbursements-to-accounts-payable ratio?

When this ratio is calculated for successive periods, especially on an automated system, the cost manager is able to determine whether accounts payable are being over- or underpaid. If a trend is detected, appropriate action can be taken to improve the company's cash flow from period to period.

HONORING TRADE PAYABLE COMMITMENTS WHILE CURTAILING EXPENSES

What is meant by "days purchasing outstanding"?

Days purchasing outstanding is a ratio used to determine whether an organization is meeting its trade payable commitments on schedule. The fewer the days purchases outstanding, the more favorable the company's debt-paying ability. From a vendor's point of view, the ratio is a measure of its customer's ability to pay debts on time.

$$\text{Days-purchases-outstanding ratio} = \frac{\text{Trades payable}}{\text{Period purchases / Days in period}}$$

Example: Data for the ABC Co. is as follows:

(in $000,000s)			
	Average Trade Payables	*Total Purchases*	*Days in Period*
19X0	$10,150	$ 90,100	360
19X1	$12,400	$113,500	360

For 19X0, the days-purchases-outstanding ratio is:

$$\begin{aligned}\text{Days-purchases-outstanding ratio} &= \frac{\text{Trades payable}}{\text{Period purchases / Days in period}} \\[6pt] &= \frac{\$10,150}{\$90,100 \text{ / } 360 \text{ days}} \\[6pt] &= \frac{\$10,150}{250.3 \text{ days}} = 40.6 \text{ days}\end{aligned}$$

For 19X1, the days-purchases-outstanding ratio is:

$$\text{Days-purchases-outstanding ratio} = \frac{\text{Trades payable}}{\text{Period purchases / Days in period}}$$

$$= \frac{\$12,400}{\$113,500 \,/\, 360 \text{ days}}$$

$$= \frac{\$12,400}{315.3 \text{ days}} = 39.30 \text{ days}$$

There were 1.3 days fewer purchases in 19X1 than in 19X0. While purchases increased by 26% ($113,500 less $90,100 equals $23,400 divided by $90,100), the payable balance increased by only 22%, which accounts for the fewer days purchases outstanding.

CONTROLLING INVENTORY LEVELS

Why are inventory ratios important?

A prime cause of business failures is an inventory that is either excessive or inadequate. While ratios do not necessarily reveal an unbalanced inventory, then can indicate whether levels are in line with industry norms or with those of other periods.

The disadvantages of excessive inventory are:

- Overuse of working capital, with the result that the organization might not be able to meet current obligations.
- Obsolescence.
- Loss of savings due to a decline in the price of raw materials.
- Creation of additional costs, such as interest on investment, storage, insurance,taxes, and possibly the need for plant expansion.

The problems with insufficient inventory are:

- Excessive out-of-stock situations.
- Delays in customer deliveries.
- Slowdowns in work activity and/or machine usage, which are inefficient.

Which inventory ratios are used the most?

The most used inventory-related ratios are:

- Inventory to cost of sales
- Sales to inventory

- Average days of sales in inventory
- Inventory to working capital

Inventory and Cost of Sales

What is the inventory-to-cost-of-sales ratio?

This is a comparison (expressed as a percentage) between the inventory value and the cost of sales.

$$\text{Inventory-to-cost-of-sales ratio} = \frac{\text{Inventory value}}{\text{Cost of sales}}$$

Example: ABC Corp.s inventory value is $260,000,000 and its cost of sales $223,900,000.

$$\text{Inventory-to-cost-of-sales ratio} = \frac{\text{Inventory value}}{\text{Cost of sales}}$$

$$= \frac{\$260,000,000}{\$223,900,000} = 116\%$$

How is the ratio of inventory to cost of sales used?

Once validated by historical data, this ratio can be used two ways. One is to estimate preliminarily the inventory levels associated with cost of sales projections. The other is to check projected inventory levels arrived at by means more conventional methods (see example).

Example: ABC Corp. projects a cost-of-sales figure of $243,300,000 for the upcoming quarter. An inventory-to-cost-of-sales ratio of 110% has been accepted as historically valid. What is a reasonable estimate of its inventory value?

$$\text{Inventory-to-cost-of-sales ratio} = \frac{\text{Inventory value}}{\text{Cost of sales}}$$

$$110\% = \frac{\text{Inventory value}}{\$243,300,000}$$

Or:

Inventory value = $243,300,000 × 1.10 = $26,763,000

ABC may expect inventory levels in the neighborhood of $26,763,000.

Is the inventory-to-cost-of-sales ratio the same or similar for each quarter as it is for the year?

No. While inventory levels remain more or less constant throughout the year, cost of sales accumulates. So the ratio of inventory to cost of sales for each quarter is normally higher than for the year.

Example: ABC Corp. shows the following data for the year:

(in $000,000s)

	Quarter				Annual Period
	First	Second	Third	Fourth	
Inventory sales	$260.0	$268.5	$256.9	$243.4	$257.2
Cost of sales	$223.9	$243.3	$248.1	$247.7	$963.0
Inventory-to-cost-of-sales ratio	116%	110%	104%	98%	27%

Note that the annual ratio is much lower than the quarterly versions, due to the accumulation of cost of sales over the year to a total of $963,000,000.

Can the inventory-to-cost-of-sales ratio be annualized?

Yes. For a rough approximation of the annualized ratio, simply divide the quarterly ratio by 4.

Example: See the preceding example. If each quarterly ratio is divided by 4, the results are:

(in $000,000s)

	Quarter				Annual Period
	First	Second	Third	Fourth	
Inventory sales	$260.0	$268.5	$256.9	$243.4	$257.2
Cost of sales	$223.9	$243.3	$248.1	$247.7	$963.0
Inventory-to-cost-of-sales ratio	116%	110%	104%	98%	27%
Annualized ratio	29%	28%	26%	24.5%	

Note: The annualized figure will be inaccurate if either the inventory value or cost of sales is an atypical amount. The quarterly figures should be validated as normal before making the annualization calculation.

How do you compute the ratio of cost of sales to average inventory?

Inventory can be computed on the basis of sales or cost of sales. Sales is used by many organizations for other types of turnover calculations, such as expense and profit margins. Most companies, however, use cost of sales when computing inventory turnover. The generally acceptable ratio is therefore the cost of sales to average inventory.

$$\text{Inventory turnover ratio} = \frac{\text{Cost of sales (C/S)}}{\text{Average inventory}}$$

Note: Sales can be substituted for cost of sales, if necessary, but the results tend to be less accurate due to variations in profit margin. In the retail industry, the ratio of sales to inventory at sales prices provides the same turnover ratio as the cost of sales to inventory at cost prices.

Example: XYZ Corp. has quarterly cost of sales of $223,900,000 and an average inventory of $260,000,000.

$$\text{Inventory turnover ratio} = \frac{\text{Cost of sales (C/S)}}{\text{Average inventory}}$$
$$= \frac{\$223,900,000}{\$260,000,000} = .86$$

Is the cost-of-sales-to-average-inventory ratio the same or similar for each quarter as it is for the year?

No. While inventory levels remain more or less constant throughout the year, cost of sales accumulates. So the ratio of cost of sales to average inventory for each quarter is normally much lower than for the year.

Example: ABC Corp. shows the following data for the year:

(in $000,000s)

	First	Second	Third	Fourth	Annual Period
Cost of sales	$223.9	$243.3	$248.1	$247.7	$963.0
Average inventory	$260.0	$268.5	$256.9	$243.4	$257.2
Annualized C/S	$895.6	$973.2	$992.4	$990.8	
Cost-of-sales-to-average-inventory ratio	.86	.91	.96	1.0	3.7

Note that the annual ratio is much higher than the quarterly versions, due to the accumulation of cost of sales over the year to a total of $963,000,000.

Can the cost-of-sales-to-average-inventory ratio be annualized?

Yes. For a rough approximation of the annualized ratio, simply multiply the quarterly ratio by 4.

Example: See the preceding example. If each quarterly ratio is multiplied by 4, the results are:

(in $000,000s)

| | Quarter | | | | Annual |
	First	Second	Third	Fourth	Period
Cost of sales	$223.9	$243.3	$248.1	$247.7	$963.0
Average inventory	$260.0	$268.5	$256.9	$243.4	$257.2
Annualized C/S	$895.6	$973.2	$992.4	$990.8	
Cost-of-sales-to-average-inventory ratio	.86	.91	.96	1.0	3.7
Annualized ratio	3.4	3.6	3.8	4.0	

Note: The annualized figure will be inaccurate if either the inventory value or cost of sales is an atypical amount. The quarterly figures should be validated as normal before making the annualization calculation.

Should inventory turnover ratios be computed without regard to the type of inventory?

They may be, but the preferred approach is to determine turnover ratios by category of inventory. The generally accepted categories are:

$$\text{Finished goods} = \frac{\text{Annualized cost of sales}}{\text{Average finished products inventory}}$$

$$\text{Work in process} = \frac{\text{Cost of products manufactured}}{\text{Work in process average inventory}}$$

$$\text{Raw materials} = \frac{\text{Cost of materials used}}{\text{Raw material average inventory}}$$

Average Days of Inventory

What is the average-days-of-inventory ratio?

The average number of days that inventory remains on hand is considered an indicator of how effectively inventory is being managed. Generally, the fewer days that inventory is on hand, the better its the cost manager.

$$\text{Average days of inventories} = \text{Number of days in period} \times \frac{\text{Period-end inventory balances}}{\text{Total cost of sales}}$$

"Period-end inventory balances" the combined inventory amounts, including finished goods, work in process, and raw materials. "Total cost of sales" is also the combined figure.

Note: Use 90 days for a quarter, 360 for a year.

Example: ABC Corp.'s inventory and cost of sales figures are:

(in $000,000s)

	Quarter				Annual Period
	First	Second	Third	Fourth	
Inventory balances	$260.0	$268.5	$256.9	$243.4	$257.2
Cost of sales	$223.9	$243.3	$248.1	$247.7	$963.0
Days in period	90	90	90	90	360
Average age of inventories	104	99	94	88	96

The average days of inventories for the first quarter is calculated as follows:

$$\begin{array}{c} \text{Average days} \\ \text{of} \\ \text{inventories} \end{array} = \begin{array}{c} \text{Number of} \\ \text{days in} \\ \text{period} \end{array} \times \frac{\text{Period-end inventory balance}}{\text{Total cost of sales}}$$

$$= 90 \text{ days} \times \frac{\$260,000,000}{\$223,900,000}$$

$$= 90 \text{ days} \times 1.16 = 104.5 \text{ days}$$

Note: Quarterly ratios do not have to be annualized.

Other quarters are computed in the same way. In ABC's case, the average age, in days, of inventories declined from quarter to quarter. This is a favorable trend.

How can the average age of inventories be used?

Given a projected cost of sales, a validated average age of inventories can be used to estimate an inventory balance for the period in question. The period may be annual, quarterly, or monthly.

$$\begin{array}{c} \text{Estimate} \\ \text{inventory} \\ \text{balance} \end{array} = \begin{array}{c} \text{Projected} \\ \text{cost of} \\ \text{sales} \end{array} \times \frac{\text{Average age of inventory}}{\text{Days in period}}$$

Example: ABC Corp. projects annual cost of sales of $963,000,000, and it uses a validated average age of inventory of 91 days.

$$\begin{array}{c} \text{Estimate} \\ \text{inventory} \\ \text{balance} \end{array} = \begin{array}{c} \text{Projected} \\ \text{cost of} \\ \text{sales} \end{array} \times \frac{\text{Average age of inventory}}{\text{Days in period}}$$

$$= \$963,000,000 \times \frac{91 \text{ days}}{360 \text{ days}}$$

$$= \$963,000,000 \times 0.253 = \$24,363,900$$

ABC may expect to have an average inventory balance during the year of approximately $24,000,000.

Sales and Inventory

What is the sales-to-inventory ratio?

By comparing inventory to sales volume, this ratio indicates whether there is too little or too much inventory to support the given level of sales. It is a measure of sales efficiency. The objective is to have the smallest level of inventory while still meeting sales requirements efficiently.

The ratio of sales to inventory is considered a rough measure of performance. Comparing sales and inventory is difficult because the two amounts have different bases. Inventory is valued at cost or market, whichever is lower; sales at selling price (that is, cost plus gross margin). Further, to compare periods, you must take into account prevailing business conditions. For example, a change in the price level at which new stock is acquired changes the relationship between sales and inventory. The dollar relationship could vary markedly without any actual change in the physical volume of sales or inventory. Finally, seasonal fluctuations in inventory values can also throw calculations off.

Note: Cost of sales is generally used for this estimate, but sale may substitute for it.

$$\text{Sales-to-inventory ratio} = \frac{\text{Sales}}{\text{Average inventory balance}}$$

Example: ABC Corp. shows the following data:

(in $000,000s)

	First	Quarter Second	Third	Fourth	Annual Period
Sales volume	$ 252.8	$ 274.9	$ 276.2	$ 273.1	$1,077.0
Annualized sales	$1,011.2	$1,099.6	$1,104.8	$1,092.4	$1,077.0
Inventory balances	$ 260.0	$ 268.5	$ 256.9	$ 243.4	$ 257.2
Sales-to-inventory ratio	.97	1.0	1.1	1.1	4.2
Annualized ratio	3.9	4.1	4.3	4.5	4.2

The sales-to-inventory ratio for the first quarter is computed as follows:

$$\text{Sales-to-inventory ratio} = \frac{\text{Sales}}{\text{Average inventory balance}}$$

$$= \frac{\$252,800,000}{\$260,000,000} = 0.97$$

Ratios for the other quarters and the year are computed in the same way.

Does the sales-to-inventory ratio have to be annualized?

Yes, because sales accumulate over the year and inventory balances remain more or less constant from quarter to quarter. There are two ways to annualize the quarterly ratio.

1. Multiply it by 4:

$$\text{Annual ratio} = \text{Quarterly ratio} \times 4$$

2. Multiply the quarterly sales volume by 4 and use the ratio formula.

$$\frac{\text{Annual sales-to-}}{\text{inventory ratio}} = \frac{\text{Quarterly sales} \times 4}{\text{Average inventory balance}}$$

Example: ABC Corp.'s quarterly ratios are:

		Quarter			Annual
	First	*Second*	*Third*	*Fourth*	*Period*
Sales volume	$ 252.8	$ 274.9	$ 276.2	$ 273.1	$1,077.0
Annualized sales	$1,011.2	$1,099.6	$1,104.8	$1,092.4	$1,077.0
Inventory balances	$ 260.0	$ 268.5	$ 256.9	$ 243.4	$ 257.2
Sales-to-inventory ratio	.97	1.0	1.1	1.1	4.2
Annualized ratio	3.9	4.1	4.3	4.5	4.2

(in $000,000s)

Method 1: Multiply the ratio by 4: Use the first quarter's figures as an example.

$$\text{Annual ratio} = \text{Quarterly ratio} \times 4$$
$$= .97 \times 4 = 3.9$$

Method 2: Multiply the quarterly sales volume by 4 and use the ratio formula. Again, use the first quarter.

$$\frac{\text{Annual sales-to-}}{\text{inventory ratio}} = \frac{\text{Quarterly sales} \times 4}{\text{Average inventory balance}}$$
$$= \frac{\$252,800,000 \times 4}{\$257,200,000}$$
$$= \frac{\$1,011,200,000}{\$257,200,000} = 3.9$$

Working Capital and Inventory

What is working capital?

Working capital, sometimes known as net working capital or net current assets, is equal to the difference between current assets and current liabilities, both balance sheet entries. The more working capital a company has, the greater is its liquidity.

Working capital = Current assets − Current liabilities

Example: Portions of ABC Co.'s balance sheet are as follows:

	Amount
Current Assets	
Cash	$ 3,500,000
Marketable securities	3,300,000
Accounts receivable	28,700,000
Inventories	
Raw materials	26,800,000
Work in process	10,700,000
Finished goods	7,300,000
Subtotal	44,800,000
Prepaid expenses	250,000
Total current assets	**$80,550,000**
• • •	
Current Liabilities	
Notes payable	$ 1,400,000
Current portion—LT debt	2,500,000
Accrued payroll	3,600,000
Accounts payable	20,850,000
Income tax payable	2,600,000
Total current liabilities	**$30,950,000**

Working capital = Current assets − Current liabilities
= $80,550,000 − $30,950,000
= $49,600,000

ABC Co. has working capital of $49,600,000.

What is the inventory-to-working-capital ratio?

This comparison relates the average inventory value (a balance sheet item) to average working capital.

$$\text{Inventory-to-working-capital ratio} = \frac{\text{Inventory}}{\text{Working capital}}$$

Example: ABC Co.'s working capital is $49,600,000. The current assets part of the company's balance sheet is as follows:

	Amount
Current Assets	
Cash	$ 3,500,000
Marketable securities	3,300,000
Accounts receivable	28,700,000
Inventories	
Raw materials	**26,800,000**
Work in process	**10,700,000**
Finished goods	**7,300,000**
Subtotal	**44,800,000**
Prepaid expenses	250,000
Total current assets	$80,550,000

$$\text{Inventory-to-working-capital ratio} = \frac{\text{Inventory}}{\text{Working capital}}$$

$$= \frac{\$44,800,000}{\$49,600,000} = 0.903, \text{ or } 90.3\%$$

ABC's inventory represents about 90% of its working capital.

What is the significance of the inventory-to-working-capital ratio?

This ratio, by showing the percentage of working capital invested in inventory, demonstrates the part of current assets that are the least liquid. Inventories that greatly exceed working capital indicate that current liabilities exceed liquid current assets (cash and cash equivalents). The company might want to consider decreasing the proportion of its inventory.

HOW COSTS RELATE TO SALES VOLUME AND PROFIT

What is the operating leverage ratio?

The operating leverage ratio assesses the effect of fluctuating sales on operating profits.

$$\text{Operating leverage ratio} = \frac{\text{Sales} - \text{Variable expenses}}{\text{Sales} - \text{Total expenses}}$$

Since the operating income equals sales less the sum of variable and fixed expenses, then:

$$\text{Operating leverage ratio} = \frac{\text{Sales} - \text{Variable expenses}}{\text{Operating expenses}}$$

Example: With first-quarter sales at $300,000, MNO Corp. incurs variable costs of $234,000 and fixed expenses of $36,000.

$$\begin{aligned}
\text{Operating leverage ratio} &= \frac{\text{Sales} - \text{Variable expenses}}{\text{Sales} - \text{Fixed expenses}} \\
&= \frac{\$300,000 - \$234,000}{\$300,000 - (\$234,000 + \$36,000)} \\
&= \frac{\$300,000 - \$234,000}{\$300,000 - \$270,000} \\
&= \frac{\$66,000}{\$30,000} = 2.2
\end{aligned}$$

The first-quarter operating leverage factor is 2.2.

Why is the operating leverage factor important?

Operating leverage is the leverage a company gains from sales volume. High sales volumes give an organization income with which to operate. Decreased sales volumes creates situations in which operating income is spread thin, posing a threat to a company's operating ability. The operating leverage ratio enables the cost manager to evaluate this so-called "income risk." The operating leverage factor says that income from operations changes "so many times" the percentage change sales volume. Note in the following formula that the factor is inversely proportional to operating income (income from operations):

$$\text{Operating leverage ratio} = \frac{\text{Sales} - \text{Variable expenses}}{\text{Operating expenses}}$$

Note: Income risk is distinguished from financial risk, which is posed by the heavy use of debt support by creditors.

Example: See the preceding example. An operating leverage factor of 2.2 means that operating income ($30,000 in the example) will change 2.2 times the percentage change in sales. If sales increase by 15%, then income from operations will increase by approximately 33%, or $9,900 (15% times 2.2): $30,000 times 0.33. For a decrease of 15% in sales, operating income would drop by $9,900.

Does the operating leverage factor change?

The operating leverage factor changes with fluctuations in sales volume and in expenses.

Example: In the second quarter of operation, MNO Corp. increases 15% to $345,000; in the third quarter, it drops by 15% to $255,000. Assume the rare occurrence that variable expenses remain at $234,000 and fixed expenses at $36,000.

For the increase in sales volume:

$$\text{Operating leverage ratio} = \frac{\text{Sales} - \text{Variable expenses}}{\text{Sales} - \text{Fixed expenses}}$$

$$= \frac{\$345,000 - \$234,000}{\$345,000 - (\$234,000 + \$36,000)}$$

$$= \frac{\$345,000 - \$234,000}{\$345,000 - \$270,000}$$

$$= \frac{\$111,000}{\$75,000} = +1.48$$

For the decrease in sales volume:

$$\text{Operating leverage ratio} = \frac{\text{Sales} - \text{Variable expenses}}{\text{Sales} - \text{Fixed expenses}}$$

$$= \frac{\$255,000 - \$234,000}{\$255,000 - (\$234,000 + \$36,000)}$$

$$= \frac{\$255,000 - \$234,000}{\$255,000 - \$270,000}$$

$$= \frac{\$21,000}{-\$15,000} = -1.40$$

When the sales volume changes (up or down), so did the operating leverage factor. At each of the revised sales levels, the operating factors change.

IS THE COMPANY MAKING MONEY? COSTS AND THE BREAK-EVEN POINT

What is the break-even point?

In business, the break-even point is the sales volume level at which the business neither profits nor loses money; sales and total costs are exactly equal. It is a function of sales volume, and fixed and variable expenses.

$$\text{Break-even point} = \frac{\text{Fixed expenses}}{1 - \dfrac{\text{Variable expenses}}{\text{Sales}}}$$

Example: MNO Corp. has first-quarter sales for Product A of $300,000. Its quarterly fixed expenses are $36,000, its variable expenses $234,000.

$$\text{Break-even point} = \frac{\text{Fixed expenses}}{1 - \dfrac{\text{Variable expenses}}{\text{Sales}}}$$

$$= \frac{\$36,000}{1 - \dfrac{\$234,000}{\$300,000}}$$

$$= \frac{\$36,000}{1 - 0.78}$$

$$= \frac{\$36,000}{0.22} = \$163,636$$

MNO's break-even point is $163,636. That is, before the dollar volume of sales reaches this point, MNO loses money; after it, MNO makes a profit. Precisely at that level, no profit or loss results.

When is the break-even point calculation made?

This computation is made to enable the cost manager to know the point at which a product, a product line, or the business itself becomes profitable.

Example: See the preceding example. MNO Corp. knows that the break-even point for Product A is $163,636. If the unit price for Product A is $20, then a little over 8,180 units must be sold for the product to break even: $163,636 divided by $20 equals 8,181.8 units. Management can then compare that requirement with sales estimates. Can enough units be sold to make Product A a profitable venture for the organization?

Does the break-even point change?

Yes. The break-even point changes with:

● Fixed expenses
● Variable expenses
● Sales volume

How do fixed expenses affect the break-even point?

Expenses drive the break-even point up. Since some fixed expenses remain the same regardless of sales volume, these expenses particularly affect break-even: The greater the total fixed expenses, the higher the break-even point will be.

Example: See the preceding example. Assume that MNO Corp. has first-quarter sales for Product A of $300,000 and variable expenses of $234,000, but fixed expenses rise $14,000 (from $36,000 to $50,000).

$$\text{Break-even point} = \cfrac{\text{Fixed expenses}}{1 - \cfrac{\text{Variable expenses}}{\text{Sales}}}$$

$$= \cfrac{\$50,000}{1 - \cfrac{\$234,000}{\$300,000}}$$

$$= \cfrac{\$50,000}{1 - 0.78}$$

$$= \frac{\$50,000}{0.22} = \$227,272$$

MNO's break-even point increases from $163,636 to $227,272. For Product A to break even, sales have to increase by $63,636 ($227,272 less $163,636).

How do sales affect the break-even point?

The break-even point generally declines with increased sales volume, assuming fixed expenses do not rise (or rise disproportionately) and that variable expenses increase only as necessary to keep pace with orders.

Example: See the preceding example. Assume that in the second-quarter:

- Sales for Product A rise by 20%:
($300,000 times 0.20 equals $60,000) $360,000
- Variable expenses increase by 15.38%:
($234,000 times 0.1538 equals $36,000) $270,000
- Fixed expenses remain the same. $ 36,000

$$\text{Break-even point} = \cfrac{\text{Fixed expenses}}{1 - \cfrac{\text{Variable expenses}}{\text{Sales}}}$$

$$= \cfrac{\$36,000}{1 - \cfrac{\$270,000}{\$360,000}}$$

$$= \cfrac{\$36,000}{1 - 0.75}$$

$$= \frac{\$36,000}{0.25} = \$144,000$$

MNO's break-even point decreases from $163,636 to $144,000.

Can you estimate how much variable expenses will change with sales?

Yes. The variable expense per unit of production can be calculated by means of the following formula:

$$\begin{array}{c} \text{Variable} \\ \text{expense per} \\ \text{unit} \end{array} = \dfrac{\begin{array}{c}\text{Total expense}\\\text{allowance}\end{array} - \begin{array}{c}\text{Total fixed}\\\text{expense}\end{array}}{\text{Production volume}}$$

- Total expense allowance is the total variable allowance for the period.
- Total fixed expense is the sum of fixed costs for the period.
- Production volume is the number of units slated to be produced within the period.

Example: MNO Corp. plans to produce 9,000 units this week. It allows $2,000 for variable expenses and $875 for fixed expenses.

$$\begin{array}{c} \text{Variable} \\ \text{expense per} \\ \text{unit} \end{array} = \dfrac{\begin{array}{c}\text{Total expense}\\\text{allowance}\end{array} - \begin{array}{c}\text{Total fixed}\\\text{expense}\end{array}}{\text{Production volume}}$$

$$= \dfrac{\$2,000 - \$875}{9,000 \text{ units}}$$

$$= \dfrac{\$1,125}{9,000 \text{ units}} = \$0.125 \text{ per unit}$$

For every unit produced, MNO spends $0.125 in variable costs.

What purpose does the per-unit variable cost serve?

If the cost manager knows what each unit of production costs in terms of variable expense, it can arrive at a fairly accurate estimate of the total variable expense that will accompany sales. Once actual figures are on hand, they can be compared with the projected amounts to see whether corrective action is required for upcoming periods.

$$\text{Variable expenses} = \text{Sales in units} \times \text{Per-unit variable cost}$$

Example: MNO Corp. the cost manager has established, over a number of accounting periods, that its per-unit variable cost is $0.125. It estimates sales of 24,000 units in the second quarter.

$$\text{Variable expenses} = \text{Sales in units} \times \text{Per-unit variable cost}$$

$$= 24,000 \times \$0.125$$

$$= \$3,000$$

MNO's second-quarter variable expenses will be approximately $3,000. Management can go on to calculate the break-even point for the quarter.

Can per-unit fixed costs be computed?

Yes. However, fixed costs vary with the number of units produced (whereas variable costs are constant).

$$\frac{\text{Fixed costs}}{\text{per unit}} = \frac{\text{Total fixed costs for the period}}{\text{Units produced in the period}}$$

Note: Over the long term, fixed costs may vary. Short-term, they can generally be assumed to remain level.

Example: MNO Corp. the cost manager has ordered 9,000 units to be produced this coming week. Fixed costs for this period are $875.

$$\frac{\text{Fixed costs}}{\text{per unit}} = \frac{\text{Total fixed costs for the period}}{\text{Units produced in the period}}$$

$$= \frac{\$875}{9,000 \text{ units}} = \$0.0972 \text{ per unit}$$

This week, MNO spends $0.0972 in fixed costs for every unit produced. If the cost manager orders 7,000 units for next week, the total amount of fixed cost remains the same, while the number of units decreases. The fixed cost per unit therefore rises:

$$\frac{\text{Fixed costs}}{\text{per unit}} = \frac{\text{Total fixed costs for the period}}{\text{Units produced in the period}}$$

$$= \frac{\$875}{7,000 \text{ units}} = \$0.125 \text{ per unit}$$

Can the "break-even" plant capacity be calculated?

The approximate plant capacity at which an organization is breaking even ("BE plant capacity") can be computed by means of the following formula:

$$\frac{\text{BE}}{\text{plant}} = \frac{\text{Fixed expenses} \times \text{Current \% of plant capacity}}{\text{Sales} - \text{Variable expenses}}$$

Example: ABC Co.'s plant is currently operating at 80% of full capacity, with fixed expenses at $72,000 and variable costs at $282,074. Sales are $474,074. For purposes of illustration, assume that the relationship between dollar sales and plant capacity is constant.

$$\begin{matrix}\text{BE} \\ \text{plant} \\ \text{capacity}\end{matrix} = \frac{\text{Fixed expenses} \times \text{Current \% of plant capacity}}{\text{Sales} - \text{Variable expenses}}$$

$$= \frac{\$72,000 \times 0.80}{\$474,074 - \$282,074}$$

$$= \frac{\$57,600}{\$192,000} = 0.30, \text{ or } 30\%$$

At the current sales and expense levels, the plant would operate at a break-even level at 30% of capacity.

CHAPTER 5

MONITORING CASH RECEIPTS: THE ACCOUNTS RECEIVABLE MANAGER

WORDS TO KNOW

Accounts-payable-turnover. A ratio that indicates the number of times the accounts payable "turned over"—that is, were paid—in a period.

Accounts receivable (receivables). A balance sheet entry indicating amounts owed to a company by customers for product sold or services rendered.

Accounts receivable turnover. The ratio of total credit sales to receivables (also known as the sales-to-receivables ratio).

Aging procedure. *See* Aging receivables procedure.

Aging receivables (aging) procedure. Accounts receivable are grouped according to their ages, usually under 30 days, 31-60 days, 61-90 days, and over 90 days. For each group, the beginning-of-period and end-of-period amounts are compared, to see whether it is taking the organization more or less time to receive payment.

Average collection period. The average number of days between the day the invoice is sent out and the day the customer pays the bill.

Average receivables. The sum of the beginning and ending balances for a period divided by 2. The period may be a month, quarter, year, or any period.

Backlog. The number of, or the dollar value of, unfilled orders.

Beginning balance. The balance for an accounting entry at the start of the accounting period.

Billed sales. Sales for which orders have been filled and invoices sent out.

Cash disbursement. *See* Disbursement.

Cash flow. The difference between cash receipts and cash disbursements.

Cash flow ratio. A comparison between an individual receipt or disbursement item and its related total.

Cash flow statement. A financial statement consisting of two breakdowns: cash receipts and disbursements, with a summary for the organization's net cash position.

Cash receipt. *See* Receipt.

Credit sales. *See* Sales.

Current period. The present accounting period.

Current period collections. The receivables collected in the present accounting period.

Current ratio. Current assets divided by current liabilities.

Days-of-sales-in-receivables ratio (or factor). The ratio between sales and receivables reflects the normal number of days of uncollected sales in receivables.

Current-period-collection rate. A gauge of how fast an organization recoups expenditures made to fill orders.

Current ratio. Current assets divided by current liabilities.

Days-purchases-in-payables ratio. The amounts payable to an organization's total purchases for a given period.

Days-purchases-in-disbursements ratio. A ratio that relates how much a company purchases to how much cash it actually disburses in a given period.

Disbursement. A cash amount paid out by the company.

Ending (end-of-period) balance. The balance of a given accounting entry at the end of the accounting period.

End-of-period balance. *See* Ending balance.

Financial risk. The risk posed by the heavy use of debt support by creditors.

Fixed expenses. Expenses that do not vary with levels of production, such as plant costs or executives' salaries.

Income risk. The risk of having insufficient income to carry on operations.

Interest plus funded debt ratio. This ratio assesses an organization's capacity to meet scheduled interest plus debt repayments.

Lagged (prior period) costs. Costs incurred by the company in the preceding account period to fill orders.

Liquidation limit. The percentage of billed sales that will be collected in the same period as they are billed.

Liquidation lag value. The numerical complement of the liquidation limit.

Net credit sales. *See* Sales.

Operating leverage ratio. A ratio that assesses the effect of fluctuating sales on operating profits.

Prior period. The preceding accounting period.

Prior period billings. Billings made during the preceding accounting period.

Progress payment. The partial payment by a customer against a receivable.

Receipt. A cash amount received by the company.

Receivables. *See* Accounts receivable.

Sales. Sales revenues less a calculated allowance for returned goods and bad debt.

Sales backlog. *See* Backlog.

Sales-to-receivables ratio. *See* Accounts receivable turnover.

Times-interest-earned ratio. A ratio that focuses on the number of times interest is covered by operating profits. The higher the ratio, the better off the company.

Times-preferred-dividend ratio. A ratio that indicates how able a company is to meet its preferred dividend obligations.

Total (credit) sales. *See* Sales.

Variable expenses. Expenses that fluctuate with the level of production.

Velocity method. A method for calculating an organization's debt-paying capability, used primarily for liquidation assessment.

Working capital ratio. Working capital divided by liabilities.

ASSESSING THE COMPANY'S CASH POSITION

What is cash flow?

Cash flow is the difference between disbursements and cash receipts.

Cash flow = Cash receipts − Cash disbursements

Note: If disbursements are greater than receipts for period, cash flow can be negative. Collection of receivables therefore contributes greatly to the company's cash position.

Example: First-quarter cash receipts for MNO Corp. are $136,900, and its cash disbursements are $144,200.

$$\text{Cash flow} = \text{Cash receipts} - \text{Cash disbursements}$$
$$= \$136,900 - \$144,200 = -\$7,300$$

In the first quarter, MNO had a negative cash flow of $7,300; that is, it paid out $7,300 more cash than it received.

What is included in cash receipts?

Cash receipts include any source, operational or other not, that results in a cash inflow for the organization. In addition to billed sales, receipts can be progress payments, customer advances, investment income, interest on loans, rents on company-owned properties, and so on.

Example: MNO Corp.'s cash receipts for the firt quarter are:

Billed sales	$ 58,500
Progress payments	47,300
Customer advances	9,100
Investment income	2,000
Interest on loan	20,000
Total cash receipts	$136,900

Which items are included in cash disbursements?

Cash disbursements are any items that result in the flow of cash out of the organization: accounts payable, payroll, federal income taxes, other taxes, deferred compensation fund payments, loan payments, interest payments, lease payments, insurance premium instalments, and so on.

Example: MNO Corp.'s cash disbursement for the first quarter are as follows:

Accounts payable	$ 85,100
Gross payroll	51,000
Income and other taxes	3,400
Retirement fund	3,500
Interest payment	1,100
Total cash disbursements	$144,100

How are cash flow ratios calculated?

Cash flow ratios are comparisons between individual receipt or disbursement items and their related totals.

$$\text{Cash flow ratio} = \frac{\text{Individual receipt item}}{\text{Total receipt}}$$

$$\text{Cash flow ratio} = \frac{\text{Individual disbursement item}}{\text{Total disbursements}}$$

Example: MNO Corp.'s cash receipts for the first quarter are:

Billed sales	$ 58,500
Progress payments	47,300
Customer advances	9,100
Investment income	2,000
Interest on loan	20,000
Total cash receipts	$136,900

Each item of cash receipt can be expressed as a percentage or decimal portion of total receipts. For billed sales:

$$\text{Cash flow ratio} = \frac{\text{Individual receipt item}}{\text{Total receipt}}$$
$$= \frac{\$58,500}{\$136,900}$$
$$= 0.427, \text{ or } 42.7\%$$

Billed sales represent 42.7% of MNO's first-quarter cash receipts. Each item of receipt can be expressed as a ratio and displayed as a cash receipt schedule:

	$	%
Billed sales	$ 58,500	42.7
Progress payments	47,300	34.6
Customer advances	9,100	6.6
Investment income	2,000	1.5
Interest on loan	20,000	14.6
Total cash receipts	$136,900	100.0

The same can be done for disbursements (using the formula above):

	$	%
Accounts payable	$ 85,100	59.0
Gross payroll	51,000	35.5
Income and other taxes	3,400	2.3
Retirement fund	3,500	2.4
Interest payment	1,100	0.8
Total cash disbursements	$144,100	100.0

What is a cash flow statement?

A cash flow statement consists of two breakdowns: cash receipts and disbursements, with a summary for the organization's net cash position.

Example: On the last day of the prior year's last quarter, MNO Corp. had a cash balance of $8,900. This is the beginning cash balance for this year's first quarter. The company's cash flow statement for the first quarter is as follows:

	$	%
Billed sales	$ 58,500	42.7
Progress payments	47,300	34.6
Customer advances	9,100	6.6
Investment income	2,000	1.5
Interest on loan	20,000	14.6
Total cash receipts	$ 136,900	100.0
Accounts payable	$ 85,100	59.0
Gross payroll	51,000	35.5
Income and other taxes	3,400	2.3
Retirement fund	3,500	2.4
Interest payment	1,100	0.8
Total cash disbursements	$ 144,100	100.0
Net cash increase (decrease)	$ (7,200)	
Beginning balance	8,900	
Ending balance	$ 1,700	

MNO Corp. had a first-quarter net cash position of $1,700. This becomes the beginning balance for the second quarter.

What do cash flow ratios do for the accounts receivable manager?

Cash ratios enable the accounts receivable manager to determine the sources of greatest cash inflow and outflow, and possibly to take steps to improve the organization's overall cash position.

Example: Given MNO Corp.'s cash flow statement (see the preceding example), several observations can be made:

- The company came dangerously close to a negative net cash position in the first quarter.

- Billed sales and progress payments represent the major portion (approximately 88%) of receipts. Remedial measures are probably best focused on these areas, as opposed to areas with lesser contributions to a positive cash position. Steps must be taken to increase billings and/or collections in the next quarter.

- Measures might also be considered that will limit or defer second-quarter disbursements.

- Borrowed funds to meet short-term cash needs are a possibility too.

How are cash flow ratios analyzed for reasonableness?

Cash ratios may be compared to industry standards or to the organization's annual figures. The rational is that, the year being statistically a larger "sample" of historical data than a month or a quarter, it may act as a norm for shorter periods.

Example: Part of MNO Corp.'s annual cash flow statement is as follows:

	First Quarter		Annual	
	$	%	$	%
Billed sales	$ 58,500	42.7	$318,000	50.1
Progress payments	47,300	34.6	240,500	37.8
Customer advances	9,100	6.6	44,600	7.0
Investment income	2,000	1.5	7,800	1.2
Interest on loan	20,000	14.6	25,000	3.9
Total cash receipts	$ 136,900	100.0	$635,900	100.0
Accounts payable	$ 85,100	59.0	$367,600	60.8
Gross payroll	51,000	35.5	213,100	35.2
Income and other taxes	3,400	2.3	6,400	1.1
Retirement fund	3,500	2.4	10,700	1.8
Interest payment	1,100	0.8	6,500	1.1
Total cash disbursements	$ 144,100	100.0	$604,300	100.0
Net cash increase (decrease)	$ (7,200)		$ 31,600	
Beginning balance	8,900		8,900	
Ending balance	$ 1,700		$ 22,700	

- Year-end billed sales collections (50.1%) are 7.4% greater than those of the first quarter (42.7%).

- Year-end progress payment collections (37.8%) also lead first-quarter receipts (34.6%).

- The annual accounts payable and gross payroll ratios (58.0% and 33.7%) are lower than the first quarter levels (59.0% and 35.5%).

All-in-all, MNO Corp. had a weak first quarter, compared to the company's annual figures.

Are there other ways to analyze a company's cash position?

There are significant relationships among an organization's billed sales, cash receipts, and accounts receivable. The accounts receivable manager can learn much by monitoring the relevant ratios, which are:

- Cash receipts to billed sales and progress payments

- Ending accounts receivable to billed sales and progress payments

- Ending accounts receivable to the sum of billed sales, progress payments, and the beginning cash balance

- Ending accounts receivable to cash receipts

- Cash receipts to ending accounts receivable

Any of them may be used, if proven valid over time, to assist in projecting cash positions in upcoming periods.

What is the ratio of cash receipts to billed sales and progress payments?

To arrive at this ratio for a given period, divide cash receipts by the sum of billed sales and progress payments.

$$\text{Cash-receipts-to-billed-sales-plus-progress-payments ratio} = \frac{\text{Cash receipts}}{\text{Billed sales} + \text{Progress payments}}$$

Example: MNO Corp.'s annual billed sales and progress payments are $560,000; its cash receipt, $558,200.

$$\text{Cash-receipts-to-billed-sales-plus-progress-payments ratio} = \frac{\text{Cash receipts}}{\text{Billed sales} + \text{Progress payments}}$$

$$= \frac{\$558,200}{\$560,000} = 0.997, \text{ or } 99.7\%$$

Cash receipts represent over 99% of billed sales and progress payments.

How do you compute the ratio between the ending accounts receivable balance and the sum of billed sales and progress payments?

To calculate this ratio for a non-annual period, divide the end-of-period accounts receivable balance by the sum of billed sales and progress payments.

$$
\begin{array}{l}
\text{Ending-receivables-} \\
\text{to-billed-sales-} \\
\text{plus-progress-} \\
\text{payments ratio}
\end{array}
=
\frac{\text{Ending accounts receivable}}{\dfrac{\text{Billed}}{\text{sales}} + \dfrac{\text{Progress}}{\text{payments}}}
$$

For an annual period, the billed sales and progress payments have to be converted to an average quarterly figure, that is, divided by 4. The annual total represents the sum of 4 quarters' worth of cash inflow, while the ending accounts receivable balance is the same as the fourth-quarter ending balance.

$$
\begin{array}{l}
\text{Ending-receivables-} \\
\text{to-billed-sales-} \\
\text{plus-progress-} \\
\text{payments ratio}
\end{array}
=
\frac{\text{Ending accounts receivable}}{\left(\dfrac{\text{Billed}}{\text{sales}} + \dfrac{\text{Progress}}{\text{payments}} \right) /4}
$$

Example: MNO Corp.'s annual billed sales and progress payments are $560,000; its end-of-year accounts receivable balance, $34,400.

$$
\begin{array}{l}
\text{Ending-receivables-} \\
\text{to-billed-sales-} \\
\text{plus-progress-} \\
\text{payments ratio}
\end{array}
=
\frac{\text{Ending accounts receivable}}{\left(\dfrac{\text{Billed}}{\text{sales}} + \dfrac{\text{Progress}}{\text{payments}} \right) /4}
$$

$$
= \frac{\$34,400}{\$560,000} /4
$$

$$
= \frac{\$34,400}{\$140,000} = 0.246, \text{ or } 24.6\%
$$

The end-of-year accounts receivable balance represents almost 25% of the average quarterly sales billings and progress payments.

How do you compute the ratio between the ending accounts receivable balance and the sum of billed sales, progress payments, and beginnng balance?

To calculate this ratio for a nonannual period, divide the end-of-period accounts receivable balance by the sum of billed sales, progress payments, and the beginning cash balance.

$$
\begin{array}{c}
\text{Ending-receivables-} \\
\text{to-billed-sales-} \\
\text{progress-payments-} \\
\text{and-beginning-} \\
\text{balance ratio}
\end{array}
=
\dfrac{\text{Ending accounts receivable}}{\underset{\text{sales}}{\text{Billed}} + \underset{\text{payments}}{\text{Progress}} + \underset{\text{cash balance}}{\text{Beginning}}}
$$

For an annual period, the total of billed sales and progress payments has to be converted to an average quarterly figure, that is, divided by 4. The annual total represents the sum of 4 quarters' worth of cash inflow, while the ending accounts receivable balance is the same as the fourth-quarter ending balance. The annual beginning cash balance is the same as the first quarter's.

$$
= \dfrac{\text{Ending accounts receivable}}{\left(\underset{\text{sales}}{\text{Billed}} + \underset{\text{payments}}{\text{Progress}} \right) /4 + \underset{\text{cash balance}}{\text{Beginning}}}
$$

Example: MNO Corp.'s annual billed sales and progress payments are $560,000, its end-of-year accounts receivable balance $34,400, and the first-quarter beginning cash balance $32,600.

$$
= \dfrac{\text{Ending accounts receivable}}{\left(\underset{\text{sales}}{\text{Billed}} + \underset{\text{payments}}{\text{Progress}} \right) /4 + \underset{\text{cash balance}}{\text{Beginning}}}
$$

$$
= \dfrac{\$34,400}{\$560,000/4 + \$32,600}
$$

$$
= \dfrac{\$34,400}{\$140,000 + \$32,600}
$$

$$
= \dfrac{\$34,400}{\$172,600} = 0.199, \text{ or } 19.9\%
$$

The end-of-year accounts receivable balance represents almost 20% of the sum of the average quarterly sales billings and progress payments plus the beginning cash balance.

What is the ratio of the ending receivable balance to cash receipts?

To compute this ratio, divide cash receipt total by the given period's ending accounts receivable balance.

$$
\begin{array}{c}
\text{Cash-receipts-to-ending-} \\
\text{receivables ratio}
\end{array}
=
\dfrac{\text{Cash receipts}}{\text{Ending receivables}}
$$

For the annual ratio, the cash receipts total must be divided by 4, so as to convert it to an average quarterly figure. (The ending receivables balance is the fourth-quarter's ending balance.)

$$\text{Cash-receipts-to-ending-receivables ratio} = \frac{\text{Cash receipts}/4}{\text{Ending receivables}}$$

Example: MNO Corp.'s end-of-year cash receipts total is $558,200, and its fourth-quarter ending accounts receivables balance, $34,400.

$$\begin{aligned}\text{Cash-receipts-to-ending-receivables ratio} &= \frac{\text{Cash receipts}/4}{\text{Ending receivables}} \\ &= \frac{\$558,200/4}{\$34,400} \\ &= \frac{\$139,550}{\$34,400} = 4.057, \text{ or } 405.7\%\end{aligned}$$

HOW ARE ACCOUNTS RECEIVABLES AFFECTING THE CASH POSITION?

How are ratios used in collecting accounts receivable?

Ratios are particularly useful when used with automated billing and collection systems. The dollar amounts entered during the course of day-to-day operations can be automatically converted, on-line, into ratios that help the accounts receivable manager monitor the rate at which receivables are being collected and, indirectly, how collections are affecting cash flow.

Accounts Receivable Turnover

What is the (accounts) receivable turnover?

The receivables turnover is the ratio of total credit sales to receivables. (It is also known as the sales-to-receivables ratio.)

$$\text{Receivables turnover} = \frac{\text{Total (credit) sales}}{\text{Receivables balance}}$$

Example: XYZ Corp.'s sales for the first quarter of 19X1 were $252,800,000, and its receivables balance $110,400,000. XYZ's receivables turnover is:

$$\begin{aligned}\text{Receivables turnover} &= \frac{\text{Total credit sales}}{\text{Receivables balance}} \\ &= \frac{\$252,800,000}{\$110,400,000} = 2.29, \text{ or } 229\%\end{aligned}$$

Note: The receivables turnover is normally expressed as an annual figure, not quarterly.

How is the receivables turnover converted to an annual figure?

There are two methods. First, the more precise procedure is to start with annualized sales and an average receivables balance.

Example: XYZ Corp.'s annual sales are $1,077,000,000, and its average receivables for the year are $107,300,000. Its annual receivables turnover is:

$$\text{Receivables turnover} = \frac{\text{Total Credit Sales}}{\text{Receivables balance}}$$

$$= \frac{\$1,077,000,000}{\$107,300,000} = 10.04, \text{ or } 1,004\%$$

Second, quarterly figures may be used and projected for the year by multiplying the resultant ratio by 4.

$$\text{Annual receivables turnover} = \text{Quarterly receivables turnover} \times 4$$

Example: XYZ Corp.'s sales for the first quarter of 19X1 were $252,800,000, and its receivables balance $110,400,000. XYZ's receivables turnover (or turnover) is:

$$\text{Receivables turnover} = \frac{\text{Total Credit Sales}}{\text{Receivables balance}}$$

$$= \frac{\$252,800,000}{\$110,400,000} = 2.29, \text{ or } 229\%$$

$$\text{Annual receivables turnover} = \text{Quarterly receivables turnover} \times 4$$

$$= 2.29, \text{ or } 229\%, \times 4$$

$$= 9.16, \text{ or } 916\%$$

How is receivables turnover best analyzed?

Receivables turnover is compared to the trends in sales and receivables over a number of time periods. Although annual periods are preferable, quarters can be compared too. One period is established as the baseline, and the sales and receivables amounts are assigned a "baseline" value of 100%.

Example: The following quarterly data is for XYZ Corp. The first quarter is the baseline period. Both the sales and the receivables turnover trends for that quarter are assigned the value of 100%.

(in $000,000s)

Qtr	Sales	% of Trend	Receivables	% of Trend	Receivables-to-Sales Ratio
1	$252.8	100%	$110.4	100%	229%
2	$274.9	109%	$111.5	101%	247%
3	$276.2	109%	$102.3	93%	270%
4	$273.1	108%	$105.1	95%	260%

The sales trend clearly indicates increases in the last three quarters of 19X1. Receivables decreased in the last two quarters but slightly increased in the second quarter (101%). The receivables turnover trend is favorable because increases in sales did not result in higher receivables, which would have necessitated a greater capital investment in outstanding customer accounts.

Note: In ascertaining why sales and receivables values vary, the two main factors are price and sales volume.

Comparing Receivables to Sales

What is the receivables-to-sales ratio?

The receivables-to-sales ratio is calculated by dividing the average receivables by total credit sales for a given period. It reflects the average age or level of customer accounts outstanding for the period. This ratio may be calculated for a quarter or month, but it is generally better expressed as an annual figure.

$$\text{Receivables-to-sales ratio} = \frac{\text{Average receivables}}{\text{Net credit sales}}$$

Example: XYZ Corp.'s first quarter sales are $252,800,000. Its average receivables for the quarter are $110,400,000. The quarterly receivables-to-sales ratio is:

$$\text{Receivables-to-sales ratio} = \frac{\text{Average receivables}}{\text{Net credit sales}}$$

$$= \frac{\$110,400,000}{\$252,800,000} = 0.437, \text{ or } 43.7\%$$

Using the same data, quarterly receivables can also be compared to annualized sales amounts. (To annualize quarterly sales figures, simply multiply them by 4.)

Example: In the preceding example, XYZ's annualized total credit sales are $1,011,200,000 ($252,800,000 times 4). This figure may be used instead of the quarterly sales in the receivables-to-sales calculation:

$$
\begin{aligned}
\text{Receivables-to-sales ratio} &= \frac{\text{Average receivables}}{\text{Net credit sales (annualized)}} \\
&= \frac{\$110,400,000}{\$1,011,200,000} \\
&= .109, \text{ or } 10.9\%
\end{aligned}
$$

Why are quarterly receivables compared to annualized sales amounts?

While sales accumulate from quarter to quarter, receivables tend to fluctuate, remaining within a given range. Comparing quarterly sales with quarterly receivables therefore represents a disproportionate amount of receivables. Annualizing sales enables you to work with a more realistic figure.

Example: The following are actual figures for XYZ sales and receivables in 19X1.

(in $000,000s)

	First	Second	Third	Fourth	Annual
Sales	$ 252.8	$ 274.9	$ 276.2	$ 273.1	$1,077.0
Annualized sales	$1,011.2	$1,099.6	$1,104.8	$1,092.4	—
Receivables	$ 110.4	$ 111.5	$ 102.3	$ 105.1	$ 107.3
Receivables-to-sales ratio	43.%	40.6%	37.0%	38.5%	10.0%

The actual annual receivables-to-sales ratio in this table (10.0%) is much closer to the results of the calculation in the preceding example using the first quarter's annualized sales figure (10.9%) than to the ratio using any quarter's receivables.

How is the average receivables amount arrived at?

The average receivables is the sum of the beginning and ending balances for a period divided by 2. The period may be a month, quarter, year, or any period.

$$
\text{Average receivables} = \frac{\text{Beginning receivables} + \text{End-of-period receivables}}{2}
$$

Example: XYZ started 19X1 with receivables of $104,300,000 and ended it with $110,300,000. Its annual receivables are:

$$\text{Average receivables} = \frac{\text{Beginning receivables} + \text{End-of-period receivables}}{2}$$

$$= \frac{\$104,300,000 + \$110,300,000}{2}$$

$$= \frac{\$214,600,000}{2} = \$107,300,000$$

Average Collection Period

How is the average collection period calculated?

The average collection period is the average number of days between the day the invoice is sent out and the day the customer pays the bill. There are two ways to make the calculation:

Method 1:

$$\text{Average collection period} = \frac{\text{Receivables}}{\text{to sales ratio}} \times \text{Days in period}$$

Example: Using XYZ's annual receivables-to-sales ratio of 10.0% (see the preceding example), its annual average collection period is:

$$\text{Average collection period} = \frac{\text{Receivables}}{\text{to sales ratio}} \times \text{Days in period}$$

$$= 10.0\% \text{ (or } 0.100) \times 365 \text{ days}$$

$$= 36.5 \text{ days}$$

It takes XYZ an average of 36.5 days to collect its receivables.

Method 2: Divide average annualized receivables by average daily credit sales (which is computed by dividing the number of days in the year, 365, into annual credit sales).

$$\text{Average collection period} = \frac{\text{Average (annualized) receivables}}{\text{Average daily credit sales}}$$
$$\text{(Sales/365)}$$

Example: If XYZ's annualized receivables is $107,300 and its annual sales $1,077,000,000, its average collection period is:

$$\text{Average collection period} = \frac{\text{Average (annualized) receivables}}{\text{Average daily credit sales} \ (\text{Sales}/365)}$$

$$= \frac{\$107,300}{\$1,077,000,000 \ / \ 365}$$

$$= \frac{\$107,300}{2950} = 36.4 \text{ days}$$

XYZ takes 36.4 days, on average, to collect a bill. Compare this result with that of the first method.

What does the average collection period mean?

Under any circumstances, the shorter the collection period, the better for the company. This computation indicates the company's efficiency in enforcing its credit policy. The company's average can be compared from one period to another, or against industry standards.

What is the aging receivables procedure for estimating collections and cash flow?

In the aging receivables (or just aging) procedure, accounts receivable are grouped according to their ages, usually under 30 days, 31-60 days, 61-90 days, and over 90 days. For each group, the beginning-of-period and end-of-period amounts are compared, to see whether it is taking the organization more or less time to receive payment.

Example: The following data is available for XYZ Corp.:

Aging Procedure (in $000,000s)					
Age of Billing	Billed 12/31/X0/	% of Total	Billed 12/31/X1	% of Total	% of Variance
Under 30 days	$77.7	80	$ 89.3	85	+5
31-60 days	14.6	15	12.6	12	-3
61-90 days	4.9	5	3.2	3	-2
Totals	$97.2	100	$105.1	100	—

For each group of receivables, the percentage of variance is calculated by subtracting the percentage of total for the ending balance (12/31/X1) from that for the beginning balance (12/31/X0). For the under-30-days group, for example: 85% less 80% is 5%.

This comparison indicates a favorable trend in collections. As of 12/31/X1, outstanding receivables in the under-30-days category show a 5% increase, while the percentage of variance in each of the other two categories have declined.

In planning collections and cash flow, unfavorable trends in billing groups can trigger specific reports and/or investigations into past due accounts, with appropriate action taken.

What is the days-of-sales-in-receivables ratio (or factor)?

This ratio between sales and receivables reflects the normal number of days of uncollected sales in receivables. The calculation can be made annually for comparative purposes or monthly for greater precision. The computation itself is for the quarter:

$$\text{Days-of-sales-in-receivables ratio} = \frac{\text{Receivables balance}}{\text{Quarterly sales / 90 (days in quarter)}}$$

Note: Use 90 days for a quarter, 360 for a year.

Example: XYZ Corp.'s first quarter sales are $252,800,000, its receivables $110,400,000. The days of sales in receivables is:

$$\text{Days-of-sales-in-receivables ratio} = \frac{\text{Receivables balance}}{\text{Quarterly sales / 90 (days in quarter)}}$$

$$= \frac{\$110,400,000}{\$252,800,000 \text{ / } 90 \text{ days}}$$

$$= \frac{\$110,400,000}{\$280,888.89} = 39.3 \text{ days}$$

The ratio 39.3 reflects the average numbers of days it takes XYZ to receive payment on accounts receivable for the quarter.

How is the days-of-sales-in-receivables ratio put to use?

This ratio, if proven consistent over time, can provide at least a preliminary basis for estimating ending receivable balances, given sales projections. The process is:

$$\text{Ending receivable balance} = \text{Days-of-sales ratio} \times \frac{\text{Sales projection}}{\text{Days in period}}$$

Note: Use 90 days for a quarter, 360 for a year.

Example: XYZ projects second-quarter of $274,900,000, and a days-of-sales ratio of 36.5 has proven to be reliable over the past few years. The second quarter's ending receivable balance is estimated as follows:

$$\text{Ending receivable balance} = \text{Days-of-sales ratio} \times \frac{\text{Sales projection}}{\text{Days in period}}$$

$$= 36.5 \text{ (days)} \times \frac{\$274,900,000}{90 \text{ days}}$$

$$= 36.5 \times \$3,054,444 = \$1,114,827$$

For the second quarter, XYZ Corp. has $1,114,827—a little over $1 million—in receivables.

EVALUATING THE TIMELINESS OF BILLINGS AND COLLECTIONS

Current Period Collections and Incurred Costs

How do you compute the ratio of current period collection to incurred costs?

As the organization incurs costs to fill orders and then bills customers upon fulfillment, some receivables are collected within the same period that the costs are incurred. As payments are received from customers, the relevant part of the receivable is used to offset the cost incurred. Thus some percentage of the cost incurred is recouped in the same period as it is incurred (the current period). The rest is carried over into the next period as a unreimbursed expenditure. A lag therefore occurs between some of the incurred costs and the receipt of payment from the customer. The ratio of collected receivables (current-period collections) to total costs incurred is computed by dividing the portion collected in the same period (the current period collection) by total costs incurred.

$$\text{Current-period-collection-to-incurred-cost ratio} = \frac{\text{Current-period collections}}{\text{Total costs incurred}}$$

Example: In the first month of its fiscal year, MNO Corp. incurs $100,000 in costs. In the same month, $55,000 worth of those costs are recouped through collections. The other

$45,000 is carried over into the second month as an unreimbursed expense.

$$\text{Current-period-collection-to-incurred-cost ratio} = \frac{\text{Current-period collections}}{\text{Total costs incurred}}$$

$$= \frac{\$55,000}{\$100,000} = 0.55, \text{ or } 55\%$$

The current-period-collection rate is 55%; that is, it has recouped 55% of its total incurred costs in the same (current) period.

What does the current-period-collection rate reflect?

This ratio is a gauge of how fast an organization recoups expenditures made to fill orders. Generally, the higher this ratio, the more cash the company has to work with and better its overall cash flow picture.

Prior Period Billings and Current Period Costs

Can prior period billings be compared to current period costs?

Yes. The lagged portion of costs can be divided by current period costs.

$$\text{Prior-period-billings-to-current-period costs} = \frac{\text{Lagged costs}}{\text{Current period costs}}$$

Example: MNO Corp. carries over $45,000,000 of unreimbursed expenses from the first to the second month of operation. In the second month, it incurs $100,000 in costs.

$$\text{Prior-period-billings-to-current-period costs} = \frac{\text{Lagged costs}}{\text{Current period costs}}$$

$$= \frac{\$45,000}{\$100,000} = 0.45, \text{ or } 45\%$$

In the second month of operation, lagged costs represent 45% of current period expenses.

What can be determined from the ratio of lagged (prior period) costs to current period costs?

This ratio responds to the question, how fast are collections being made? A high ratio indicates that collections are slow; a low ratio, collections are being made quickly.

Is there another way to monitor the rate at which collections are being made?

Yes. The ratio of current and prior period billings to current costs enables the accounts receivable manager to gauge the rate of collections.

$$
\begin{array}{l}\text{Current-and-prior-} \\ \text{period-billings-to-} \\ \text{current-costs ratio}\end{array} = \frac{\begin{array}{c}\text{Current period} \\ \text{billings}\end{array} + \begin{array}{c}\text{Prior period} \\ \text{billings}\end{array}}{\text{Current costs}}
$$

Example: MNO Corp. carries over $45,000,000 of unreimbursed expenses from the first to the second month of operation. In the second month, it incurs $100,000 in costs, of which $50,000 is expected to be collected in the current period.

$$
\begin{array}{l}\text{Current-and-prior-} \\ \text{period-billings-to-} \\ \text{current-costs ratio}\end{array} = \frac{\begin{array}{c}\text{Current period} \\ \text{billings}\end{array} + \begin{array}{c}\text{Prior period} \\ \text{billings}\end{array}}{\text{Current costs}}
$$

$$
= \frac{\$50,000 + \$45,000}{\$100,000}
$$

$$
= \frac{\$95,000}{\$100,000} = 0.95, \text{ or } 95\%
$$

MNO Corp. may expect to collect 95% of the sum of prior and current period costs.

Prior Period Billings and Total Collections

How do you compare prior period billings with total collections?

Prior period billings are divided by the total collections in the current period.

$$
\begin{array}{l}\text{Prior-period-} \\ \text{billings-to-} \\ \text{total-col-} \\ \text{lections ratio}\end{array} = \frac{\text{Prior period unreimbursed expenses}}{\text{Current period total collections}}
$$

Example: MNO Corp. carries over $45,000,000 of unreimbursed expenses from the first to the second month of operation. In the second month, it collects that $45,000 and 50% of the current period's incurred costs of $100,000 (or $50,000 equals $100,000 times 0.50).

$$\begin{array}{l} \text{Prior-period-} \\ \text{billings-to-} \\ \text{total-col-} \\ \text{lections ratio} \end{array} = \frac{\text{Prior period unreimbursed expenses}}{\text{Current period total collections}}$$

$$= \frac{\$45,000}{\$45,000 + \$50,000}$$

$$= \frac{\$45,000}{\$95,000} = 0.474, \text{ or } 47.4\%$$

In the second month of operations, prior period billings represent 47.4% of current period collections.

What does the ratio of prior period billings to total collections mean to the accounts receivable manager?

This percentage is a guage of the lagging portions of billings. Normally, a rising trend in this ratio means that cash flow is being stretched. A declining trend reflects an improving cash position.

Liquidation Limit

What is the liquidation limit?

The liquidation limit is the percentage of billed sales that will be collected in the same period as they are billed. Expressed as a percentage, this limit must be determined by each organization in light of its collections history.

Example: MNO Corp. has established over a number of years that, on average, it collects 60% of its billings in the same period. The MNO liquidation limit is therefore 60%.

Note: The liquidation limit is the complement of the liquidation lag value.

What is the liquidation lag value of billed sales?

The liquidation lag value is the portion of billed sales that will be collected sometime after the billing period. Expressed as a percentage, this ratio must be determined by an organization in light of its collection record.

Example: MNO Corp. has established over a number of years that, on average, it collects 40% of its billings in the period following the billing period. The MNO liquidation lag value is therefore 40%.

Note: The liquidation lag value is the complement of the liquidation limit.

How are the liquidation limit and liquidation lag value used?

Either of these ratios can be used as a planning guideline in making cash flow projections.

Example: MNO Corp. estimates that in the upcoming year billings will average $120,000 per month. With a liquidation limit of 60%, it may reasonably expect to recoup $72,000 each month, having that amount available for cash flow purposes: $120,000 in billings times 0.60 liquidation limit equals $72,000.

Conversely, the liquidation lag value of billed sales is $48,000: $120,000 billed sales times 0.40 liquidation lag value equals $48,000.

GAUGING THE CUSTOMER'S DEBT-PAYING CAPABILITY IN THE WORST CASE

In the event of liquidation, a customer corporation must pay its creditors before its stockholders. The accounts receivable manager's question concerns the probability of payment if the customer is dissolved.

Velocity Method

What is the velocity method?

Although the velocity method is used primarily for liquidation assessment, it can also be helpful in analyzing a company's ongoing debt-paying ability to its company's financial position. The term "velocity" is used because the method assesses how quickly the organization could pay off its debt if all its assets were liquidated. The rapidity of payment depends greatly on the maturity and aging of accounts receivable, payables, and inventory—how fast its own billings can be collected, when it has to make payments on bills, and how soon inventory can be converted to cash. The velocity method evaluates the timing of a company's cash inflow compared to its outflow.

The basic model is:

			%
Current Assets:			
Cash	$_____		
Aged receivables (estimated) due in:			
30 days	$_____		—
31-60 days	_____		—
61-90 days	_____		—
Total receivables	$_____		

Aged inventory (estimated), cash sales:		
30 days	$_____	—
31-60 days	_____	—
90-day credit sales	_____	—
Total inventory	$_____	
Total all assets		$_____

Current Liabilities:		
Notes payable in 30 days	$_____	
Aged payables (estimated), due in:		
30 days	$_____	—
31-60 days	_____	—
61-90 days	_____	—
Total payables	$_____	
Total all liabilities		$_____

Example: ABC Co. shows the following financial data:

(in $000,000s)

		%
Current Assets:		
Cash	$10,000	
Aged receivables (estimated) due in:		
30 days	$41,400	69.5
31-60 days	15,000	25.1
61-90 days	3,200	5.4
Total receivables	$59,600	
Aged inventory (estimated), cash sales:		
30 days	$11,500	15.5
31-60 days	9,000	12.2
90-day credit sales	53,600	72.3
Total inventory	$74,100	
Total all assets		$143,700
Current Liabilities:		
Notes payable in 30 days	$ 8,000	
Aged payables (estimated), due in:		
30 days	$28,000	58.1
31-60 days	14,700	30.5
61-90 days	5,500	11.4
Total payables	$48,200	
Total all liabilities		$56,200

ABC is in a favorable position to meet its immediate debt commitments.

- Accounts receivable represents 41.5% of the total current assets: $59,600 divided by $143,700 equals .4147, or 41.5%.

- The aged payable commitments represent 85.7% of the total current liabilities: $48,200 divided by $56,200.
- Most of the receivables (69.5%) are due to be collected within 30 days.
- Inventory will take longer to convert to cash, with credit sales representing the lion's share (72.3%).
- A little over half of accounts payable (58.1%) is due within 30 days, with the balance not due for 31 to 90 days.
- The current ratio (current assets divided by current liabilities; see page 000 for the calculation) is 2.6 ($143,700 divided by $56,200). This seems adequate in light of industry standards.
- The working capital ratio (working capital divided by liabilities; see page 169 for the calculation) is 1.6. This indicates that the owners' equity in the current assets is 1.6 times the creditors' current contribution to capital.
- However, the estimated cash receipts within 30 days plus cash balance after 30 days just about matches payables due within 30 days.

Cash	$10,000	
30-day receivables	41,400	
30-day inventory	11,500	
Total cash in 30 days		$62,900
Less:		
Notes payable in 30 days	$ 8,000	
Accounts payable in 30 days	28,000	
Total payable 30 days		$36,000
Cash balance		$26,900
Divided by total 30-day payables		$36,000
Ratio of 30-day cash balance to 30-day payables		74.7%

Note: This data does not represent a cash budget because it does not reflect estimated expenses, tax provisions, and miscellaneous commitments.

What is the calculation for the times-interest-earned ratio?

This ratio focuses on the number of times interest is covered by operating profits. The higher the ratio, the better off the company.

$$\text{Times-interest-earned ratio} = \frac{\text{Income from operations}}{\text{Interest expense}}$$

Example: In its first quarter of 19X1, ABC Co. had income from operations of $17,100,000 and paid $800,000 in interest on debt.

$$\text{Times-interest-earned ratio} = \frac{\text{Income from operations}}{\text{Interest expense}}$$

$$= \frac{\$17,100,000}{\$800,000} = 21.4$$

For the quarter, ABC had income from operations that was 21.4 times the amount of interest it owed.

Does the times-interest-earned ratio change with time?

Yes. The primary cause of fluctuations in the ratio is a change in income from operations.

Example: ABC shows the following data for 19X1:

		Quarter			Annual
	First	Second	Third	Fourth	Period
Income from operations	$17,100	$19,600	$16,500	$12,800	$66,000
Interest earned	$ 800	$ 800	$ 900	$ 900	$ 3,400
Times interest earned	21.4	24.5	18.3	14.2	19.4

(in $000,000s)

Over the year, the time-interest-earned ratio fluctuated from 21.4 in the first quarter, through a high of 24.5 in the second, to 14.2 in the fourth, with an annual average of 19.4. Note that, while the level of interest remained for the most part constant, income from operations changed more dramatically.

What does the time-interest-earned ratio tell analysts?

This ratio answers the question, how adequately do earnings compare with the payment of bond interest? The higher the ratio, the better the organization is able to meet its interest payments.

Some organizations take a more conservative approach. They reduce the pretax income by the estimated federal income taxes before dividing the value by the bond interest.

What is the ratio for interest plus funded debt?

This ratio assesses an organization's capacity to meet scheduled interest plus debt repayments. The portion of the

long-term debt due for repayment within the current annual
period is classified as a current liability on the balance sheet.

$$\text{Debt coverage} = \frac{\text{Pretax earnings}}{\text{Interest} + \dfrac{\text{Funded debt repayment}}{1 - \text{Tax rate}}}$$

A decline in the ratio over time is an unfavorable trend
because, given stable interest expense and fixed funded debt
repayments, the reason is usually declining pretax earnings.
Such a decline serves as a warning to the organization (particularly if other debt-paying ratios are following the same
pattern), that it may encounter problems in borrowing more
money and in meeting schedule debt commitments. Trade
vendors should also be concerned since trade payments may
also be deferred.

Example: In addition to $800,000 in interest payments,
ABC Corp. is schedule to make a funded debt repayment of
$1,000,000 this quarter. Pretax earnings are $15,000,000,
and the tax rate 52%.*

$$\begin{aligned}
\text{Debt coverage} &= \frac{\text{Pretax earnings}}{\text{Interest} + \dfrac{\text{Funded debt repayment}}{1 - \text{Tax rate}}} \\[2ex]
&= \frac{\$15,000,000}{\$800,000 + \dfrac{\$1,000,000}{1 - 0.52}} \\[2ex]
&= \frac{\$15,000,000}{\$800,000 + \dfrac{\$1,000,000}{0.48}} \\[2ex]
&= \frac{\$15,000,000}{\$800,000 + \$2,083,333} \\[2ex]
&= \frac{\$15,000,000}{\$2,883,333} = 5.2 \text{ times}
\end{aligned}$$

ABC Corp. has enough pretax earnings to cover its interest
payments and debt repayments over 5 times.

---

*Federal, state, and local corporate income taxes included. This
figure is illustrative only; actual tax rates vary from state to state and
from one corporation to another.

CHAPTER 6

REGULATING THE OUTFLOW OF CASH: THE ACCOUNTS PAYABLE MANAGER

WORDS TO KNOW

Accounts-payable-turnover. A ratio that indicates the number of times the accounts payable "turned over"—that is, were paid—in a period.

Accounts receivable (receivables). A balance sheet entry indicating amounts owed to a company by customers for product sold or services rendered.

Accounts receivable turnover. The ratio of total credit sales to receivables (also known as the sales-to-receivables ratio).

Aging procedure. *See* Aging receivables procedure.

Aging receivables (aging) procedure. Accounts receivable are grouped according to their ages, usually under 30 days, 31-60 days, 61-90 days, and over 90 days. For each group, the beginning-of-period and end-of-period amounts are compared, to see whether it is taking the organization more or less time to receive payment.

Average collection period. The average number of days between the day the invoice is sent out and the day the customer pays the bill.

Average receivables. The sum of the beginning and ending balances for a period divided by 2. The period may be a month, quarter, year, or any period.

Backlog. The number of, or the dollar value of, unfilled orders.

Beginning balance. The balance for an accounting entry at the start of the accounting period.

Billed sales. Sales for which orders have been filled and invoices sent out.

Cash disbursement. *See* Disbursement.

Cash flow. The difference between cash receipts and cash disbursements.

Cash flow ratio. A comparison between an individual receipt or disbursement item and its related total.

Cash flow statement. A financial statement consisting of two breakdowns: cash receipts and disbursements, with a summary for the organization's net cash position.

Cash receipt. *See* Receipt.

Credit sales. *See* Sales.

Current period. The present accounting period.

Current period collections. The receivables collected in the present accounting period.

Current ratio. Current assets divided by current liabilities.

Days-of-sales-in-receivables ratio (or factor). The ratio between sales and receivables reflects the normal number of days of uncollected sales in receivables.

Current-period-collection rate. A gauge of how fast an organization recoups expenditures made to fill orders.

Current ratio. Current assets divided by current liabilities.

Days-purchases-in-payables ratio. The amounts payable to an organization's total purchases for a given period.

Days-purchases-in-disbursements ratio. A ratio that relates how much a company purchases to how much cash it actually disburses in a given period.

Disbursement. A cash amount paid out by the company.

Ending (end-of-period) balance. The balance of a given accounting entry at the end of the accounting period.

End-of-period balance. *See* Ending balance.

Financial risk. The risk posed by the heavy use of debt support by creditors.

Fixed expenses. Expenses that do not vary with levels of production, such as plant costs or executives' salaries.

Income risk. The risk of having insufficient income to carry on operations.

Interest plus funded debt ratio. This ratio assesses an organization's capacity to meet scheduled interest plus debt repayments.

Lagged (prior period) costs. Costs incurred by the company in the preceding account period to fill orders.

Liquidation limit. The percentage of billed sales that will be collected in the same period as they are billed.

Liquidation lag value. The numerical complement of the liquidation limit.

Net credit sales. *See* Sales.

Operating leverage ratio. A ratio that assesses the effect of fluctuating sales on operating profits.

Prior period. The preceding accounting period.

Prior period billings. Billings made during the preceding accounting period.

Progress payment. The partial payment by a customer against a receivable.

Receipt. A cash amount received by the company.

Receivables. *See* Accounts receivable.

Sales. Sales revenues less a calculated allowance for returned goods and bad debt.

Sales backlog. *See* Backlog.

Sales-to-receivables ratio. *See* Accounts receivable turnover.

Times-interest-earned ratio. A ratio that focuses on the number of times interest is covered by operating profits. The higher the ratio, the better off the company.

Times-preferred-dividend ratio. A ratio that indicates how able a company is to meet its preferred dividend obligations.

Total (credit) sales. *See* Sales.

Variable expenses. Expenses that fluctuate with the level of production.

Velocity method. A method for calculating an organization's debt-paying capability, used primarily for liquidation assessment.

Working capital ratio. Working capital divided by liabilities.

HOW ARE DISBURSEMENTS AFFECTING CASH FLOW?

What is cash flow?

Cash flow is the net amount when disbursements are deducted from cash receipts.

$$\text{Cash flow} = \text{Cash receipts} - \text{Cash disbursements}$$

Note: If disbursements are greater than receipts for period, cash flow can be negative.

Example: First-quarter cash receipts for MNO Corp. are $136,900, and its cash disbursements are $144,200.

$$\begin{aligned}\text{Cash flow} &= \text{Cash receipts} - \text{Cash disbursements}\\ &= \$136,900 - \$144,200 = -\$7,300\end{aligned}$$

In the first quarter, MNO had a negative cash flow of $7,300; that is, it paid out $7,300 more cash than it received.

What is included in cash receipts?

Cash receipts include any source, operational or other not, that results in a cash inflow for the organization. In addition to billed sales, receipts can be progress payments, customer advances, investment income, interest on loans, rents on company-owned properties, and so on.

Example: MNO Corp.'s cash receipts for the firt quarter are:

Billed sales	$ 58,500
Progress payments	47,300
Customer advances	9,100
Investment income	2,000
Interest on loan	20,000
Total cash receipts	$136,900

What are cash disbursements?

Cash disbursements are any items that result in the flow of cash out of the organization: accounts payable, payroll, federal income taxes, other taxes, deferred compensation fund payments, loan payments, interest payments, lease payments, insurance premium instalments, and so on.

Example: MNO Corp.'s cash disbursement for the first quarter are as follows:

Accounts payable	$ 85,100
Gross payroll	51,000
Income and other taxes	3,400
Retirement fund	3,500
Interest payment	1,100
Total cash disbursements	$144,100

What are cash flow ratios?

Cash flow ratios are comparisons between individual receipt or disbursement items and their related totals.

$$\text{Cash flow ratio} = \frac{\text{Individual receipt item}}{\text{Total receipt}}$$

$$\text{Cash flow ratio} = \frac{\text{Individual disbursement item}}{\text{Total disbursements}}$$

Example: MNO Corp.'s cash receipts for the first quarter are:

Billed sales	$ 58,500
Progress payments	47,300
Customer advances	9,100
Investment income	2,000
Interest on loan	20,000
Total cash receipts	$136,900

Each item of cash receipt can be expressed as a percentage or decimal portion of total receipts. For billed sales:

$$\text{Cash flow ratio} = \frac{\text{Individual receipt item}}{\text{Total receipt}}$$

$$= \frac{\$58,500}{\$136,900} = 0.427, \text{ or } 42.7\%$$

Billed sales represent 42.7% of MNO's first-quarter cash receipts. Each item of receipt can be expressed as a ratio and displayed as a cash receipt schedule:

	$	%
Billed sales	$ 58,500	42.7
Progress payments	47,300	34.6
Customer advances	9,100	6.6
Investment income	2,000	1.5
Interest on loan	20,000	14.6
Total cash receipts	$136,900	100.0

The same can be done for disbursements (using the formula above):

	$	%
Accounts payable	$ 85,100	59.0
Gross payroll	51,000	35.4
Income and other taxes	3,400	2.4
Retirement fund	3,500	2.4
Interest payment	1,100	0.8
Total cash disbursements	$144,100	100.0

What is a cash flow statement?

A cash flow statement consists of two breakdowns: cash receipts and disbursements, with a summary for the organization's net cash position.

Example: On the last day of the prior year's last quarter, MNO Corp. had a cash balance of $8,900. This is the beginning cash balance for this year's first quarter. The company's cash flow statement for the first quarter is as follows:

	$	%
Billed sales	$ 58,500	42.7
Progress payments	47,300	34.6
Customer advances	9,100	6.6
Investment income	2,000	1.5
Interest on loan	20,000	14.6
Total cash receipts	$ 136,900	100.0
Accounts payable	$ 85,100	59.0
Gross payroll	51,000	35.4
Income and other taxes	3,400	2.4
Retirement fund	3,500	2.4
Interest payment	1,100	0.8
Total cash disbursements	$ 144,100	100.0
Net cash increase (decrease)	$ (7,200)	
Beginning balance	8,900	
Ending balance	$ 1,700	

MNO Corp. had a first-quarter net cash position of $1,700. This becomes the beginning balance for the second quarter.

What do cash ratios do for the accounts payable manager?

Cash ratios enable the accounts payable manager to determine the sources of greatest cash inflow and outflow, and possibly to take steps to improve the organization's overall cash position.

Example: Given MNO Corp.'s cash flow statement (see preceding example), several observations can be made:

- The company came dangerously close to a negative net cash position in the first quarter.

- Billed sales and progress payments represent the major portion (approximately 88%) of receipts. Remedial measures are probably best focused on these areas, as opposed to areas with lesser contributions to a positive cash position. Steps must be taken to increase billings and/or collections in the next quarter.

- Measures might also be considered that will limit or defer second-quarter disbursements.

- Borrowed funds to meet short-term cash needs are a possibility too.

How are cash ratios analyzed for reasonableness?

Cash ratios may be compared to industry standards or to the organization's annual figures. The rational is that, the year being statistically a larger "sample" of historical data than a month or a quarter, it may act as a norm for shorter periods.

Example: Part of MNO Corp.'s annual cash flow statement is as follows:

| | First Quarter | | Annual | |
	$	%	$	%
Billed sales	$ 58,500	42.7	$318,000	50.1
Progress payments	47,300	34.6	240,500	37.8
Customer advances	9,100	6.6	44,600	7.0
Investment income	2,000	1.5	7,800	1.2
Interest on loan	20,000	14.6	25,000	3.9
Total cash receipts	$ 136,900	100.0	$635,900	100.0
Accounts payable	$ 85,100	59.0	$367,600	58.0
Gross payroll	51,000	35.5	213,100	33.7
Income and other taxes	3,400	2.3	6,400	1.0
Retirement fund	3,500	2.4	10,700	1.7
Interest payment	1,100	0.8	6,500	1.0
Total cash disbursements	$ 144,100	100.0	$604,300	100.0
Net cash increase (decrease)	$ (7,200)		$ 31,600	
Beginning balance	8,900		8,900	
Ending balance	$ 1,700		$ 22,700	

- Year-end billed sales collections (50.1%) are 7.4% greater than those of the first quarter (42.7%).
- Year-end progress payment collections (37.8%) also lead first-quarter receipts (34.6%).
- The annual accounts payable and gross payroll ratios (58.0% and 33.7%) are lower than the first quarter levels (59.0% and 35.5%).

All-in-all, MNO Corp. had a weak first quarter, compared to the company's annual figures.

BALANCING PURCHASES, PAYABLES, AND DISBURSEMENTS

What is the days-purchases-in-payables ratio?

This ratio relates the amounts payable to an organization's total purchases for a given period. When vaildated by historical data, this factor acts as a guideline in verifying the reasonableness of payables figures that are developed by other means.

$$\text{Days-purchases-in-payables ratio} = \frac{\text{Accounts payable, ending balance}}{\text{Period purchases / Days in period}}$$

Note: Accounts payable, ending balance is calculated as follows:

	Accounts payable, beginning balance
+	Purchases for the period
−	Cash disbursements for the period
	Accounts payable, ending balance

Example: ABC Co. started the quarter with an accounts payable of $42,000,000. During the quarter, the company made purchases of $78,300,000, and cash disbursements of $79,600,000.

	Accounts payable, beginning balance	$42,000,000
+	Purchases for the period	78,300,000
−	Cash disbursements for the period	79,600,000
	Accounts payable, ending balance	$40,700,000

$$\text{Days-purchases-in-payables ratio} = \frac{\text{Accounts payable, ending balance}}{\text{Period purchases / Days in period}}$$

$$= \frac{\$40,700,000}{\$78,300,000 \text{ / } 90 \text{ days}}$$

$$= \frac{\$40,700,000}{\$870,000 \text{ per day}} = 46.8 \text{ days}$$

For the quarter, ABC has 46.8 days' worth of purchases payable.

What is the ratio of daily purchases versus daily disbursements?

Called the days-purchases-in-disbursements ratio, this relates how much a company purchases to how much cash it actually disburses in a given period. It is expressed in terms of days' worth of purchase.

$$\text{Days-purchases-in-disbursements} = \frac{\text{Cash disbursements}}{\text{Period purchases / days in period}}$$

Example: During the quarter, ABC Co. made purchases of $78,300,000 and cash disbursements of $79,600,000.

$$\text{Days-purchases-in-disbursements} = \frac{\text{Cash disbursements}}{\text{Period purchases / days in period}}$$

$$= \frac{\$79,600,000}{\$78,300,000 \text{ / } 90 \text{ days in period}}$$

$$= \frac{\$79,600,000}{\$870,000} = 91.5 \text{ days}$$

91.5 days' worth of a quarter's purchases have resulted in cash disbursements. In effect, its purchases and cash disbursements are running just about one for one: 91.5 days' worth of disbursements versus 90 days' worth of purchases. If this factor is historically consistent, ABC can expect to pay for all its purchases within a quarter.

What is the accounts-payable-turnover ratio?

This ratio indicates the number of times the accounts payable "turned over"—that is, were paid—in a period.

$$\text{Accounts-payable-turnover ratio} = \frac{\text{Period purchases}}{\text{Accounts payable, ending balance}}$$

Example: ABC Co. ended the quarter with an accounts payable balance of $40,700,000. During the quarter, it made purchases of $78,300,000.

$$\frac{\text{Accounts-payable}}{\text{turnover ratio}} = \frac{\text{Period purchases}}{\text{Accounts payable, ending balance}}$$

$$= \frac{\$78,300,000}{\$40,700,000} = 1.9$$

During the quarter, ABC made purchases that were 1.9 its ending accounts payable amount.

How is the accounts-payable-turnover ratio used?

This ratio can be used not only for comparative purposes (from period to period or with industry standards), but also for estimating ending payable balances, given estimated sales.

Example: ABC Co.'s accounts-payable-turnover ratio has been validated by historical data to be 1.9. For the upcoming quarter, purchases are projected at $77,100,000. The end-of-quarter accounts payable balance is estimated as follows:

$$\frac{\text{Accounts-payable-}}{\text{turnover ratio}} = \frac{\text{Period purchases}}{\text{Accounts payable, ending balance}}$$

$$1.9 = \frac{\$77,100,000}{\text{Accounts payable, ending balance}}$$

Or:

$$\frac{\text{Accounts payable,}}{\text{ending balance}} = \frac{\$77,100,000}{1.9} = \$40,578,947$$

ABC's estimated accounts payable ending balance is about $40,600,000.

How is the ratio of disbursements to accounts payable computed?

To calculate this ratio for a given period, divide actual disbursements by the accounts payable during the period.

$$\frac{\text{Disbursements-to-accounts-}}{\text{payable ratio}} = \frac{\text{Disbursements}}{\text{Accounts payable}}$$

Example: During the first quarter of its fiscal year, MNO Corp. made actual cash disbursements of $85,100, against an accounts payable total of $82,200.

$$\text{Disbursements-to-accounts-payable ratio} = \frac{\text{Disbursements}}{\text{Accounts payable}}$$

$$= \frac{\$85,100}{\$82,200} = 1.04, \text{ or } 104\%$$

MNO Corp. overpaid is obligations by 4% in the first quarter.

What is the purpose of the disbursements-to-accounts-payble ratio?

When this ratio is calculated for successive periods, especially on an automated system, the accounts payable manager is able to determine whether accounts payable are being over- or underpaid. If a trend is detected, appropriate action can be taken to improve the company's cash flow from period to period.

HONORING TRADE PAYABLE COMMITMENTS

What is meant by "days purchasing outstanding"?

Days purchasing outstanding is a ratio used to determine whether an organization is meeting its trade payable commitments on schedule. The fewer the days purchases outstanding, the more favorable the company's debt-paying ability. From a vendor's point of view, the ratio is a measure of its customer's ability to pay debts on time.

$$\text{Days-purchases-outstanding ratio} = \frac{\text{Trade payables}}{\text{Period purchases / Days in period}}$$

Example: Data for the ABC Co. is as follows:

(in $000,000s)

	Average Trade Payables	Total Purchases	Days in Period
19X0	$10,150	$ 90,100	360
19X1	$12,400	$113,500	360

For 19X0, the days-purchases-outstanding ratio is:

$$\text{Days-purchases-outstanding ratio} = \frac{\text{Trade payables}}{\text{Period purchases / Days in period}}$$

$$= \frac{\$10,150}{\$90,100 \text{ / } 360 \text{ days}}$$

$$= \frac{\$10,150}{250.3 \text{ days}} = 40.6 \text{ days}$$

For 19X1, the days-purchases-outstanding ratio is:

$$\text{Days-purchases-outstanding ratio} = \frac{\text{Trade payables}}{\text{Period purchases / Days in period}}$$

$$= \frac{\$12,400}{\$113,500 / 360 \text{ days}}$$

$$= \frac{\$12,400}{315.3 \text{ days}} = 39.33$$

There were 1.3 days fewer purchases in 19X1 than in 19X0. While purchases increased by 26% ($113,500 less $90,100 equals $23,400 divided by $90,100), the payable balance increased by only 22%, which accounts for the fewer days purchases outstanding.

CAN THE COMPANY MEET ITS CASH OBLIGATIONS? LIQUIDITY RATIOS

What is a liquidity ratio?

The liquidity of a business is its capability to meet current debt obligations. A reasonably sound liquidity position enables an organization to obtain the financing to take advantage of investment opportunities and respond to operational emergencies. Liquidity ratios measure how well a corporation is able to meet its obligations. The liquidity ratios in which the accounts payable manager might be interested are:

● Current (working capital) ratio

● Acid test ratio

● Cash ratio

● Cash turnover ratio

What is the current ratio?

Sometimes known as the working capital ratio, the current ratio compares current assets to current liabilities.

$$\text{Current ratio} = \frac{\text{Current assets}}{\text{Current liabilities}}$$

Note: The current ratio is expressed as a multiple.

Example: Parts of ABC's balance sheet are as follows:

	Amount
Current Assets	
Cash	$ 3,500,000
Marketable securities	3,300,000
Accounts receivable	28,700,000
Inventories	
Raw materials	26,800,000
Work in process	10,700,000
Finished goods	7,300,000
Subtotal	44,800,000
Prepaid expenses	250,000
Total current assets	**$80,550,000**
• • •	
Current Liabilities	
Notes payable	$ 1,400,000
Current portion—LT debt	2,500,000
Accrued payroll	3,600,000
Accounts payable	20,850,000
Income tax payable	2,600,000
Total current liabilities	**$30,950,000**

$$\frac{\text{Current}}{\text{ratio}} = \frac{\text{Current assets}}{\text{Current liabilities}}$$

$$= \frac{\$80,550,000}{\$30,950,000} = 2.60$$

ABC's current ratio is 2.60; that is, its assets are worth 2.60 times its liabilities.

What is the significance of the current ratio?

The current ratio indicates the number of times current assets will pay off current liabilities. Historically, a 2:1 ratio has been considered the ideal minimum. Of course, there are exceptions. Some corporations with a 2:1 ratio or more may have hidden financial problems.

How is the acid test ratio calculated?

This ratio compares the company's current liabilities with its quick assets—cash, marketable securities, and accounts receivable. These assets are considered "quick" because they either are cash or can be converted to cash virtually overnight. Other types of assets, such as inventory, work in process, and the like, take much longer to convert to cash and are therefore excluded from this calculation.

$$\text{Acid test ratio} = \frac{\text{Cash} + \text{Marketable securities} + \text{Accounts receivable}}{\text{Current liabilities}}$$

Or:

$$\text{Acid test ratio} = \frac{\text{Quick assets}}{\text{Current liabilities}}$$

Note: The acid test ratio is expressed as a multiple.

Example: Portions of ABC Co.'s balance sheet are as follows:

	Amount
Current Assets	
Cash	**$ 3,500,000**
Marketable securities	**3,300,000**
Accounts receivable	**28,700,000**
Inventories	
Raw materials	26,800,000
Work in process	10,700,000
Finished goods	7,300,000
Subtotal	44,800,000
Prepaid expenses	250,000
Total current assets	$80,550,000
• • •	
Current Liabilities	
Notes payable	$ 1,400,000
Current portion—LT debt	2,500,000
Accrued payroll	3,600,000
Accounts payable	20,850,000
Income tax payable	2,600,000
Total current liabilities	**$30,950,000**

$$\text{Acid test ratio} = \frac{\$3,500,000 + \$3,300,000 + \$28,700,000}{\$30,950,000}$$

Or:

$$\text{Acid test ratio} = \frac{\$35,500,000}{\$30,950,000} = 1.15$$

ABC Co. can cover its current liabilities 1.15 times over within a few days' notice.

What does the acid test ratio say about an organization?

The acid test determines how well a corporation can meet its current obligations immediately—within days. It tells the accounts payable manager and analysts whether the company could, in the worst case, pay all its current obligations. Normally, the ratio should be no less than 1.

How does the cash ratio differ from the acid test?

The cash ratio includes even fewer assets than the acid test; it leaves out accounts receivable. The only two types of assets figured in are cash and marketable securities, on the assumption that cash is on hand and securities can be liquidated with a phone call. (Marketably securities are considered "cash equivalents.")

$$\text{Cash ratio} = \frac{\text{Cash} + \text{Marketable securities}}{\text{Current liabilities}}$$

Note: The cash ratio is usually expressed as decimal or percentage.

Example: Portions of ABC Co.'s balance sheet are as follows:

	Amount
Current Assets	
Cash	**$ 3,500,000**
Marketable securities	**3,300,000**
Accounts receivable	28,700,000
Inventories	
Raw materials	26,800,000
Work in process	10,700,000
Finished goods	7,300,000
Subtotal	44,800,000
Prepaid expenses	250,000
Total current assets	$80,550,000
• • •	
Current Liabilities	
Notes payable	$ 1,400,000
Current portion—LT debt	2,500,000
Accrued payroll	3,600,000
Accounts payable	20,850,000
Income tax payable	2,600,000
Total current liabilities	**$30,950,000**

$$\frac{\text{Cash}}{\text{ratio}} = \frac{\text{Cash} + \text{Marketable securities}}{\text{Current liabilities}}$$

$$= \frac{\$3,500,000 + \$3,300,000}{\$30,950,000} = 0.2197, \text{ or } 22\%$$

ABC Co.'s cash and cash equivalents can meet 22% of its current obligations.

Is there a "good" cash ratio?

There is no "normal" cash ratio applicable to all companies in all industries. Management must evaluate its company's own ratio in light of corporate objectives and policies, as well as industry norms.

What is the cash turnover ratio?

The cash turnover ratio relates sales (the "top line" on the income statement) to a company's cash balance (an entry in the current assets section of the balance sheet).

$$\text{Cash turnover} = \frac{\text{Sales}}{\text{Cash}}$$

Example: With sales of $240,000,000, ABC Co.'s current assets section is as follows:

	Amount
Current Assets	
Cash	**$ 3,500,000**
Marketable securities	3,300,000
Accounts receivable	28,700,000
Inventories	
Raw materials	26,800,000
Work in process	10,700,000
Finished goods	7,300,000
Subtotal	44,800,000
Prepaid expenses	250,000
Total current assets	$80,550,000

$$\text{Cash turnover} = \frac{\text{Sales}}{\text{Cash}} = \frac{\$240,000,000}{\$3,500,000} = 68.6$$

ABC Co. sales are over 68 times its cash balance.

What does the cash turnover indicate?

With this ratio, you can analyze and assess the effectiveness of an organization's use of its cash position to generate revenue. Generally, the higher the ratio, the more effective use the accounts payable manager is making of cash.

Also, the turnover rate is helpful in determining preliminary cash balance forecasts based on sales projections.

Note: For best results an average cash position should be used.

Example: ABC Co. has ascertained that its cash position is historically 1/65 of its sales volume. Management projects a sales volume of $252,000,000 for the upcoming year.

$$\frac{1}{65} = \frac{\text{Sales}}{\text{Cash}} = \frac{\$252,000,000}{\text{Cash}}$$

Or:

$$\text{Cash} = \frac{\$252,000,000}{65} = \$3,876,923$$

ABC Co. can look for a cash position in the neighborhood of $38,000,000 or $39,000,000.

CHAPTER 7

MEETING SALES DEMAND EFFICIENTLY AND EFFECTIVELY: THE PRODUCTION MANAGER

WORDS TO KNOW

Break-even point. The sales volume level at which the business neither profits nor loses money; sales and total costs are exactly equal.

Break-even plant capacity. The approximate plant capacity at which an organization is breaking even ("BE plant capacity").

COGS. *See* cost of sales.

Cost of goods sold (COGS). *See* Cost of sales.

Cost of sales (cost of goods sold, COGS, direct cost). The cost of making or buying a product sold, or of providing a service rendered, consisting of direct personnel, direct materials (and other direct costs), and factory overhead.

Direct cost. *See* Cost of sales.

Direct material. An element of cost of sales, the cost of materials used in making a product or in rendering a service.

Direct personnel (labor). Employees directly involved in the making of a product or in the rendering of a service. This payroll falls into the category of direct costs (cost of sales, cost of goods sold).

Factory overhead. An element of cost of sales, the part of factory overhead directly attributable to making a product. (Some fixed factory costs may be regarded as indirect costs.)

Fixed expenses. Expenses that do not vary with production volume, such as plant costs and executives' salaries.

G&A. *See* General and administrative expenses.

General and administrative (G&A) expenses. Costs associated with general the production manager, controller's staffs, and procurement.

Indirect cost. A cost that cannot be directly attributed to production, such as selling expenses or general and administrative (G&A) costs.

Indirect expenses (operating expense). Sometimes collectively referred to as "overhead," expenses that are incurred to operate a business but that do not relate directly to the making of the company's product. Examples are administrative, sales, and accounting staff, or office equipment, company cars, and benefit plans.

Indirect personnel (labor). Employees who are necessary for running a business but who are not directly involved in production or service. Indirect labor wages and salaries are indirect costs.

Machine hour rate method. The cost per hour of running the company's production equipment.

Material and other direct costs (ODC). Materials and other direct expenses directly related to the making of the company product.

Material and other direct costs. A direct cost (cost of sale), the materials and other items needed to make the company's product.

OIC. *See* Other indirect costs.

Other indirect costs (OIC). Expenses that cannot be attributed to the making of a specific product. Examples are depreciation on a plant in which many products are made, utility and heating expenses, or delivery fleet lease payments and maintenance costs.

Operating expenses. *See* Indirect expense.

Overhead. Expenses that represent indirect services and support for operational activities; they do not contribute directly – or they cannot be identified as directly contributing – to the manufacture of a product.

Prime cost. The sum of direct labor plus material and other direct costs.

Production volume. The number of units slated to be produced within the period.

Product unit cost rate. The application of overhead on the basis of the product quantities produced, expressed as a rate of dollars spent per units produced (either actual or estimated figures).

Selling expenses. An indirect cost associated with sales, selling expenses include the costs of marketing and contract administration.

Total expense allowance. The total variable allowance for the period.

Total fixed expense. The sum of fixed costs for the period.

Variable expenses. Expenses that fluctuate with production levels, such as materials.

HOW PRODUCTION VOLUME AFFECTS COSTS AND PROFITS

The Break-Even Point

What is the break-even point?

In business, the break-even point is the sales volume level at which the business neither profits nor loses money; sales and total costs are exactly equal. It is a function of sales volume, and fixed and variable expenses.

$$\text{Break-even point} = \frac{\text{Fixed expenses}}{1 - \dfrac{\text{Variable expenses}}{\text{Sales}}}$$

Example: MNO Corp. has first-quarter sales for Product A of $300,000. Its quarterly fixed expenses are $36,000, its variable expenses $234,000.

$$\begin{aligned}
\text{Break-even point} &= \frac{\text{Fixed expenses}}{1 - \dfrac{\text{Variable expenses}}{\text{Sales}}} \\[2ex]
&= \frac{\$36,000}{1 - \dfrac{\$234,000}{\$300,000}} \\[2ex]
&= \frac{\$36,000}{1 - 0.78} \\[2ex]
&= \frac{\$36,000}{0.22} = \$163,636
\end{aligned}$$

MNO's break-even point is $163,636. That is, before the dollar volume of sales reaches this point, MNO loses money; after it, MNO makes a profit. Precisely at that level, no profit or loss results.

When is the break-even point calculation made?

This computation is made to enable the production manager to know the point at which a product, a product line, or the business itself becomes profitable.

Example: See the preceding example. MNO Corp. knows that the break-even point for Product A is $163,636. If the unit price for Product A is $20, then a little over 8,180 units must be sold for the product to break even: $163,636 divided by $20 equals 8,181.8 units. The production manager can then compare that requirement with sales estimates. Can enough units be sold to make Product A a profitable venture for the organization?

Does the break-even point change?

Yes. The break-even point changes with:

- Fixed expenses
- Sales volume
- Variable expenses

How do fixed expenses affect the break-even point?

Expenses drive the break-even point up. Since some fixed expenses remain the same regardless of sales volume, these expenses particularly affect break-even: The greater the total fixed expenses, the higher the break-even point will be.

Example: See the preceding example. Assume that MNO Corp. has first-quarter sales for Product A of $300,000 and variable expenses of $234,000, but fixed expenses rise $14,000 (from $36,000 to $50,000).

$$
\begin{aligned}
\text{Break-even point} &= \cfrac{\text{Fixed expenses}}{1 - \cfrac{\text{Variable expenses}}{\text{Sales}}} \\[2ex]
&= \cfrac{\$50,000}{1 - \cfrac{\$234,000}{\$300,000}} \\[2ex]
&= \frac{\$50,000}{1 - 0.78} \\[2ex]
&= \frac{\$50,000}{0.22} = \$227,272
\end{aligned}
$$

MNO's break-even point increases from $163,636 to $227,272. For Product A to break even, sales have to increase by $63,636 ($227,272 less $163,636).

How do sales affect the break-even point?

The break-even point generally declines with increased sales volume, assuming fixed expenses do not rise (or rise disproportionately) and that variable expenses increase only as necessary to keep pace with orders.

Example: See the preceding example. Assume that in the second-quarter:

- Sales for Product A rise by 20%:
  ($300,000 times 0.20 equals $60,000) $360,000
- Variable expenses increase by 15.38%:
  ($234,000 times 0.1538 equals $36,000) $270,000
- Fixed expenses remain the same. $ 36,000

$$\text{Break-even point} = \frac{\text{Fixed expenses}}{1 - \dfrac{\text{Variable expenses}}{\text{Sales}}}$$

$$= \frac{\$36,000}{1 - \dfrac{\$270,000}{\$360,000}}$$

$$= \frac{\$36,000}{1 - 0.75}$$

$$= \frac{\$36,000}{0.25} = \$144,000$$

MNO's break-even point decreases from $163,636 to $144,000.

Variable Expenses

Can you estimate how much variable expenses will change with sales?

Yes. The variable expense per unit of production can be calculated by means of the following formula:

$$\frac{\text{Variable}}{\text{expense per}} = \frac{\dfrac{\text{Total expense}}{\text{allowance}} - \text{Total fixed expense}}{\text{Production volume}}$$

- Total expense allowance is the total variable allowance for the period.
- Total fixed expense is the sum of fixed costs for the period.
- Production volume is the number of units slated to be produced within the period.

Example: MNO Corp. plans to produce 9,000 units this week. It allows $2,000 for variable expenses and $875 for fixed expenses.

$$\frac{\text{Variable}}{\text{expense per}} = \frac{\dfrac{\text{Total expense}}{\text{allowance}} - \text{Total fixed expense}}{\text{Production volume}}$$

$$= \frac{\$2,000 - \$875}{9,000 \text{ units}}$$

$$= \frac{\$1,125}{9,000 \text{ units}} = \$0.125 \text{ per unit}$$

For every unit produced, MNO spends $0.125 in variable costs.

What purpose does the per-unit variable cost serve?

If the production manager knows what each unit of production costs in terms of variable expense, it can arrive at a fairly accurate estimate of the total variable expense that will accompany sales. Once actual figures are on hand, they can be compared with the projected amounts to see whether corrective action is required for upcoming periods.

Variable expenses = Sales in units × Per-unit variable cost

Example: MNO Corp. the production manager has established, over a number of accounting periods, that its per-unit variable cost is $0.125. It estimates sales of 24,000 units in the second quarter.

$$\begin{aligned} \text{Variable expenses} &= \text{Sales in units} \times \text{Per-unit variable cost} \\ &= 24{,}000 \times \$0.125 \\ &= \$3{,}000 \end{aligned}$$

MNO's second-quarter variable expenses will be approximately $3,000. The production manager can go on to calculate the break-even point for the quarter.

Can per-unit fixed costs be computed?

Yes. However, fixed costs vary with the number of units produced (whereas variable costs are constant).

$$\frac{\text{Fixed costs}}{\text{per unit}} = \frac{\text{Total fixed costs for the period}}{\text{Units produced in the period}}$$

Note: Over the long term, fixed costs may vary. Short-term, they can generally be assumed to remain level.

Example: MNO Corp. the production manager has ordered 9,000 units to be produced this coming week. Fixed costs for this period are $875.

$$\begin{aligned} \frac{\text{Fixed costs}}{\text{per unit}} &= \frac{\text{Total fixed costs for the period}}{\text{Units produced in the period}} \\ &= \frac{\$875}{9{,}000 \text{ units}} = \$0.0972 \text{ per unit} \end{aligned}$$

This week, MNO spends $0.0972 in fixed costs for every unit produced. If the production manager orders 7,000 units for next week, the total amount of fixed cost remains the same, while the number of units decreases. The fixed cost per unit therefore rises:

$$\text{Fixed costs per unit} = \frac{\text{Total fixed costs for the period}}{\text{Units produced in the period}}$$

$$= \frac{\$875}{7,000 \text{ units}} = \$0.125 \text{ per unit}$$

Sales Volume

Can the break-even calculation be used to determine the sales volume necessary to achieve a given level of operating income?

Yes. Given a break-even point, the production manager can calculate the sales volume required to maintain a predetermined level of operating income if a variable changes. Use the complement of the factor derived for the denominator of the break-even formula in the following equation, and solve for Sales:

$$\text{Sales} = \frac{\text{Fixed expenses} + \text{Operating income}}{\text{Complement}}$$

Example: ABC Co. has first-quarter sales for Product × of $400,000. Its quarterly fixed expenses are $42,000, its variable expenses $238,000. The production manager is looking for operating income of $120,000 on this product.

$$\text{Break-even point} = \frac{\text{Fixed expenses}}{1 - \dfrac{\text{Variable expenses}}{\text{Sales}}}$$

$$= \frac{\$42,000}{1 - \dfrac{\$238,000}{\$400,000}}$$

$$= \frac{\$42,000}{1 - 0.595}$$

$$= \frac{\$42,000}{0.405} = \$103,703$$

Product × breaks even at $103,703 worth of sales. The factor in the denominator of the break-even formula is 0.405.

In the second quarter, plant expansion causes fixed expenses to rise by $30,000 to $72,000. The production manager must now know the sales level at which operating income of $120,000 can be maintained.

$$\text{Sales} = \frac{\text{Fixed expenses} + \text{Operating income}}{\text{Complement}}$$

$$= \frac{\$72,000 + \$120,000}{0.405}$$

$$= \frac{\$192,000}{0.405} = \$474,074$$

With increase plant (fixed) costs, sales must increase to $474,074 for Product $\times$ to yield $120,000 in operating income.

Plant Capacity

Can the "break-even" plant capacity be calculated?

The approximate plant capacity at which an organization is breaking even ("BE plant capacity") can be computed by means of the following formula:

$$\begin{array}{c}\text{BE}\\ \text{plant}\\ \text{capacity}\end{array} = \frac{\text{Fixed expenses} \times \text{Current \% of plant capacity}}{\text{Sales} - \text{Variable expenses}}$$

Example: ABC Co.'s plant is currently operating at 80% of full capacity, with fixed expenses at $72,000 and variable costs at $282,074. Sales are $474,074. For purposes of illustration, assume that the relationship between dollar sales and plant capacity is constant.

$$\begin{array}{c}\text{BE}\\ \text{plant}\\ \text{capacity}\end{array} = \frac{\text{Fixed expenses} \times \text{Current \% of plant capacity}}{\text{Sales} - \text{Variable expenses}}$$

$$= \frac{\$72,000 \times 0.80}{\$474,074 - \$282,074}$$

$$= \frac{\$57,600}{\$192,000} = 0.30, \text{ or } 30\%$$

At the current sales and expense levels, the plant would operate at a break-even level at 30% of capacity.

MONITORING AND ESTIMATING DIRECT EXPENSES (COST OF SALES)

What is cost of sales?

Sometimes known as cost of goods sold, cost of sales consists of the expenses that can be directly attributed to the making of the company's product or the rendering of its service. Examples of such "direct" costs are assembly line workers, raw materials that go into the product, equipment used to produce goods, and so on.

Does the cost of sales bear a relationship to sales?

Yes. The total cost of sales can be divided by the "top line," sales or revenues, to arrive at a factor.

$$\text{Cost-of-sale-to-sale ratio} = \frac{\text{Cost of sales}}{\text{Sales}}$$

Example: The following monthly data is available for XYZ Corp.

(in $000,000s)

	Jan.
Sales	$44.0
Direct labor	9.6
Overhead	13.0
Material & ODC	15.8
Cost of sales	$38.4
Gross profit	5.6
G&A/selling expenses	2.7
Income from operations	$ 2.9

$$\begin{aligned}\text{Cost-of-sale-} \atop \text{to-sale ratio} &= \frac{\text{Cost of sales}}{\text{Sales}} \\ &= \frac{\$38,400,000}{\$44,000,000} = 0.8727, \text{ or } 87.3\%\end{aligned}$$

How is the cost-of-sales-to-sales ratio used?

The ratio is useful to the production manager as an estimating tool. A validated average ratio provides a fairly reliable planning statistic to "ballpark" a total cost of sales value based on the company's projected sales volume.

How is this ratio used to evaluate actual data?

With actual data on hand and a valid historical ratio, an organization can compare them to determine whether the actual figure is above or below average.

Example: XYZ Corp. uses an historically validated cost-of-sales-to-sales ratio of 88.1%. That is, on average, its cost of sales runs 88.1% of total sales volume. For the month of January, XYZ's cost-of-sales-to-sales ratio is 87.3% (see preceding example). This is 0.8% less than the average (88.1% less 87.3%).

How would the cost-of-sales-to-sales ratio assist production managers in making projections?

Production planners can apply the organization's historically average ratio to the projected sales volume for a given upcoming period, to arrive at an estimated cost of sales.

Example: XYZ Corp.'s sales manager projects $36,500,000 in sales for the month of February. The company's average cost-of-sales-to-sales ratio is 88.1%.

$$\text{Cost-of-sale-to-sale ratio} = \frac{\text{Cost of sales}}{\text{Sales}}$$

$$0.881 = \frac{\text{Cost of sales}}{\$36,500,000}$$

Or:

$$\text{Cost of sales} = 0.881 \times \$36,500,000 = \$32,156,500$$

For the month of February, XYZ can expect cost of sales in the neighborhood of $32,156,500.

Can types of costs of sales be evaluated like overall cost of sales?

Yes. In fact, in many cases it is generally more useful to compare individual types of costs to sales, rather than the overall cost of sales. For each category, however, the formula is the same.

Cost of sales consists of several categories:

- Direct labor (personnel)
- Overhead (factory overhead)
- Material and other direct costs (ODC)

$$\text{Cost-of-sales-to-sale ratio} = \frac{\text{Cost of sales}}{\text{Sales}}$$

Example: The following monthly data is available for XYZ Corp.;

(in $000,000s)

	Jan.
Sales	$44.0
Direct labor	9.6
Overhead	13.0
Material & ODC	15.8
Cost of sales	$38.4
Gross profit	5.6
G&A/selling expenses	2.7
Income from operations	$ 2.9

$$\text{Cost-of-sales-to-sale ratio} = \frac{\text{Cost of labor}}{\text{Sales}}$$

$$= \frac{\$9,600,000}{\$44,000,000} = 0.2181, \text{ or } 21.8\%$$

$$\text{Cost-of-sales-to-sale ratio} = \frac{\text{Cost of overhead}}{\text{Sales}}$$

$$= \frac{\$13,000,000}{\$44,000,000} = 0.2954, \text{ or } 29.6\%$$

$$\text{Cost-of-sales-to-sale ratio} = \frac{\text{Cost of material \& ODC}}{\text{Sales}}$$

$$= \frac{\$15,800,000}{\$44,000,000} = 0.3590, \text{ or } 35.9\%$$

Any of the individual cost elements may be used to check the reasonableness of sales projections and/or to estimate costs for upcoming periods.

Can an individual cost be expressed as a ratio of the overall cost of sale?

Yes. To monitor cost elements, each type of expense may be expressed as a percentage of overall cost of sales.

$$\text{Direct-cost-to-cost-of-sales ratio} = \frac{\text{Individual direct cost}}{\text{Cost of sales}}$$

Example: XYZ Corp. shows the following monthly data:

(in $000,000s)

	Jan.
Sales	$44.0
Direct labor	9.6
Overhead	13.0
Material & ODC	15.8
Cost of sales	$38.4

$$\text{Direct-cost-to-cost-of-sales ratio} = \frac{\text{Direct labor}}{\text{Cost of sales}}$$

$$= \frac{\$9,600,000}{\$38,400,000} = .250, \text{ or } 25\%$$

$$\text{Direct-cost-to-cost-of-sales ratio} = \frac{\text{Overhead expenses}}{\text{Cost of sales}}$$

$$= \frac{\$13,000,000}{\$38,400,000} = .339, \text{ or } 33.9\%$$

$$\text{Direct-cost-to-cost-of-sales ratio} = \frac{\text{Material \& ODC}}{\text{Cost of sales}}$$

$$= \frac{\$15,800,000}{\$38,400,000} = .411, \text{ or } 41.1\%$$

What use is it to monitor individual cost-of-sale elements?

While the overall ratio of cost of sales to sales may remain in line with the historical average, an individual cost element may be increasing disproportionately. Also, given a dollar amount for cost of sales, individual elements can be estimated according to the percentage each represents of the whole.

Example: XYZ Corp. shows the following monthly and six-month data:

(in $000,000s)

	Jan.	Jan. Ratios*	Six-Month Average
Sales	44.0	___	225.3
Direct labor	9.6	0.25	59.0
Overhead	13.0	0.34	51.0
Material & ODC	15.8	0.41	86.9
Cost of sales	$38.4		$196.9
Cost-of-sales-to-sales ratio	0.87		

*See preceding example for calculations.

The six-month ratios for cost-of-sale elements are calculated and compared to January's:

$$\text{Direct-cost-to-cost-of-sales ratio} = \frac{\text{Direct labor}}{\text{Cost of sales}}$$

$$= \frac{\$59,000,000}{\$196,900,000} = 0.299, \text{ or } 30\%$$

$$\text{Direct-cost-to-cost-of-sales ratio} = \frac{\text{Overhead expenses}}{\text{Cost of sales}}$$

$$= \frac{\$51,000,000}{\$196,900,000} = 0.259, \text{ or } 26\%$$

$$\text{Direct-cost-to-cost-of-sales ratio} = \frac{\text{Material \& ODC}}{\text{Cost of sales}}$$

$$= \frac{\$86,900,000}{\$196,900,000} = .441, \text{ or } 44\%$$

Note: Individual cost rates add up to 100% (30 plus 26 plus 44).

	Jan.	Jan. Ratios*	Six-Month Average	Six-Month Ratios
Sales	44.0		225.3	
Direct labor	9.6	0.25	59.0	0.30
Overhead	13.0	0.34	51.0	0.26
Material & ODC	15.8	0.41	86.9	0.44
Cost of sales	$38.4		$196.9	
Cost-of-sales-to-sales ratio	0.87			

(in $000,000s)

*See preceding example for calculations.

While direct labor and materials for January (0.25 and 0.41) were lower than the six-month ratios (0.30 and 0.44), overhead showed an 8-point jump (0.34 in January compared to 0.26 for the half-year).

This increase in overhead would not be detected if only the cost-of-sales-to-sales ratio were computed:

$$\text{Cost-of-sales-to-sale ratio} = \frac{\text{Cost of sales}}{\text{Sales}}$$

$$= \frac{\$196,900,000}{\$225,300,000} = 0.874, \text{ or } 87\%$$

The January ratio (0.87) matches the six-month ratio exactly, leading one to believe that cost of sales is well in hand.

Can the total cost of sales be compared to product units?

Yes. An organization can compute how much in total cost of sales (or cost of goods sold) is represented by each unit produced.

$$\text{Cost of sales per unit} = \frac{\text{Cost of sales}}{\text{Units produced}}$$

Example: In February, Hudson Co. produced 7,400 widgets, and its cost of sales were:

	(in $000s)
Direct labor dollars	$ 8,000
Overhead expense	10,900
Material and ODC	13,100
Cost of sales	$32,000

$$\text{Cost of sales per unit} = \frac{\text{Cost of sales}}{\text{Units produced}}$$

$$= \frac{\$32,000}{7,400 \text{ units}} = \$4.32 \text{ per unit}$$

Hudson pays $4.32 in cost of sales per unit.

Can individual elements of cost of sales be compared to units produced?

Yes. The formula is similar to the one for total cost of sales.

$$\text{Cost of sales per unit} = \frac{\text{Individual cost of sales}}{\text{Units produced}}$$

Example: In February, Hudson Co. produced 7,400 widgets, and its cost of sales were:

	(in $000s)
Direct labor dollars	$ 8,000
Overhead expense	10,900
Material and ODC	13,100
Cost of sales	$32,000

For direct labor dollars:

$$\text{Cost of sales per unit} = \frac{\text{Individual cost of sales}}{\text{Units produced}}$$

$$= \frac{\$8,000}{7,400 \text{ units}} = \$1.08 \text{ per unit}$$

Hudson pays $1.08 in direct labor dollars per unit produced. Other cost of sale elements are computed in the same way:

(in $000s)

	$	$ Per Unit
Direct labor dollars	$ 8,000	$1.08
Overhead expense	10,900	1.47
Material and ODC	13,100	1.77
Cost of sales	$32,000	$4.32

ANALYZING AND UTILIZING THE WORK FORCE

Direct and Indirect Labor

What is the difference between direct and indirect labor?

Direct labor includes employees directly involved in the making of a product or in the rendering of a service. Direct labor payroll falls into the category of direct costs (cost of sales, cost of goods sold).

Examples: In a manufacturing firm, direct labor would consist of, among others, the assembly line workers; in a fast-food service chain, the cooks and counter attendants.

Indirect labor is made up of employees who are necessary for running a business but who are not directly involved in production or service. Indirect labor wages and salaries are indirect costs.

Examples: Receptionists, accounting department clerks, or maintenance workers.

How are direct labor and indirect labor compared?

These types of costs can be compared in terms of their headcounts.

$$\text{Indirect-to-direct-labor ratio} = \frac{\text{Indirect labor headcount}}{\text{Direct labor headcount}}$$

Generally, a low ratio is assumed to be an indicator of productive and effective use of indirect personnel. Further, if indirect manpower is reasonably reduced and controlled, the effect on total overhead epxenses and rate (relative to product cost and competitive sales price) can be significant.

Example: In January XYZ Corp. has 32,909 employees. Of that total, 22,312 were classified as direct labor, 10,597 as indirect labor.

$$\text{Indirect-to-direct-labor ratio} = \frac{\text{Indirect labor headcount}}{\text{Direct labor headcount}}$$

$$= \frac{10,597}{22,312} = 0.475, \text{ or } 47.5\%$$

Of XYZ's total workforce, 47.5% is indirect labor.

Can this ratio be expressed in terms of payroll dollars?

Yes. Instead of headcounts, use the same formula with the amounts spent on wages.

$$\text{Indirect-to-direct personnel ratio} = \frac{\text{Indirect personnel cost}}{\text{Direct personnel cost}}$$

Example: This quarter, ABC Corp. incurred an indirect personnel cost of $16,522,000 and a direct personnel cost of $34,737,000.

$$\text{Indirect-to-direct personnel ratio} = \frac{\text{Indirect personnel cost}}{\text{Direct personnel cost}}$$

$$= \frac{\$16,522,000}{\$34,737,000} = .4756, \text{ or } 47.6\%$$

How is the indirect-to-direct-personnel ratio used?

This ratio is used to project indirect personnel requirements by multiplying direct personnel costs by an average ratio.

$$\begin{array}{ccc}
\text{Indirect} & \text{Direct} & \text{Average indirect-} \\
\text{personnel} = & \text{personnel} \times & \text{to-direct-} \\
\text{requirements} & \text{costs} & \text{personnel ratio}
\end{array}$$

Example: If ABC Corp. accepts 47.6% as a valid ratio, it can be applied to the next quarter's projected direct personnel costs (of $37,500,00) to estimate indirect labor expenses.

$$\begin{array}{ccc}
\text{Indirect} & \text{Direct} & \text{Average indirect-} \\
\text{personnel} = & \text{personnel} \times & \text{to-direct-} \\
\text{requirements} & \text{costs} & \text{personnel ratio}
\end{array}$$

$$= \$37,500,000 \times .476 = \$17,850,000$$

ABC may expect indirect labor costs to be in the neighborhood of $17,850,000 in the upcoming quarter.

Also, trends in this ratio indicate to the production manager whether indirect personnel expenses are growing in or out of proportion to the production workforce. Inasmuch as indirect labor costs generally represent the largest percentage of all individual overhead costs, this is an area that bears close monitoring. Small percentage reductions can mean large dollar contributions to the profit margin.

Example: The following data is available for XYZ Corp.:

	(in $000,000s)			
Expense	*19X1* $	*19X0* $	*Variance* $	%
Total overhead	269.8	253.8	16.0	6.3
Direct labor $	198.0	181.6	16.4	9.0
Indirect labor $	125.0	120.0	5.0	4.2
Indirect-to-direct-labor ratio	63.1	66.1	3.0	4.5

The decrease in the ratio from 66.1% to 63.1% (a 3-point, or 4.5% decrease) is favorable, reflecting control over overhead costs. Indirect labor expenses are growing at a slightly slower pace than those of direct labor.

Can direct and indirect labor be compared to total labor?

Yes. Either type of labor cost can be expressed as a ratio or percentage of total labor cost, measured in terms of head count.

$$\text{Direct-labor-to-total-labor ratio} = \frac{\text{Direct labor headcount}}{\text{Total labor headcount}}$$

Or:

$$\text{Indirect-labor-to-total-labor ratio} = \frac{\text{Indirect labor headcount}}{\text{Total labor headcount}}$$

Example: In January XYZ Corp. has 32,909 employees. Of that total, 22,312 were classified as direct labor, 10,597 as indirect labor.

$$\text{Direct-labor-to-total-labor ratio} = \frac{\text{Direct labor headcount}}{\text{Total labor headcount}}$$

$$= \frac{22,312}{32,909} = 0.678, \text{ or } 67.8\%$$

$$\text{Indirect-labor-to-total-labor ratio} = \frac{\text{Indirect labor headcount}}{\text{Total labor headcount}}$$

$$= \frac{10,957}{32,909} = 0.333, \text{ or } 33.3\%$$

In January, XYZ's direct labor is about two-thirds (67.8%) of its total payroll, its indirect labor about one-third (33.2%).

Direct Personnel and Sales

What is the sales-to-direct-personnel relationship?

Preliminary sales projections can be made, or sales projections arrived at by other means may be cross-checked, by means of the relationship between sales and direct personnel. Sales is divided by the number of direct personnel employed, the result being a per-capita distribution of the sales volume.

$$\text{Sales per direct personnel} = \frac{\text{Sales volume}}{\text{Number of direct personnel}}$$

Example: ABC Corp.'s sales manager projects next quarter's sales volume at $252,800,000, and it will employ 34,737 direct laborers. Historically, the sales per direct personnel average has been $7,750. How reasonable is it to expect to support that sales level with the projected number of direct personnel?

$$\text{Sales per direct personnel} = \frac{\text{Sales volume}}{\text{Number of direct personnel}}$$

$$= \frac{\$252,800,000}{34,737 \text{ workers}} = \$7,278 \text{ per worker}$$

Compared to the historical average of $7,750, $7,278 is a little low but not dramatically so. The lower-than-average projection may be the effect of below-average sales projections.

Can total cost of sales be expressed in terms of labor hours?

Yes. The total cost of sales is divided by direct labor hours.

$$\text{Cost-of-sales-per-direct-labor-hour ratio} = \frac{\text{Total cost of sales}}{\text{Direct labor hours}}$$

Example: For the month of February, XYZ Corp. incurred total cost of sales of $32,000, and paid for 3,000 direct labor hours.

$$\begin{aligned} \text{Cost-of-sales-} \\ \text{per-direct-labor-} \\ \text{hour ratio} \end{aligned} = \frac{\text{Total cost of sales}}{\text{Direct labor hours}}$$

$$= \frac{\$32,000}{3,000 \text{ direct labor hours}}$$

$$= \$10.67 \text{ per direct labor hour}$$

In February, for every direct labor hour worked, XYZ spent $10.67 in total cost of sales.

ALLOCATING INDIRECT ("OVERHEAD") COSTS TO PRODUCTION

What are indirect expenses?

Indirect costs, sometimes collectively referred to as "overhead," are expenses that are incurred to operate a business but that do not relate directly to the making of the company's product. Examples are administrative, sales, and accounting staff, or office equipment, company cars, and benefit plans. Usually indirect expenses consist of:

- General and administrative (G&A) costs, such as the cost of payroll computer systems, the wages of bookkeepers, or retainers for corporate attorneys.

- Selling expenses, such as general advertising, a salesperson's company car, or commissions.

- Other indirect costs (OIC), which cannot be attributed to the making of a specific product. Examples are depreciation on a plant in which many products are made, utility and heating expenses, or delivery fleet lease payments and maintenance costs.

- Overhead, or indirect expenses other than those listed above.

Indirect expenses = G&A + selling expenses + OIC + Overhead

Example: Hudson Co.'s annual selling expenses are $5,400,000, and its G&A costs $4,900,000. It also incurs depreciation and other types of expenses that cannot be attributed to specific products to the tune of $2,300.000.

$$\text{Indirect expenses} = \text{G\&A} + \text{selling expenses} + \text{OIC}$$
$$= \$4,900,000 + \$5,400,000 + \$2,300,000$$
$$= \$12,600,000$$

Selling, General, and Administrative (G&A) Expenses

What are selling, general, and administrative expenses?

General and administrative costs are those associated with general the production manager, controller's staffs, and procurement. Selling expenses are those related to marketing and administering contracts. Selling, general, and administrative expenses are listed as operating expenses (along with cost of goods sold and depreciation) on the income statement. In many companies, they are itemized as part and parcel of the overall expense reporting format.

Example: XYZ Corp.'s overall cost reporting format for 19X1 is as follows:

(in $000,000s)

Expense	$	% of Total Expense*
Indirect labor	$27.0	47.4
Misc. labor benefits	3.7	6.5
Retirement plan	1.3	2.3
Management incentive	**0.7**	**1.2**
Supplies	5.4	9.5
Taxes & insurance	2.7	0.6
Depreciation	0.8	1.4
Equipment rentals	2.2	3.9
Utilities	0.8	1.4
Telephone & telegraph	2.7	4.7
Travel	1.4	2.5
Professional/outside services	2.0	3.5
Entertainment	0.6	1.0
Dues and donations	0.5	0.9
Miscellaneous	0.6	1.1
Advertising/promotion	**3.0**	**5.3**
Sales commissions	**1.2**	**2.1**
Total expenses	$56.60	100.0

*Individual expenses are calculated as ratios of overall expenses; see preceding section.

In the preceding listing, "Management incentive" is a G&A expense, while "advertising/promotion" and "Sales commissions'' are selling expenses. The company choose to isolate other G&A expenses, such as executives' compensation.

How are selling/G&A expenses compared to product units?

Indirect expenses may be compared to product units by means of the so-called ''labor hour approach.'' This is a quick way to estimate total cost based on the labor rate (assuming the dollar-per-hour rate is reliable).

$$\text{Indirect cost per unit} = \frac{\text{Selling/G\&A expenses}}{\text{Units produced}}$$

Example: Hudson Co.'s annual selling expenses are $5,400,000, its G&A costs $4,900,000, and other indirect costs $2,300,000. The company produced 20,100,000 widgets during the year.

$$\text{Indirect cost per unit} = \frac{\text{Selling/G\&A expenses}}{\text{Units produced}}$$
$$= \frac{\$12,600,000}{20,100,000 \text{ units}} = \$.626 \text{ per unit}$$

For every unit produced in 19X1, Hudson paid $.626 in indirect costs.

How are indirect costs per product unit used in connection with direct costs per product?

Along with direct costs per product unit (see pages 000-000), indirect costs per product provide projections of total cost and operating income. They can also be used in pricing and customer quotations.

$$\text{Total cost per unit} = \frac{\text{Indirect cost}}{\text{per unit}} + \frac{\text{Direct cost}}{\text{per unit}}$$

Example: Hudson's indirect costs per product are $.626. (See preceding example.) The company's direct costs (cost of sales) per product are $4.32. (See page 000 for the computation.)

$$\text{Total cost per unit} = \frac{\text{Indirect cost}}{\text{per unit}} + \frac{\text{Direct cost}}{\text{per unit}}$$
$$= \$.626 + \$4.32 = \$4.946 \text{ per unit}$$

For every unit produced, Hudson pays total cost of $4.95.

How is the rate of selling/G&A expense per direct labor hour computed?

The sum of selling, general, and administrative expenses is divided by the total number of direct labor hours performed within the period. The result is a rate, expressed as dollars per direct labor hour.

$$\text{Selling-G\&A-per-direct-labor-hour rate} = \frac{\text{Selling, G\&A}}{\text{Direct labor hours}}$$

Example: In 19X1, XYZ Corp. incurred G&A expenses of $1,200,000 and selling expenses of $4,200,000. During the year, it paid for 39,400,000 direct labor hours.

$$\begin{aligned}
\text{Selling-G\&A-per-direct-labor-hour rate} &= \frac{\text{Selling, G\&A}}{\text{Direct labor hours}} \\
&= \frac{\$4,200,000 + \$1,200,000}{39,400,000} \\
&= \frac{\$5,400,000}{39,400,000} = 0.137, \text{ or } \$0.13/\text{hour}
\end{aligned}$$

For every direct labor hour performed, XYZ Corp. spends 13 cents on selling, general, and administrative expenses.

Of what benefit is the rate of selling/G&A per direct labor hour?

As direct labor hours and sales activity increase, they affect G&A and selling expenses. If a combined G&A and selling expense "rate" can be historically validated, it can express what these expenses "should" be as a dollar rate per direct labor hour. Companies can use this rate per hour or the ratio of selling/G&A to direct labor *dollars* (see next section). But the comparison to direct labor *hours* is more commonly used because an increase in hourly labor rate does not act as a "hidden" source of higher labor costs.

Can selling/G&A expenses be compared to direct labor dollars?

Yes. The sum of selling and G&A costs can be divided by the total direct labor dollars spent in a period. The result is a ratio, expressed as a decimal or percentage.

$$\text{Selling-G\&A-to-direct-labor-dollars ratio} = \frac{\text{Selling, G\&A (\$)}}{\text{Direct labor dollars}}$$

Example: In 19X1, XYZ Corp. incurred G&A expenses of $1,200,000 and selling expenses of $4,200,000. During the year, it paid $198,000,000 in direct labor costs.

$$
\begin{aligned}
\text{Selling-G\&A-per-direct-labor-dollar rate} &= \frac{\text{Selling, G\&A (\$)}}{\text{Direct labor dollars}} \\
&= \frac{\$4,200,000 + \$1,200,000}{\$198,000,000} \\
&= \frac{\$5,400,000}{\$198,000,000} \\
&= 0.027, \text{ or } 2.7\%
\end{aligned}
$$

The ratio of selling, general, and administrative expenses to direct labor dollars is 2.7%. Expressed another way: For every direct labor dollar spent, XYZ Corp. spends 2.7% (or 2.7 cents) on selling, general, and administrative expenses.

What purpose is served by the ratio of selling/G&A to direct labor dollars?

If the ratio can be accepted as a guideline, it enables the production manager to insert an estimated dollar figure in expense projections.

Example: XYZ Corp. estimates that it will spend $205,000,000 on direct labor dollars in the coming year. Also, the ratio of selling, general, and administrative costs to direct labor dollars has been, on average, 2.7%.

$$
\begin{aligned}
\text{Selling-G\&A-to-direct-labor-dollars ratio} &= \frac{\text{Selling, G\&A (\$)}}{\text{Direct labor dollars}} \\
0.027 &= \frac{\text{Selling, G\&A (\$)}}{\$205,000,000}
\end{aligned}
$$

Or:

Selling, G&A ($) = 0.027 × $205,000,000 = $5,535,000

XYZ can reasonably expect to pay $5,535,000 in selling, general, and administrative expenses in the year to come.

Can individual selling/G&A costs be related to units produced?

Yes. Any one cost can be monitored by dividing it by the number of product units.

$$\text{Indirect cost per unit} = \frac{\text{Individual cost element}}{\text{Units produced}}$$

Example: Hudson Co.'s annual selling expenses are $5,400,000, and its G&A costs $4,900,000. It also incurs depreciation and other indirect costs (OIC) that cannot be attributed to specific products to the tune of $2,300,000.

For selling expenses:

$$\text{Indirect cost per unit} = \frac{\text{Individual cost element}}{\text{Units produced}}$$

$$= \frac{\$5,400,000}{20,100,000 \text{ units}} = \frac{\$.269}{\text{per unit}}$$

Other indirect cost elements are computed in the same way:

(in $000s)		
	$	*$ Per Unit*
Selling expenses	$ 5.4	$.269
G&A	$ 4.9	$.244
OIC	$ 2.3	$.114
Total cost	$12.6	$.627

Overhead

What are overhead expenses?

Overhead expenses represent indirect services and support for operational activities; they do not contribute directly—or they cannot be identified as directly contributing—to the manufacture of a product. Typical overhead expenses are:

● Retirement plans
● Fringe benefits
● The production manager incentives
● Supplies
● Taxes
● Insurance
● Repair and maintenance
● Depreciation
● Equipment rentals
● Utilities
● Telephone
● Travel

- Professional/outside services
- Entertainment
- Dues and donations
- Miscellaneous expenses

Such expenses can be elusive to monitor, plan, and control. Yet they need not present a problem if you (a) accumulate accurate source data and (b) make use of overhead expense ratios.

Some of these overhead expenses are categorized as "general and administrative (G&A) expenses," others as "selling expenses."

Can individual expenses be compared to total overhead expenses?

Yes. Any of the individual expenses listed in the preceding section can be expressed as a ratio to total overhead.

$$\text{Individual-to-total-overhead-expense ratio} = \frac{\text{Individual overhead expense (\$)}}{\text{Total overhead expense}}$$

Example: XYZ Corp. shows the following overhead expense data for 19X1:

(in $000,000s)

Expense	19X1 $	Ratio to Total (%)
Indirect labor	$125.0	46.3
Misc. labor benefits	50.0	18.5
Retirement plan	12.5	4.6
Management incentive	2.5	0.9
Supplies	18.5	6.9
Taxes & insurance	14.2	5.3
Repair & maintenance	12.5	4.6
Depreciation	13.2	4.9
Equipment rentals	2.4	0.9
Utilities	4.2	1.6
Telephone	4.0	1.5
Travel	3.8	1.4
Professional/outside services	4.7	1.8
Entertainment	0.9	0.3
Dues and donations	0.8	0.3
Miscellaneous	0.6	0.2
Total overhead	269.8	100.0

Each of these individual overhead expense ratios was calculated in the same way. Take Indirect labor as an example:

$$\frac{\text{Individual-to-total-}}{\text{overhead-expense ratio}} = \frac{\text{Individual overhead expense (\$)}}{\text{Total overhead expense}}$$

$$\frac{\text{Individual-to-total}}{\text{overhead-expense ratio}} = \frac{\text{Indirect labor (\$)}}{\text{Total overhead expense}}$$

$$= \frac{\$125,000,000}{\$269,800,000} = .4633, \text{ or } 46.3\%$$

Can overhead costs be applied to product?

Indirect costs may be applied to a product on the basis of ratios, either before or after the expenditures are ascertained.

How are indirect costs applied to a product before the expenses are known?

Indirect (overhead) expenses are applied to a product before expenses are incurred by means of the application rate. The unit of measurement may be units, direct labor hours, or dollars.

$$\text{Application rate} = \frac{\text{Overhead expenses}}{\text{Production}}$$

To calculate a predetermined rate, divide the estimated overhead by the estimated production (again in units, direct labor hours, or dollars).

$$\text{Predetermined rate} = \frac{\text{Estimated overhead}}{\text{Estimated production}}$$

These formulas are, however, conceptual. In actuality, overhead may be expressed as a rate or percentage of:

- Direct labor dollars
- Direct labor hour
- Prime costs
- Machine hour
- Unit cost rate

Note: The ratios of overhead to sales and cost of sales are explained on page 289.

How is overhead compared to direct labor dollars?

Direct labor dollars are the dollars paid to employees directly engaged in the making of the product or in the rendering of the service. Expressed as so many dollars per direct labor dollar, this ratio reflects how much the company spends on overhead for every dollar it spends on direct labor.

$$\text{Overhead-to-direct-labor-dollars ratio} = \frac{\text{Overhead (\$)}}{\text{Direct labor (\$)}}$$

Example: For the first six months of 19X1, XYZ Corp. incurred $79,600,000 in overhead expenses and $59,000,000 in direct labor dollars.

$$\text{Overhead-to-direct-labor-dollars ratio} = \frac{\text{Overhead (\$)}}{\text{Direct labor (\$)}}$$

$$= \frac{\$79,600,000}{\$59,000,000} = 1.349$$

For every dollar spent on direct labor, XYZ spent $1.35 on overhead. If this rate can be validated as accurate, it can serve as a guideline in planning and as a tool in checking actual figures, once on hand.

What does the production manager learn from the ratio of total overhead to direct labor dollars?

This ratio may be useful in bidding an estimating contract costs.

Example: The following data applies to XYZ Corp.:

	(in $000,000s)			
	19X1	19X0	Variance	
Expense	$	$	*Diff.*	%
Total overhead	269.8	253.8	16.0	6.3
Direct labor dollars	198.0	181.6	16.4	9.0
Ratio of total overhead to direct labor dollars	136.2	139.7	(3.5)	2.5

In 19X1, the ratio of total overhead to direct labor dollars is 136.2%; in 19X0, 137.9%. The variance of 3.5% represents a 2.5% decrease. The rate reduction is attributed largely to a 9.0% increase in direct labor dollars ($181,600,000 to $198,000,000) versus an offsetting increase of only 6.3% in total overhead ($253,800,000 to $269,800,000).

How is overhead compared to direct labor hours?

Direct labor hours are the hours spent by employees directly engaged in the making of the product or in the rendering of the service.

$$\text{Overhead-to-direct-labor-hours ratio} = \frac{\text{Overhead (\$)}}{\text{Direct labor hours}}$$

Example: For the first six months of 19X1, XYZ Corp. incurred $79,600,000 in overhead expenses and paid for 20,101,010 direct labor hours.

$$\text{Overhead-to-direct-labor-hours ratio} = \frac{\text{Overhead (\$)}}{\text{Direct labor hours}}$$

$$= \frac{\$79,600,000}{20,100,000 \text{ hours}} = \frac{\$3.96}{\text{per hour}}$$

For every direct labor hour worked, XYZ spent $3.96 on overhead. If this rate can be validated as accurate, it can serve as a guideline in planning and as a tool in checking actual figures, once on hand.

What benefit is there to comparing overhead to direct labor hours?

With a historically validated ratio, the production manager can:

● Estimate product costs per direct labor hour.
● Develop a factory overhead budget.

How is overhead computed in terms of prime cost?

Prime cost is the sum of direct labor plus material and other direct costs.

$$\text{Overhead-to-prime-cost ratio} = \frac{\text{Overhead (\$)}}{\text{Prime cost (\$)}}$$

Or:

$$\text{Overhead-to-prime cost ratio} = \frac{\text{Overhead (\$)}}{\text{Direct labor dollars} + \text{Direct materials \& ODC}}$$

Example: In January of 19X1, XYZ Corp. incurred $38,400,000 in overhead expenses, paid $9,600,000 in direct labor, and incurred $15,800,000 in materials and other direct costs.

$$\text{Overhead-to-prime cost ratio} = \frac{\text{Overhead (\$)}}{\text{Direct labor dollars} + \text{Direct materials \& ODC}}$$

$$= \frac{\$38,400,000}{\$9,600,000 + \$15,800,000}$$

$$= \frac{\$38,400,000}{\$25,400,000} = 1.512, \text{ or } 151.2\%$$

For every dollar spent on prime costs, XYZ spent $1.51 on overhead. If this rate can be validated as accurate, it can serve as a guideline in planning and as a tool in checking actual figures, once on hand.

What is the machine hour rate method?

The machine hour rate is the cost per hour of running the company's production equipment. The rate includes:

- Specific charges to each machine, such as lease payments or depreciation, maintenance costs, or power requirements.
- Heating, lighting, and building costs.
- All other general and service costs, including indirect supplies and miscellaneous labor, supervision, and engineering support.

Each of these types of costs can be generated by the affected departments.

The total of all machine-related and prorated costs are then divided by the number of hours the machinery runs over the year (or the period in question).

$$\text{Machine hour rate} = \frac{\text{Machine-related expense} + \text{Heating, light, plant} + \text{Overhead}}{\text{Annual machine hours}}$$

Example: Each of the four main presses of Acme Printing Co. run 3,300 hours in a year.

- Machine-related expenses are depreciation, $12,500; service contracts and costs, $5,000; power, $1,350.
- Prorated heating, light, and plant costs amount to $3,500.

- Supervisory labor, downtime for maintenance and repair, and service supplies and parts come to $6,700.

$$\text{Machine hour rate} = \frac{\text{Machine-related expense} + \text{Heating, light, plant} + \text{Overhead}}{\text{Annual machine hours}}$$

$$= \frac{\$18,850 + \$3,500 + \$6,700}{3,300 \text{ hours}}$$

$$= \frac{\$29,050}{3,300 \text{ hours}} = \$8.80 \text{ per hour}$$

What is the product unit cost rate?

The simplest and most direct way to apply overhead is on the basis of the product quantities produced, expressed as a rate of dollars spent per units produced. The calculations may involve actual or estimated figures, and they may be for the total plant, a department, or a cost center.

$$\text{Product unit cost} = \frac{\text{Overhead (\$)}}{\text{Units of product}}$$

Example: XYZ Corp. made 8,800 widgets in January. Its overhead $13,000,000.

$$\text{Product unit cost} = \frac{\text{Overhead (\$)}}{\text{Units of product}}$$

$$= \frac{\$13,000,000}{8,800 \text{ units}} = \$1,477.27 \text{ per unit}$$

XYZ spends $1,477 in overhead for every unit produced.

What if a firm cannot use units produced in the product unit cost method?

Units produced is only one possible factor. The rate can also be expressed in terms of pounds, gallons, feet, or other types of units.

$$\text{Product unit cost} = \frac{\text{Overhead (\$)}}{\text{Units}}$$

Example: A division of Apex, Inc. produces three products, each of a different weight but of basically the same type. Management knows that their overhead is running $2,146.49 per month. They must be able to compute their cost per unit. The units produced are as follows:

| | Product | | | |
	A	B	C	Total
Units produced	500	400	600	
Unit weight (lbs.)	3	5	2	
Weight produced	1,500	2,000	1,200	4,700

$$\text{Product unit cost} = \frac{\text{Overhead (\$)}}{\text{Pounds}}$$

$$= \frac{\$2{,}146.49}{4{,}700 \text{ lbs.}} = \$.4567 \text{ per pound}$$

Apex's overhead cost per pound is $.4567.

| | Product | | | |
	A	B	C	Total
Units produced	500	400	600	
Unit weight (lbs.)	3	5	2	
Weight produced	1,500	2,000	1,200	4,700
Cost per pound	$.4567	$.4567	$.4567	$.4567
Overhead cost applied to lbs.	$685.05	$913.50	$548.04	$2,146.49

For Product A:

$$\text{Product unit cost} = \frac{\text{Overhead (\$)}}{\text{Units of product}}$$

$$= \frac{\$685.05}{500 \text{ lbs.}} = \$1.37 \text{ per unit}$$

Apex spends $1.37 in overhead dollars for every unit of Product A. The cost per unit for Products B and C is computed in a similar fashion.

| | Product | | | |
	A	B	C	Total
Units produced	500	400	600	
Unit weight (lbs.)	3	5	2	
Weight produced	1,500	2,000	1,200	4,700
Cost per pound	$.4567	$.4567	$.4567	$.4567
Overhead cost applied to lbs.	$685.05	$913.50	$548.04	$2,146.49
Cost per unit	$ 1.37	$ 2.28	$ .91	

What is the ratio of overhead to cost of sales?

This ratio weighs overhead dollars against those spent in generating sales—"cost of sales."

$$\text{Total-overhead-to-cost-of-sales ratio} = \frac{\text{Total overhead (\$)}}{\text{Cost of sales (\$)}}$$

Note: This ratio can be used for any period—month, quarter, year, etc.

Example: For 19X1, XYZ Corp.'s total overhead came to $269,800,000, and its cost of sales to $945,000,000.

$$\text{Total-overhead-to-cost-of-sales ratio} = \frac{\text{Total overhead (\$)}}{\text{Cost of sales (\$)}}$$

$$= \frac{\$269,800,000}{\$945,000,000} = 0.286,$$

$$\text{or } 28.6\%$$

Overhead costs came to 28.6% of the cost of sales.

What good does it do to compare overhead to cost of sales?

Along with direct labor, direct material, and other direct costs, overhead is an important element in the composition of cost of sales. Variances from one period to the next can be the occasion for follow-up action.

Example: The following data is available for XYZ Corp.

(in $000,000s)					
	19X1	19X0	Variance		
Expense	$	$	$	%	
Total overhead	269.8	253.8	16.0	6.3	
Cost of sales	945.0	865.0	80.0	9.2	
Overhead-to-cost-of-sales ratio (%)	28.6	29.3	0.7	0.1	

The ratio of overhead to cost of sales decreased slightly from 29.3% to 28.6% (a variance of 0.7%). This was due to the higher cost of sales, which was only partially offset by a smaller increase in overhead. From the one year to the other, the cost of sales rose at only a little greater rate than overhead.

How is the rate of fringe benefits to direct labor hours calculated?

The total dollar cost of fringe benefits (retirement plan, the production manager incentives, and other labor benefits) is divided by total direct labor hours. The rate is expressed in terms of the dollars spent on benefits for every hour of direct labor performed.

$$\text{Fringe-benefits-to-direct-labor-hours rate} = \frac{\text{Fringe benefits (\$)}}{\text{Direct labor hours}}$$

Example: In 19X1, XYZ Corp. paid for 39,400,000 direct labor hours and spent the following on fringe benefits:

Retirement plan	$12,500,000
Management incentives	$ 2,500,000
Miscellaneous labor benefits	$50,000,000
Total fringe benefits	$65,000,000

$$\text{Fringe-benefits-to-direct-labor-hours rate} = \frac{\text{Fringe benefits (\$)}}{\text{Direct labor hours}}$$

$$= \frac{\$65,000,000}{39,400,000} = \frac{\$1.65}{\text{per hour}}$$

For every hour of direct labor performed, XYZ spends $1.65 on fringe benefits.

What does the fringe-benefit-to-direct-labor-hours rate tell the production manager?

Either comparisons of rates from period to period or comparisons of actual to estimated rates can help the production manager assess its performance in controlling these costs and in planning future fringe benefit allocations.

Example: The following data is available for XYZ Corp.:

(in $000,000s)

Expense	19X1 $	19X0 $	Variance $	%
Total overhead	269.8	253.8	16.0	6.3
Direct labor hours	39.4	37.3	2.1	5.6
Fringe benefits	65.0	58.2	6.8	11.7
Fringe-benefits-to-direct-labor-hours ratio	1.65	1.59	0.06	3.8

The rate of fringe benefits to direct labor hours increased from $1.59 in 19X0 to $1.65 in 19X1—3.8%. This compares favorably with the 5.6% rise in direct labor hours over the same timespan.

How is the ratio between fringe benefits and total labor dollars computed?

The total dollar cost of fringe benefits (retirement plan, the production manager incentives, and other labor benefits) is divided by total labor dollars. Total labor cost is the sum of direct and indirect labor. The rate is expressed in terms of the dollars spent on benefits for every hour of direct labor performed.

$$\text{Fringe-benefits-to-direct-labor-dollars rate} = \frac{\text{Fringe benefits (\$)}}{\text{Total labor \$}}$$

Note: Total labor dollars are used because both direct and indirect personnel share in the retirement and other labor benefits (vacations, sick leave, insurance, and the like).

Example: In 19X1, XYZ Corp. paid $198,000,000 in direct labor dollars, $125,000,000 for indirect labor, and the following on fringe benefits:

Retirement plan	$12,500,000
Management incentives	$ 2,500,000
Miscellaneous labor benefits	$50,000,000
Total fringe benefits	$65,000,000

$$\text{Fringe-benefits-to-direct-labor-dollars rate} = \frac{\text{Fringe benefits (\$)}}{\text{Total labor \$}}$$

$$= \frac{\$65,000,000}{\$198,000,000 + \$125,000,000}$$

$$= \frac{\$65,000,000}{\$323,000,000} = 0.201, \text{ or } 20.1\%$$

For every dollar XYZ pays for total labor, it incurs an additional $.201 cost in fringe benefits.

What does the fringe-benefit-to-total-labor-dollars rate tell the production manager?

By highlighting the proportion of fringe benefits to total labor dollars, this ratio is more useful for monitoring than for planning or control. Fringe benefits are largely beyond the control of the production manager since the pertinent guidelines are governed by the organization's policies and procedures, by law and tax codes, and by negotiations with labor.

Example: The following data is available for XYZ Corp.:

	19X1	*19X0*	*Variance*	
Expense	*$*	*$*	*$*	*%*
Total overhead	269.8	253.8	16.0	6.3
Direct labor hours	39.4	37.3	2.1	5.6
Direct labor $	198.0	181.6	16.4	9.0
Indirect labor $	125.0	120.0	5.0	4.2
Fringe benefits	65.0	58.2	6.8	11.7
Fringe-benefits-to-total-labor-dollars ratio (%)	20.1	19.3	0.8	4.1

(in $000,000s)

The rate of fringe benefits to total labor dollars increased from 19.3% in 19X0 to 20.1% in 19X1—4.1%. This rise is due primarily to the 9.0% increase in direct labor hours.

APPENDIX

TOOLS FOR FINANCIAL AND OPERATIONS ANALYSIS

WORDS TO KNOW

Arithmetic mean. Calculated two ways: algebraically and by the deviation method. (1) Arithmetic mean: The sum of the values of all items in a series divided by the number of those items. (2) Deviation mean: An arbitrary midpoint value is selected, and assigned a value of 0. The frequency deviation of each group from the midpoint (0) is calculated. Given this data, an estimated mean is produced.

Arithmetic median. A position average. Each item in the series is assigned a range of values (the class inverval) and a frequency (the number of events occurring within the class interval).

Arithmetic mode. The value that occurs most frequently in a series (assuming enough data is available for a "smooth," that is, ideal distribution).

Average. A measure for "central tendency"—that is, a typical value around which other figures congregate or which divides their number in half; an overall value.

Cyclical variation. A fluctuation related to such conditions as prosperity, recession, and depression.

Deviation analysis. Analysis of deviations, or variations, to determine how well an average represents the data.

Extrapolation. The projection of known values.

Freehand method. Also known as the inspection or estimate method, the projection of trends by freehand plotting known data on a graph and then extending the curve along its historical direction.

Geometric mean. Used primarily for averaging ratios and for computing the average rates of increase/decrease among data sets, this mean is a value whose calculation depends on the sizes of all the values.

Graph. A diagrammatic ratio. The vertical axis is calibrated for one set of values, and the horizontal axis is calibrated for another set of values. By plotting points according to these two sets of values, you can compare one value to another.

Industry norms. For every industry, there is a set of normal ratios, which reflect the average value for the given type of business.

Mean. *See* Arithmetic mean, Geometric mean.

Mean deviation. In deviation analysis, variations measured on an absolute basis.

Mode. *See* Arithmetic mode.

Moving average. An average of values associated with successive periods; every time the average is calculated, the first-period value is dropped and the latest-period value is added.

Ratio. A numerical relationship that compares one magnitude with another in the form of a multiple, such as 2:1. The multiple may also be expressed as a fraction (2/1), percentage (200%), or rate (2 per 1).

Seasonal variation. A movement that occurs at a regular time intervals during a business period.

Semiaveraging method. Time series data is segregated into into two equal parts and the arithmetic mean calculated for each part of the series. Two points are plotted on a graph and a connecting line drawn to represent the trend.

Standard deviation. In deviation analysis, variables measure on a relative basis. (standard deviation).

Statistical forecasting. Projecting a time series.

Time series. A sequential arrangement of selected statistical data according to its occurrence in time.

Time series trend. *See* Trend.

Trend: A long-term movement, either upward or downward.

AVERAGING

What is an average?

An average is a measure for "central tendency"—that is, a typical value around which other figures congregate or which divides their number in half. It is an overall value.

There are different types of averages, of which four are the most common:

1. Arithmetic mean
2. Median
3. Mode
4. Geometric mean

How is the arithmetic mean calculated?

The arithmetic mean can be calculated in two ways: algebraically and by the deviation method.

What is the algebraic method of calculating the arithmetic mean?

The algebraic method of calculating the arithmetic mean is the sum of the values of all items in a series divided by the number of those items.

$$\text{Mean} = \frac{\text{Sum of the values}}{\text{Number of items}}$$

Example: ABC Co. had sales over four quarters as follows. What is the arithmetic mean of the four quarters' worth of sales volume?

	(in $000s)		
	Quarter		
First	*Second*	*Third*	*Fourth*
$520	$530	$525	$535

The number of items in the series is 4 (4 quarters).

$$
\begin{aligned}
\text{Mean} &= \frac{\text{Sum of the values}}{\text{Number of items}} \\
&= \frac{\$520,000 + \$530,000 + \$525,000 + \$535,000}{4} \\
&= \frac{\$2,110,000}{4} = \$527,500
\end{aligned}
$$

The arithmetic mean—the "average"—of ABC's quarterly sales volume is $527,500.

What is the deviation method for calculating the arithmetic mean?

The deviation method may be used when each item in a series represents a range of values (a class interval), in which an event occurs with a given frequency. An arbitrary midpoint value is selected, and assigned a value of 0. The frequency deviation of each group from the midpoint (0) is calculated. Given this data, an estimated mean is produced.

$$\text{Arithmetic mean} + \frac{\text{Estimated Sum of all frequency deviations}}{\text{Total frequency of all items}} = \text{Mean}$$

Example: Current ratios may be grouped into four categories: 0-1.99, 2.0-2.99, 3.00-3.99, 4.0-5.99. (See page 313 for the definition of current ratio.) The number of items in the series is 4. Within each category (or item) is the number of organizations with current ratios within the range. The number of organizations is the frequency of the category, or item. The midpoint is a current ratio of 3.00. The data is:

Ratios (Class Interval	Midpoint (MP)	Frequency (Number of Organizations)	Deviation	Frequency Deviation
0 -1.99	1	20	-2	-40
2.00-2.99	2	50	-1	-50
3.00-3.99	3	40	0	0
4.00-5.99	4	30	$+1$	30
Totals		140		-60

$$\text{Arithmetic mean} + \frac{\text{Estimated Sum of all frequency deviations}}{\text{Total frequency of all items}} = \text{Mean}$$

$$= 3.00 + \frac{-60}{140} = 3.00 + (-0.428) = 2.57$$

The arithmetic mean of current ratios is 2.57.

How is the median calculated?

The median is a position average. Each item in the series is assigned a range of values (the class inverval) and a frequency (the number of events occurring within the class interval). To calculate the median, first prepare an array of data showing the class intervals, the frequencies for the intervals, and the cumulative frequencies. Then select a median class and apply the following formula:

$$\text{Median} = \begin{array}{c}\text{Median}\\\text{class}\\\text{lower}\\\text{limit}\end{array} + \cfrac{\begin{array}{c}\text{Total number}\\\text{in all}\\\text{classes}\end{array} - \begin{array}{c}\text{Sum of}\\\text{frequency}\\\text{cumulations}\\\text{before}\\\text{median}\\\text{class}\end{array}}{\text{Median class frequency}} \times \begin{array}{c}\text{Median}\\\text{class}\\\text{interval}\end{array}$$

Example: Following are sales volume categories, in each of which a number of organizations fall.

Sales (in $000s)	Number of Organizations	Cumulative Frequency
0-199.0	40	40
200.0-299.0	60	100
300.0-399.0	100	200
400.0-499.0	100	300
500.0-599.0	100	400
600.0 and over	80	480
	480	

The class intervals are the ranges of sales volumes in the left-hand column. The number of organizations in each class is the frequency (middle column). In the right-hand column are the cumulative frequencies; each new frequency is added to the total of the others preceding. The median class is 400.0-499.0 because it is the middle item in the column. Its lower limit is 400.0 and its interval 100. The cumulative frequencies before the median class is 200, and the total accumulated frequency (the total number in all classes) is 480.

$$\text{Median} = \begin{array}{c}\text{Median}\\\text{class}\\\text{lower}\\\text{limit}\end{array} + \cfrac{\begin{array}{c}\text{Total number}\\\text{in all}\\\text{classes}\end{array} - \begin{array}{c}\text{Sum of}\\\text{frequency}\\\text{cumulations}\\\text{before}\\\text{median}\\\text{class}\end{array}}{\text{Median class frequency}} \times \begin{array}{c}\text{Median}\\\text{class}\\\text{interval}\end{array}$$

$$= 400 + \left(\frac{\frac{480}{2} - 200}{100} \times 100 \right)$$

$$= 400 + \left(\frac{240 - 200}{100} \times 100 \right)$$

$$= 400 + \left(\frac{40}{100} \times 100 \right)$$

$$= 400 + (0.40 \times 100) = 400 + 40.0 = 440.0$$

Median sales for this series are $440,000.

What is the mode, and how is it computed?

The mode is the value that occurs most frequently in a series (assuming enough data is available for a "smooth," that is, ideal distribution). To calculate the mode, prepare an array of the available data. On the left is a list of the classes, each with a constant interval; on the right, a list of the frequencies corresponding to the classes. The middle class is then considered the modal class, for which you must note the lower limit and the difference in frequencies between its lower and upper limit. The postmodal class is the next class "up" in the series; note the difference in frequencies. Then apply the formula for the modal value.

$$\text{Modal value} = \begin{array}{c}\text{Modal}\\\text{class}\\\text{lower}\\\text{limit}\end{array} + \dfrac{\text{Frequency in modal class}}{\begin{array}{c}\text{Modal class}\\\text{difference}\\\text{in frequency}\end{array} + \begin{array}{c}\text{Postmodal}\\\text{class differ-}\\\text{ence in}\\\text{frequency}\end{array}} + \begin{array}{c}\text{Size of}\\\text{each}\\\text{class}\\\text{interval}\end{array}$$

Example: In the following array, note that the classes (categories of period income) are arranged so that the one with the greatest frequency is in the middle. This is the modal class. Since each class has to have a constant interval, the available data had to be broken into two 3,000-3,500 classes; the one with the greater frequency was chosen as the modal class.

Period Income ($) (Class)	Sales Volume (in $000s)
2,000-2,500	100.0
3,000-3,500	120.0
3,000-3,500	150.0
2,500-3,000	130.0
2,200-2,700	100.0

The size of the class interval is $500. The lower limit of the modal class is $3,000, and the difference between its lower and upper frequencies is 30 (150.0 less 120.0). The postmodal class is the $2,500-$3,000 class, and difference between the lower and upper frquencies is 20.0 (150.0 less 130.0).

$$\text{Modal value} = \begin{array}{c}\text{Modal}\\\text{class}\\\text{lower}\\\text{limit}\end{array} + \dfrac{\text{Frequency in modal class}}{\begin{array}{c}\text{Modal class}\\\text{difference}\\\text{in frequency}\end{array} + \begin{array}{c}\text{Postmodal}\\\text{class differ-}\\\text{ence in}\\\text{frequency}\end{array}} + \begin{array}{c}\text{Size of}\\\text{each}\\\text{class}\\\text{interval}\end{array}$$

$$= \$3,000 + \left(\frac{30.0}{30.0 + 20.0}\right)\$500$$

$$= \$3,000 + \left(\frac{30.0}{50.0}\right)\$500$$

$$= \$3,000 + (0.60) \times \$500 = \$3,000 + \$300 = \$3,300$$

$3,300 is the modal income value.

What is the geometric mean?

The geometric mean is used primarily for averaging ratios and for computing the average rates of increase/decrease among data sets. This type of mean is a value whose calculation depends on the sizes of all the values.

$$\text{Geometric mean} = \sqrt{\text{Product of all data set values}}$$

Example: In 19X1, a firm increased its sales volume over 19X0 by 40%, while another company increased sales by 50%. The first company's 19X1 sales are expressed as 140% of 19X0, the second company's as 150% of 19X0. If all other factors for each firm are equal, then the geometric mean may be used.

$$\begin{aligned}
\text{Geometric mean} &= \sqrt{\text{Product of all data set values}} \\
&= \sqrt{140\% \times 150\%} \\
&= \sqrt{21,000\%} = 144.9\%
\end{aligned}$$

The average rate of increase between the two firms is 144.9% of the previous year, or 44.9%.

DEVIATION ANALYSIS

Why is a measure of deviation important?

Deviations, or variations, indicate how well an average represents the data. Variations can be measured on an absolute basis (mean deviation) or on a relative basis (standard deviation). Of the two, standard deviation is the more important.

What is mean deviation?

If the data points in a set can be pictured as dots scattered around a point representing their arithmetic mean, then how far each "dot" is from the mean point is its mean deviation.

How is mean deviation calculated?

To determine the mean deviation of a data series, (1) take the average of data points:

$$\text{Average of data points} = \frac{\text{Total value of all data points}}{\text{Total number of all data points}}$$

and (2) divide it into the total deviation value:

$$\text{Mean deviation} = \frac{\text{Total of all deviation values}}{\text{Average of data points}}$$

The total deviation value is the sum of the deviations of all data points from the mean.

Notes: Since the sum of all the deviations surrounding the arithmetic mean is zero, ignore all signs in the calculation.

The lower the average mean deviation, the smaller the "scatter," or dispersion, of the points.

Example: ABC Co. has logged the following sales figures for the first eight months of 19X1.

Monthly Periods	Sales Volume (in $000s)	Deviation from Monthly Average (in $000s)
January	500.0	7.25
February	496.0	11.25
March	508.0	.75
April	510.0	2.75
May	512.0	4.75
June	507.0	.25
July	515.0	7.75
August	510.0	2.75
Totals	4,058.0	37.50

1. Calculate the average volume (average of data points):

$$\text{Average of data points} = \frac{\text{Total value of all data points}}{\text{Total number of all data points}}$$
$$= \frac{\$4,058,000}{8 \text{ months}} = \$507,250 \text{ per month}$$

The average monthly sales volume is $507,250.

2. Calculate the mean deviation:

$$\text{Mean deviation} = \frac{\text{Total of all deviation values}}{\text{Average of data points}}$$
$$= \frac{\$37,500}{\$507,250} \quad \begin{array}{l} .074, \text{ or } \$74,000 \\ \text{mean deviation} \end{array}$$

The mean deviation from the average monthly sales volume is $74,000.

How is standard deviation computed?

Standard deviation is a measure of the tendency of data to disperse. There are two formulas:

1. The long method:

$$\text{Standard deviation} = \sqrt{\left(\frac{\text{Sum of deviations}}{\text{Number of data sets}}\right)^2}$$

2. The short method:

$$\text{Standard deviation} = \sqrt{\frac{\text{Data set values, squared}}{\text{Number of data sets}} + \left(\frac{\text{Sum of data sets}}{\text{Number of data sets}}\right)^2}$$

Example: The following data has been prepared in anticipation of calculating the standard deviation in income.

Period	Net Income in $000s)	Deviations from Average (in $000s)	Net Income (squared in $000s)	Deviations squared (in $000s)
1	25	−3	625	9
2	28	—	784	—
3	29	+1	841	1
4	26	−2	676	4
5	29	+1	841	1
6	31	+3	961	9
	168		4,728	24

Notes: The sum of all the deviations surrounding the arithmetic mean is zero (as in the third column above). Therefore ignore all signs in the calculation (as in the last column above).

1. The long method:

$$\text{Standard deviation} = \sqrt{\left(\frac{\text{Sum of deviations}}{\text{Number of data sets}}\right)^2}$$

$$= \sqrt{\frac{\$24,000 \text{ (the sum of the last column)}}{6 \text{ periods}}}$$

$$= \sqrt{\$4,000} = \$2,000 \text{ per period}$$

The standard deviation of income per period is $2,000.

2. The short method:

$$\text{Standard deviation} = \sqrt{\dfrac{\text{Data set values, squared}}{\text{Number of data sets}} + \left(\dfrac{\text{Sum of data sets}}{\text{Number of data sets}}\right)^2}$$

$$= \sqrt{\dfrac{\$4,728,000}{6 \text{ periods}} - \left(\dfrac{\$168,000}{6 \text{ periods}}\right)^2}$$

$$= \sqrt{\$788.000 - (\$28,000)^2}$$

$$= \sqrt{\$788,000 - \$784,000}$$

$$= \sqrt{\$4,000} = \$2,000 \text{ per period}$$

DETERMINING TRENDS

A trend is a long-term movement, upward or downward. Because by its nature it is long term, a trend is more realistically determined over a long time span. Shot-term analysis may not be significant. Forecasting a trend, or extending it into the future, is accomplished by means of extrapolation (the projection of known values).

Trend forecasting can be done by two methods:

1. Inspection or estimate (the freehand method)
2. Calculation (semiaveraging or moving average methods)

What is the freehand method?

Also known as the inspection or estimate method, projecting trends by freehand consists of preparing a graph from the known data and extending the curve along its historical direction.

Example: For the past six years, ABC Co. has recorded the following sales revenues.

(in $000,000)					
19X1	19X2	19X3	19X4	19X5	19X6
$110	$150	$140	$170	$160	$200

This data can be plotted on a graph, and a line drawn to indicate the trend of sales over the last six years, as follows:

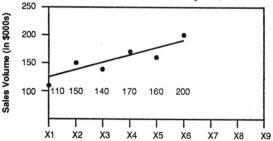

By extrapolation, the line can be extended for another several years (19X7-19X9). Note that even the year-to-year sales volumes indicated an up-and-down movement over the past six years, so that specific levels can be estimated for the upcoming three years.

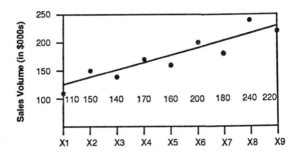

How is the semiaveraging method used?

In this method, you segregate the time series data into two equal parts and calculate the arithmetic mean for each part of the series. Then plot two points on a graph and draw a connecting line that represents the trend.

$$\text{Average} = \frac{\text{Sum of data set values}}{\text{Number of data sets}}$$

Example: For the past six years, ABC Co. has recorded the following sales revenues.

		(in $000,000)			
19X1	*19X2*	*19X3*	*19X4*	*19X5*	*19X6*
$110	$150	$140	$170	$160	$200

The time series data—sales volumes for six years—is divided into two equal parts, three years and three years, and an average is taken for each.

Years 19X1-19X3:

$$\begin{aligned}
\text{Average} &= \frac{\text{Sum of data set values}}{\text{Number of data sets}} \\
&= \frac{\$110,000,000 + \$150,000,000 + \$140,000,000}{3} \\
&= \frac{\$400,000,000}{3} = \$133,333,333
\end{aligned}$$

Years 19X4-19X6:

$$\text{Average} = \frac{\text{Sum of data set values}}{\text{Number of data sets}}$$

$$= \frac{\$170,000,000 + \$160,000,000 + \$200,000,000}{3}$$

$$= \frac{\$530,000,000}{3} = \$176,666,666$$

Then these two points are plotted on a graph, and the two points connected by a straight line (as shown by the solid line below). The straight line may then be extended into future years, as in the freehand method (dashed line).

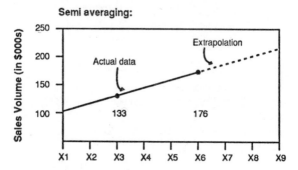

Semi averaging:

What is the moving average procedure?

A moving average is an average of values associated with successive periods; every time the average is calculated, the first-period value is dropped and the latest-period value is added. The number of periods can be however many you choose. Moving averages for sales volume, for instance, can be computed on 3 years, 5 years, 10 years. The more periods that are included in the moving average, the more reliable it becomes. Otherwise, the formula for computing the average is the standard one.

$$\text{Average} = \frac{\text{Sum of data set values}}{\text{Number of data sets}}$$

A moving average line is plotted alongside the actual data line, to show deviations from the average. Example: The following sales volume information is available for XYZ Corp.:

(in $000,000)

Year	19X1	19X2	19X3	19X4	19X5	19X6	19X7	19X8	19X9
Sales volume	150	160	170	160	180	190	200	190	200
Moving total (3 years)	—	480	490	510	530	570	580	590	—
Moving average (3 years)	—	160	163	170	177	190	193	196	

For 19X1, no moving average is calculated because the average is the same as the average. The average of 19X2 is calculated in 19X3, when 3 years' worth of data is on hand. The last year, 19X9, is not filled in because it is the last point in the trend line, and it cannot be computed until 2 more years' worth of data is avaialble.

For 19X2, the 3-year moving average is calculated as follows:

$$\text{Average} = \frac{\text{Sum of data set values}}{\text{Number of data sets}} = \frac{19X1 + 19X2 + 19X3}{3}$$

$$= \frac{\$170,000,000 + \$160,000,000 + \$200,000,000}{3}$$

$$= \frac{\$530,000,000}{3} = \$176,666,666$$

For 19X3, the data for 19X1 is dropped off, and the data for 19X4 is tacked on:

$$\text{Average} = \frac{\text{Sum of data set values}}{\text{Number of data sets}} = \frac{19X2 + 19X3 + 19X4}{3}$$

$$= \frac{\$160,000,000 + \$170,000,000 + \$160,000,000}{3}$$

$$= \frac{\$490,000,000}{3} = \$163,333,333$$

And so on. The data shown in the table above can then plotted, as follows:

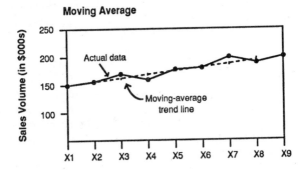

Moving Average

RATIOS

What are ratios?

A ratio is a numerical relationship that compares one magnitude with another in the form of a multiple.

Example: 2:1

The multiple may also be expressed as a fraction, percentage, or rate.

Examples: Fraction, 2/1
            Percentage, 200%
            Rate, 2 per 1, 2 for 1

How are ratios used?

In business, ratios can be used to compare:

1. A part or segment to the whole
2. One part or segment to another within the whole
3. One whole to another

Examples: ABC Co. puts out three products.

1. A part or segment to the whole: Product A sales are calculated to be 40% of total sales, Product B 35%, and Product C 25%. Expressed as percentages, the three products' shares of total sales add up to 100%.

2. One part or segment to another within the whole: Product A brought in $8,000,000, Product B $5,000,000. The relationship between the two products' sales may be expressed as a ratio: Product B sales are 62.5% of Product A sales ($5,000,000 divided by $8,000,000 times 100).

3. One whole to another: ABC Co.'s sales are 60% of XYZ Corp.'s sales. When using ratios to compare one whole to another, such as two companies, take steps to be sure that the circumstances and conditions for both companies are compatible.

PREPARING GRAPHS

What is a graph?

A graph is a diagrammatic ratio. The vertical axis is calibrated for one set of values, and the horizontal axis is calibrated for another set of values. By plotting points according to these two sets of values, you can compare one value to another. To prepare a graph you must:

- Decide on the values of the vertical and horizontal axes.
- Plot the points on the graph.
- Relate the points in some graphic way. There are three basic types of graphs: linear, bar, and scatter.

Note: In trend analysis, the horizontal axis very often represents time, so that each point reflects a vertical-axis value at a given point (of time) on the horizontal axis.

Example: XYZ Corp.'s management has found that the ratio of overhead expense to direct labor ("DL") dollars averages 1.36. They wish to compare the monthly ratios against the average:

	Ratio	Variance from Average (1.36)
January	1.38	+0.02
February	1.38	+0.02
March	1.36	0
April	1.31	−0.05
May	1.43	+0.07
June	1.31	−0.05
July	1.40	+0.04
August	1.32	−0.04
September	1.39	+0.03
October	1.32	−0.04
November	1.36	0
December	1.41	+0.05

- Decide on the values of the vertical and horizontal axes. The vertical axis is calibrated in terms of ratio values, the horizontal axis in terms of months of the year.

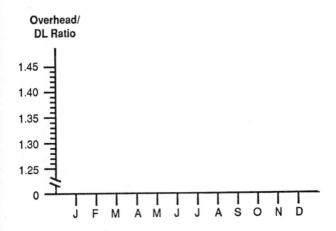

- Plot the points on the graph. The ratio for each month is marked by a dot on the graph. (Note also that the variance from the average ratio can be noted above the dot.)

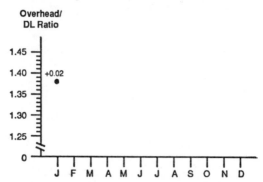

- Relate the points in some graphic way. When all the values are plotted, they should be related in some way. The simplest method is to connect them all with a line. This is a linear graph.

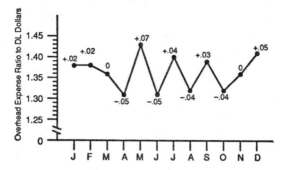

They can also be used to create bars, for a bar graph.

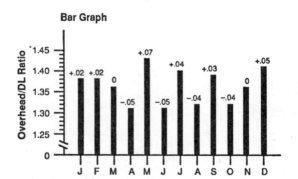

You can also leave the points unconnected, but draw a line representing the average, or baseline. This is a scatter-graph.

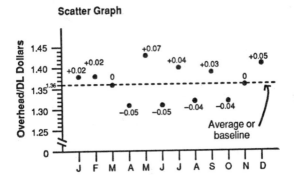

How does a graph assist in analysis?

A graph enables you to visualize data that might otherwise be difficult to grasp. Trends and deviations become clearly evident. With computer-generated graphs, management can often pinpoint trouble areas, make projections, and decide on action to be taken much more quickly than if the data is in tabular form.

Example: Using the linear graph of the preceding example, management can locate deviations from the average, deter-mine reasons for them, and take whatever action is neces-sary. They may find out, for instance, that the largest positive deviation (0.07 in May) resulted from the increase in ex-penses for that period, while direct labor dollars remained stable. Why did overhead go up?

The negative ratios of April and June, on the other hand, do not necessarily mean that overhead was kept down. In fact, the ratios dropped only because more direct labor dol-lars were spent. Why did direct labor dollars jump for these two months?

Getting the answers to these and similar questions assists management in understanding the dynamics of the organiza-tion and in planning more effective controls in the future.

COMPARISONS WITH INDUSTRY NORMS

What are industry norms?

For every industry, there is a set of normal ratios, which reflect the average value for the given type of business.

Example: The price-earnings (PE) ratio is calculated by dividing a common stock's market price by its earnings per share. Texas Instruments common stock might be expected to trade at a market price roughly 25 times its earnings per common share. In other words, its PE ratio is, on average, 25. Texas Instruments is considered in the Electronic Components, industry whose average PE ratio is 21. By comparison, Texas Instruments, with its PE ratio of 25, is above the industry norm of 21.

Where can industry norms be obtained?

Normal industry ratios can be procured from:

- Dun & Bradstreet, Inc.
- Standard & Poor's Corporation
- Moody's Manual of Investments
- Robert Morris Associates
- Value Line
- Various trade associations for their members

Which ratios are published?

The primary ratios are:

- Current (working capital) ratio
- Net income return on sales
- Net income as a percentage of working capital
- Net income as a percentage of net worth
- Sales as a percentage of working capital
- Receivable collection period (the length of)
- Sales to inventory
- Fixed assets to tangible net worth
- Debt to tangible net worth
- Debt to tangible net worth (equity ratio)
- Inventory to working capital
- Current liabilities to inventory
- Funded debt to working capital

GLOSSARY

Accounting equation. The equation reflected in the balance sheet: assets − liabilities = stockholders' equity.

Accounts payable. Cash amounts that the corporation owes to others.

Accounts-payable-turnover. A ratio that indicates the number of times the accounts payable "turned over"—that is, were paid—in a period.

Accounts receivable (receivables). A balance sheet entry indicating dollar amounts owed to a company by customers for product sold or services rendered.

Accounts receivable turnover. The ratio of total credit sales to receivables (also known as the sales-to-receivables ratio).

Acid test ratio. A ratio that compares the company's current liabilities with its quick assets—cash, marketable securities, and accounts receivable.

Accumulated depreciation. The total of all depreciation taken on a fixed asset since the year it was purchased through the current year.

Aging procedure. *See* Aging receivables procedure.

Aging receivables (aging) procedure. Accounts receivable are grouped according to their ages, usually under 30 days, 31-60 days, 61-90 days, and over 90 days. For each group, the beginning-of-period and end-of-period amounts are compared, to see whether it is taking the organization more or less time to receive payment.

Arithmetic mean. Calculated in two ways: algebraically and by the deviation method. (1) Arithmetic mean: The sum of the values of all items in a series divided by the number of those items. (2) Deviation mean: An arbitrary midpoint value is selected, and assigned a value of 0. The frequency deviation of each group from the midpoint (0) is calculated. Given this data, an estimated mean is produced.

Arithmetic median. A position average. Each item in the series is assigned a range of values (the class inverval) and a frequency (the number of events occurring within the class interval).

Arithmetic mode. The value that occurs most frequently in a series (assuming enough data is available for a "smooth," that is, ideal distribution).

Asset. Something of value that is owned by or owed to the corporation.

Average. A measure for "central tendency"—that is, a typical value around which other figures congregate or which divides their number in half; an overall value.

Average collection period. The average number of days between the day the invoice is sent out and the day the customer pays the bill.

Average receivables. The sum of the beginning and ending balances for a period divided by 2. The period may be a month, quarter, year, or any period.

Backlog. The number of, or the dollar value of, unfilled orders.

Balance sheet. A financial statement that contains the three primary elements of a business enterprise: assets, liabilities, and stockholders' (shareholders', owners') equity. The three elements must "balance" out according to the so-called accounting equation: Assets = Liabilities + Equity.

Beginning balance. The balance for an accounting entry at the start of the accounting period.

Billed sales. Sales for which orders have been filled and invoices sent out.

Bottom line. *See* Net income.

Break-even point. The sales volume level at which the business neither profits nor loses money; sales and total costs are exactly equal.

Break-even plant capacity. The approximate plant capacity at which an organization is breaking even ("BE plant capacity").

Capital. *See* Stockholders' equity.

Capitalization. *See* Stockholders' equity.

Capitalization structure. *See* Capital structure.

Capital structure. How a company's capital is derived, such as from investors or from lenders (e.g., bondholders).

Cash disbursement. *See* Disbursement.

Cash flow. The difference between cash receipts and cash disbursements.

Cash flow ratio. A comparison between an individual receipt or disbursement item and its related total.

Cash flow statement. A financial statement consisting of two breakdowns: cash receipts and disbursements, with a summary for the organization's net cash position.

Cash ratio. A ratio that is calculated like the acid test ratio but that includes fewer assets. It leaves out accounts receivable and includes only cash and marketable securities.

Cash receipt. *See* Receipt.

Cash turnover ratio. The ratio that relates sales (the "top line" on the income statement) to a company's cash balance (an entry in the current assets section of the balance sheet).

COGS. *See* cost of sales.

Common stock. Shares reflecting ownership in a corporation that are bought and sold in the open market by investors. The common stock entry on the balance sheet reflects the par value only.

Cost of goods sold. *See* Cost of sales.

Costs. *See* Expenses.

Cost of sales (cost of goods sold, COGS, direct cost). The cost of making or buying a product sold, or of providing a service rendered, consisting of direct personnel, direct materials (and other direct costs), and factory overhead.

Credit sales. *See* Total credit sales.

Current asset. An asset whose useful life is less than one year, such as cash, securities, accounts receivable.

Current period. The present accounting period.

Current period collections. The receivables collected in the present accounting period.

Current-period-collection rate. A gauge of how fast an organization recoups expenditures made to fill orders.

Current ratio. Current assets divided by current liabilities.

Cyclical variation. A fluctuation related to such conditions as prosperity, recession, and depression.

Days-of-sales-in-receivables ratio (or factor). The ratio between sales and receivables reflects the normal number of days of uncollected sales in receivables.

Days-purchases-in-payables ratio. A ratio that relates the amounts payable to an organization's total purchases for a given period.

Days-purchases-in-disbursements ratio. A ratio that relates how much a company purchases to how much cash it actually disburses in a given period.

Days purchasing outstanding. A ratio used to determine whether an organization is meeting its trade payable commitments on schedule. The fewer the days purchases outstanding, the more favorable the company's debt-paying ability.

Debt issue. A bond issued by a corporation. A bond represents monies loaned to the corporation by bondholders, unlike a share of stock which reflects ownership.

Deferred charges. An expense that has been incurred but whose payment, for whatever reasons, has been put off until some time in the future.

Depreciation. Distribution of the original cost of a fixed asset, such as a building or fleet of cars, over the number of years in the asset's useful life.

Deviation analysis. Analysis of deviations, or variations, to determine how well an average represents the data.

Direct cost. *See* Cost of sales.

Direct expenses. *See* Cost of sales.

Direct labor. *See* Direct personnel cost.

Direct material. An element of cost of sales, the cost of materials used in making a product or in rendering a service.

Direct personnel (labor). Employees directly involved in the making of a product or in the rendering of a service. This payroll falls into the category of direct costs (cost of sales, cost of goods sold).

Disbursement. A cash amount paid out by the company.

Disbursements-to-accounts-payable ratio. The ratio between actual disbursements and the accounts payable during the period.

Ending (end-of-period) balance. The balance of a given accounting entry at the end of the accounting period.

End-of-period balance. *See* Ending balance.

Equity (capital, net worth). The difference between the value of a company's assets and the amount of its liabilities (both balance sheet totals). The interest of owners in a business. See also Stockholders' equity.

Expenses. The costs of doing business. *See* Direct expenses, Indirect expenses.

Factory overhead. An element of cost of sales, the part of factory overhead directly attributable to making a product. (Some fixed factory costs may be regarded as indirect costs.)

Extrapolation. The projection of known values.

Factory overhead. An element of cost of sales, the part of factory overhead directly attributable to making a product. (Some fixed factory costs may be regarded as indirect costs.)

Financial risk. The risk posed by the heavy use of debt support by creditors.

Finished goods. Product that has been completed and is awaiting shipment.

Fixed asset. An asset whose useful life is greater than one year, such as a manufacturing plant, an office building, or heavy equipment.

Fixed expenses. Expenses that do not vary with levels of production, such as plant costs or executives' salaries.

Freehand method. Also known as the inspection or estimate method, the projection of trends by freehand plotting known data on a graph and then extending the curve along its historical direction.

G&A. *See* General and administrative expense.

General and administrative (G&A) expense. An indirect cost associated with running a business, other than production or sales.

Geometric mean. Used primarily for averaging ratios and for computing the average rates of increase/decrease among data sets, this mean is a value whose calculation depends on the sizes of all the values.

Graph. A diagrammatic ratio. The vertical axis is calibrated for one set of values, and the horizontal axis is calibrated for another set of values. By plotting points according to these two sets of values, you can compare one value to another.

Gross margin. *See* Gross profit.

Gross profit (margin). Sales less cost of sales (direct costs).

Income (earnings) before taxes. *See* Pretax earnings.

Income from operations. *See* Operating income.

Income risk. The risk of having insufficient income to carry on operations.

Income (profit and loss) statement (P&L). A financial statement showing a company's net income—the profit after deducting all expenses—over a period.

Indirect cost (operating expense). A cost that cannot be directly attributed to production, such as selling expenses or general and administrative (G&A) costs.

Indirect expense. *See* Indirect cost.

Indirect personnel (labor). Employees who are necessary for running a business but who are not directly involved in production or service. Indirect labor wages and salaries are indirect costs.

Industry norms. For every industry, there is a set of normal ratios, which reflect the average value for the given type of business.

Interest plus funded debt ratio. This ratio assesses an organization's capacity to meet scheduled interest plus debt repayments.

Inventory. Goods owned by the corporation, in the form of raw materials, work in process, or finished goods.

Investors' capital. *See* Stockholders' equity.

Lagged (prior period) costs. Costs incurred by the company in the preceding account period to fill orders.

Liability. A debt or obligation of the corporation.

Liquidation limit. The percentage of billed sales that will be collected in the same period as they are billed.

Liquidation lag value. The numerical complement of the liquidation limit.

Long-term (funded) debt. Debt whose term is greater than one year, such as a ten-year bank loan or a thirty-year corporate bond issue.

Machine hour rate method. The cost per hour of running the company's production equipment.

Marketable security. A security that is easily traded, such as a stock or bond.

Material and other direct costs (ODC). Materials and other direct expenses directly related to the making of the company product.

Material and other direct costs. A direct cost (cost of sale), the materials and other items needed to make the company's product.

Mean. *See* Arithmetic mean, Geometric mean.

Mean deviation. In deviation analysis, variations measured on an absolute basis.

Mode. *See* Arithmetic mode.

Moving average. An average of values associated with successive periods; every time the average is calculated, the first-period value is dropped and the latest-period value is added.

Net credit sales. *See* Sales.

Net fixed assets. Fixed assets less accumulate depreciation.

Net income (bottom line, net profit). All revenues (operating and nonoperating) less all expenses (direct, indirect, taxes, etc.).

Net income before taxes. *See* Pretax earnings.

Net profit. *See* Net income.

Net sales. *See* Sales.

Net worth. *See* Equity.

OIC. *See* Other indirect costs.

Operating expenses. *See* Indirect expense.

Operating income (factory income, income from operations). Sales less cost of sales (direct costs) and operating (indirect) expenses. It excludes peripheral income, such as interest on investments, and nonoperating expenses, such as taxes.

Operating leverage ratio. A ratio that assesses the effect of fluctuating sales on operating profits.

Other direct costs (ODC). Costs, other than labor or materials, that are directly attributable to the making of the company product—e.g., factory-related expenses.

Other indirect costs (OIC). Expenses that cannot be attributed to the making of a specific product. Examples are depreciation on a plant in which many products are made, utility and heating expenses, or delivery fleet lease payments and maintenance costs.

Overhead. Expenses that represent indirect services and support for operational activities; they do not contribute directly—or they cannot be identified as directly contributing—to the manufacture of a product.

Owners' equity. *See* Stockholders' equity.

Paid-in Capital. Money taken in by the corporation for the sale of stock.

P&L. *See* Income statement.

Preferred stock. Shares reflecting ownership in a corporation that pay fixed dividends.

Prepaid expenses. An asset in the form of an expense, such as rent or insurance premiums, that has been paid in advance.

Pretax earnings (pretax income, pretax profit, net income before taxes). Earnings left after adding operating income to nonoperating income (e.g., interest earned on loans), and then deducting nonoperating expenses (e.g., extraordinary costs)—but not taxes.

Prime cost. The sum of direct labor plus material and other direct costs.

Prior period. The preceding accounting period.

Prior period billings. Billings made during the preceding accounting period.

Production volume. The number of units slated to be produced within the period.

Product unit cost rate. The application of overhead on the basis of the product quantities produced, expressed as a rate of dollars spent per units produced (either actual or estimated figures).

Profit and loss statement. *See* Income statement.

Progress payment. The partial payment by a customer against a receivable.

Ratio. A numerical relationship that compares one magnitude with another in the form of a multiple, such as 2:1. The multiple may also be expressed as a fraction (2/1), percentage (200%), or rate (2 per 1).

Raw materials. Materials used the making of finished goods.

Receipt. A cash amount received by the company.

Receivables. *See* Accounts receivable.

Retained earnings. The earnings that a corporation accumulates since its startup—profits that are "kept," as opposed to being distributed as dividends.

Revenue (revenues). *See* Sales.

Sales. *See* Total credit sales.

Sales. Sales revenues less a calculated allowance for returned goods and bad debt.

Sales (net sales, revenue, top line, total credit sales, etc.). Income from the sale of a company's product or service, less a deduction for returns and bad debt.

Sales backlog. *See* Backlog.

Sales-to-receivables ratio. *See* Accounts receivable turnover.

Seasonal variation. A movement that occurs at regular time intervals during a business period.

Selling expenses. An indirect cost associated with sales, selling expenses include the costs of marketing and contract administration.

Semiaveraging method. Time series data is segregated into into two equal parts and the arithmetic mean calculated for each part of the series. Two points are plotted on a graph and a connecting line drawn to represent the trend.

Shareholders' equity. *See* Stockholders' equity.

Standard deviation. In deviation analysis, variables measure on a relative basis. (standard deviation).

Statistical forecasting. Projecting a time series.

Stockholders' (shareholders', owners') equity (equity capital, investors' capital, capital, capitalization). The difference between total assets and total liabilities. It represents the investors' ownership interest in the company.

Time series. A sequential arrangement of selected statistical data according to its occurrence in time.

Time series trend. *See* Trend.

Times-interest-earned ratio. A ratio that focuses on the number of times interest is covered by operating profits. The higher the ratio, the better off the company.

Times-preferred-dividend ratio. A ratio that indicates how able a company is to meet its preferred dividend obligations.

Top line. *See* Sales.

Total (credit) sales. Total sales less allowances for returns and bad debt. Same as sales.

Total expense allowance. The total variable allowance for the period.

Total fixed expense. The sum of fixed costs for the period.

Total sales. *See* Sales.

Total overhead. *See* Other indirect costs.

Trend. A long-term movement, either upward or downward.

Variable expenses. Expenses that fluctuate with the level of production.

Velocity method. A method for calculating an organization's debt-paying capability, used primarily for liquidation assessment.

Vertical analysis. Each balance sheet entry within a total (such as cash or notes payable) is divided by the total itself (such as total assets or total current liabilities). The resulting ratio is then placed next to the dollar amount of the entry in the balance sheet.

In an income statement, the expression of each entry as a ratio or percentage of sales.

Volume. *See* Total credit sales.

Working capital ratio. Working capital divided by liabilities.

Work in process (progress). Product that is not yet completed, such as automobiles partly through the assembly line.

INDEX

E

F

G